D1482339

JOURNAL FOR THE STUDY OF THE NEW TESTAMENT
SUPPLEMENT SERIES

9

Department of Biblical Studies
The University of Sheffield
Sheffield S10 2TN
England

THE HYMNS OF LUKE'S INFANCY NARRATIVES

Their Origin, Meaning and Significance

Stephen Farris

Journal for the Study of the New Testament
Supplement Series 9

Published by
JSOT Press
Department of Biblical Studies
The University of Sheffield
Sheffield S10 2TN
England

Printed in Great Britain
by Redwood Burn Ltd.,
Trowbridge, Wiltshire.

British Library Cataloguing in Publication Data

Farris, Stephen
    The hymns of Luke's infancy narratives : their
    origin, meaning and significance.—(Journal
    for the study of the New Testament supplement series,
    ISSN 0309-0787; 9)
    1. Bible. N.T. Luke—Commentaries   2. Canticles
    I. Title   II. Series
    226'.406   BS2595.3

    ISBN 0-905774-91-4
    ISBN 0-905774-92-2 Pbk

CONTENTS

PREFACE

The student of form-criticism will find no difficulty in determining the origin of this work; it came into existence as a PhD dissertation. In this case the dissertation was presented to Cambridge University in 1982. I wish to express my gratitude to the editors of the *Journal for the Study of the New Testament* Supplement Series for accepting it for publication. Only the chapter on Raymond Martin's method of Syntax Criticism and its application to Luke 1–2 has been substantially altered. That chapter had already appeared in print in essay form in R.T. France and David Wenham, *Gospel Perspectives*, II. I am grateful for their permission to use that material, albeit in altered form, in this larger work.

Since this is substantially the same work as my PhD dissertation it is my pleasant duty to thank in print those without whose help my stay in Cambridge would have been either impossible or fruitless. I must thank first of all those who made my stay in Cambridge financially possible: the trustees of the Paulin Memorial fund of St Andrew's Presbyterian Church, Windsor, Ontario, Runnymede Presbyterian Church and the Scott Mission, Toronto, and Dr Donald MacDonald who administers several scholarship funds on behalf of the Presbyterian Church in Canada. But above all I must in this connection thank the electors of the Lewis and Gibson Scholarship of Westminster College, Cambridge, for entrusting me with that award.

I must also mention those who by their good company and support rendered my time in Cambridge so pleasant. These include the faculty and students of Westminster College, the MCR of Fitzwilliam College and the habitués of Tyndale House.

I am especially grateful to my supervisor, Professor M.D. Hooker and to Dr E. Bammel who aided me while Professor Hooker was on sabbatical leave. To these two scholars I am indebted for both challenge and encouragement.

But thanks and gratitude must chiefly go to my wife, Patty, to whom I can never adequately express my appreciation even by dedicating to here, as I now do, this work.

Abbreviations

Works cited are identified by author's surname and a short title. More complete information may be found in the bibliography at the conclusion of the work. The following abbreviations are commonly used.

AJT	*American Journal of Theology*
APOT	R. Charles, *Apocrypha and Pseudepigrapha of the Old Testament*
BD	Blass–Debrunner, *Grammar*
BJRL	*Bulletin of the John Rylands Library*
BZ	*Biblische Zeitschrift*
CBQ	*Catholic Biblical Quarterly*
CUP	Cambridge University Press
CJT	*Canadian Journal of Theology*
EvTh	*Evangelische Theologie*
ICC	International Critical Commentary
JBL	*Journal of Biblical Literature*
JQR	*Jewish Quarterly Review*
JSOT	*Journal for the Study of the Old Testament*
JSS	*Journal of Semitic Studies*
JTS	*Journal of Theological Studies*
Nov Test	*Novum Testamentum*
NTA	E. Hennecke, *New Testament Apocrypha*
NTS	*New Testament Studies*
OUP	Oxford University Press
PTR	*Princeton Theological Review*
RSR	*Recherches de Science Religieuse*
SB	Strack–Billerbeck, *Kommentar*
SBL	Society for Biblical Literature
TDNT	G. Kittel, *Theological Dictionary of the New Testament*
Vig Christ	*Vigiliae Christianae*
ZAW	*Zeitschrift für die alttestamentliche Wissenschaft*
ZNW	*Zeitschrift für die neutestamentliche Wissenschaft*

INTRODUCTION

If one were to arrange New Testament passages into a league table according to the frequency of appearance of scholarly work on them the hymns of Luke's infancy narratives would not appear at the head of the table. Passages like the Lord's prayer, the prologue of John, or the Christ hymn of Philippians 2 would probably occupy the top few places. The hymns of Luke 1–2 would, however, hardly be in danger of relegation to the lower divisions where ignored texts lie in academic darkness; a glance at the bibliography of, for example, Raymond Brown's massive study of the New Testament Birth stories, *The Birth of the Messiah*,[1] would relieve one of any such fear. So massive and magisterial is Brown's work that one scholar, on hearing the subject of my research, said to me, 'The infancy narratives? Hasn't Raymond Brown said everything there is to say?' Why then turn again to the hymns of Luke's infancy narratives?

There are, of course, many reasons for doing so, the first and simplest of which is the beauty of these poems. That the Magnificat, the Benedictus, and the Nunc Dimittis appear regularly in the offices of many Christian traditions, although not my own, bears witness to this. In their simplicity and their dignity and in the resonance of their cadences these hymns can hardly be matched. Secondly, the poems possess their own characteristic insight into the way God deals with his people. The manner in which the Magnificat is used in liberation theology and the consequent understanding of it in large portions of the Latin American church shows that this hymn in particular can still speak powerfully to the poor who hope to be filled with good things.

The words are familiar ones to us and powerful ones to those who share the powerlessness out of which the hymns were apparently written, but they are nevertheless strange for in them we hear the lingering echo of something that has passed away, of something we are not. Those who live by faith in Jesus Christ claim to be sons and daughters of faithful Abraham. By participation in the shoot from the stump of Jesse Christians are ingrafted into Abraham's family tree. But those who first sang these hymns were apparently sons and daughters of Abraham after the flesh; they called him 'father' (Lk. 1.55, 73) and they praised the God of Israel (Lk. 1.68; 2.32). Even if, as I shall argue, they, like the modern church, praised God for the coming of Jesus the Messiah, there is a huge difference between them and present-day Christians. Now there is a gap between Israel and the church, a gap forced open and spread by misunderstanding, polemic, and often by the most abominable of acts. One is a child of Abraham either by membership in Israel or by membership in the church and the one who seeks to pass from one status to the other must leave behind much of what he formerly was. In the hymns of Luke 1-2, however, we may hear the words of a community which saw in the coming of Jesus the fulfilment of God's purposes with Israel and of his promises to their ancestors. They did not leave behind their former lives when they became followers of Jesus; their past was fulfilled. In the hymns of Luke 1-2 we may hear the praise of an early Jewish-Christian community. This is the third reason for examining the hymns.

There remains a further question: 'Why did Luke include these hymns?' One can hardly deny that the hymns stand in a striking position in Luke–Acts—at the very head of the two-volume work. Do they anticipate themes which reappear later in Luke's works or is their position, and perhaps even their presence, fortuitous? To consider the purpose of the inclusion of the hymns in Luke–Acts is a fourth reason for studying them.

It is at this point that I may be able to begin to justify my choice of subject. There have been, as I have implied, many studies of the Lucan nativity hymns, some of the very highest quality. There has not been, as far as I know, a comprehensive attempt to consider all these questions. Certain studies have dealt with particular questions concerning these hymns, their original language, their community of origin, etc., but none, to the best of my knowledge, has attempted to fit the various answers to these questions into a consistent whole. It is my intention, therefore, to trace as completely as possible the history of the hymns of the infancy narratives from their origins to their final use in Luke–Acts. This, if adequately done, would be a worthwhile contribution to scholarship.

Definition of Terms
The terms used in the title of this work, *The Hymns of Luke's Infancy
Narratives* require definition. It is easy enough to define Luke's
infancy narratives. These are the stories about the events surrounding
the birth and childhood of John the Baptist and Jesus of Nazareth
which may be found in Luke 1.5–2.52.

The word 'hymn' requires more careful definition. The most
succinct definition is probably that of the great form-critic, Hermann
Gunkel. A hymn, he wrote, is 'a song of praise'.[2] One might add for
our present purposes that the praise of a hymn is directed towards
God.[3] The word 'song' in Gunkel's definition implies that the praise
is couched in a lyrical or poetic form. Using this basic definition it is
easy enough to identify the hymns of Luke's infancy narratives. They
are those poems known as the Magnificat (Lk. 1.46-55), the Benedictus
(Lk. 1.68-79), and the Nunc Dimittis (Lk. 2.29-32). Each of these
poems exhibits the parallelism which is so characteristic of Hebrew
poetry and the burden of each is the praise of God. If one uses
Gunkel's definition these poems are hymns.

But when the reader comes to the chapter on the form of the
hymns he will notice that I have rejected Gunkel's identification of
these poems as eschatological hymns, that is, poems which display
the structure of hymns but look forward to a great saving act of
God.[4] A more accurate description of these hymns, I shall argue, is
that of C. Westermann who called them 'declarative psalms of
praise'.[5] Westermann considered the term 'hymn' inadequate or
even misleading, for it cannot describe the simple one-sentence
ejaculation of praise in response to a saving act of God which lies at
the heart of the declarative psalm of praise.[6] Furthermore the word
'hymn' most naturally corresponds not to declarative praise, praise
for what God has done, but to descriptive praise, praise of what God
is, the other great category of praise in Westermann's system.[7] The
word 'hymn', it might seem, ought to disappear from the pages of this
book.

For two reasons it will remain, however. First, when Westermann
used the word 'hymn' he meant 'a fine, cultivated, artistic creation
with harmony and euphony, that is, . . . a literary unit'.[8] To describe,
for example, the Song of the Sea, Exodus 15.21, in this way might be
unjustified; to apply these words to the Magnificat, Benedictus, and
Nunc Dimittis is not. At the heart of those three poems one can
certainly see the one-sentence ejaculation of praise characteristic of

the declarative psalm of praise but those single sentences have grown
into 'fine, cultivated, artistic creations'. The word hymn, therefore, is
not entirely inapplicable. Secondly, the word 'hymn' is far more
convenient that the cumbersome phrase 'declarative psalm of praise'.
The latter would doubtless be the more precise designation of these
poems, but its repeated use would be wearisome.

By the word 'hymn', therefore, I mean those poems in Luke 1–2
which could reasonably be called songs of praise of God. Although I
have adopted Gunkel's simple definition of the word 'hymn' I do not
imply by its use acceptance of Gunkel's classification of the poems.
Furthermore, by defining the word in this manner I exclude from
consideration other passages in Luke 1–2 which have sometimes
been called hymns.[9] Other elements in the infancy stories, the three
angelic pronouncements, to Zechariah (Lk. 1.13ff.), to Mary (Lk.
1.28ff.) and to the shepherds (Lk. 2.10ff.), Elizabeth's greeting to
Mary (Lk. 1.42ff.) and Simeon's prophecy (Lk. 2.34f.), display certain
poetic characteristics. Since these passages do not praise God,
however, they cannot be considered hymns.

The reader will have noticed that another brief piece of poetry in
Luke 1–2 has also been excluded from consideration. This is the
Gloria in excelsis, Luke 2.14. While this too is a short song in praise
of God it differs markedly from the Magnificat, Benedictus and Nunc
Dimittis. Those have grown into extended poems; the Gloria has
remained a brief shout of praise, a 'Siegesruf.[10] The Gloria must be
compared with the 'victory shouts' of Revelation and the many
doxologies that appear in early Christian literature. The Magnificat,
Benedictus and Nunc Dimittis, on the other hand, seem close kin to
OT and intertestamental Jewish psalms. The Gloria in excelsis,
therefore, requires a separate study for which there is simply not
room in this work. Regretfully, it must be laid aside.

In this book, therefore, the expression 'hymns of Luke's infancy
narratives' means, quite simply, the Magnificat, Benedictus, and
Nunc Dimittis. These are 'declarative psalms of praise' or more
simply, 'songs of praise' or, more simply still, 'hymns'. From time to
time the hymns will be called poems, or psalms, or canticles. These
differing expressions are used only for the sake of variety.

There are many fascinating questions which have to do with other
parts of the birth stories which cannot be considered in these pages.
Areas such as source criticism of the narrative sections of Luke 1–2,
the possibility of a baptist document there, questions of historicity,

etc., can be dealt with only when they directly affect the understanding of the hymns themselves.

Like Gaul, this work is divided into three parts. Its three sections correspond to the three nouns in its sub-title: *The Hymns of Luke's Infancy Narratives: their Origin, Meaning and Significance.* The first section, on the origin of the hymns, deals with the various problems that cluster around that question, the possibility of Lucan authorship, the question of language of composition and of community from which they originated. The second section, on the meaning of the hymns, is an exegesis of the texts. The third and final section, on the significance of the hymns, is a brief, concluding essay which concerns itself with the purposes for which Luke used these hymns, that is, the role which the hymns play within Luke–Acts.

The tasks undertaken in the three sections are not entirely separable; one can hardly study the questions involved in the first section, for example, without already having done at least a preliminary exegesis of the texts and without considering the uses to which Luke puts them. Nevertheless, this structure will, I trust, enable the reader to follow, with the minimum of confusion, the history of the hymns from their origin to their present use in Luke–Acts.

It remains only to add that the name 'Luke' is used in this work only as a term of convenience for the composer of the third Gospel and Acts. By using that name I do not intend to commit myself to any particular theory of authorship.

PART ONE

THE ORIGIN OF THE HYMNS

A great deal of careful scholarship has concerned itself with one simple question, 'Where did the hymns of Luke 1-2 come from?' There are three possible answers to this question: 1. that they were composed by the persons to whom they are attributed in the narrative; 2. that Luke composed them himself in order to enrich his narrative; 3. that the hymns came to Luke from some source which may be identified more precisely at a later point. All three have, at one time or another, been advanced.

The first possibility, although widely held among conservative scholars[1], need not detain us long. Let me quote briefly from a scholar whose conservative credentials can hardly be questioned, I.H. Marshall: 'the hymns attributed to some of the principal actors are unlikely to have been spontaneous compositions, but serve, like the speeches in ancient histories, to express the significance of the moment in appropriate language'.[2] To insist that the Magnificat was spoken by Mary, the Benedictus by Zechariah, the Nunc Dimittis by Simeon, in the words we find in our New Testaments may be to misinterpret the purpose for which the hymns appear in the narrative. Furthermore, several objections to the theory of Lucan composition of the hymns, the martial tone of the hymns, the non-specific nature of the praise in them, the evidence of their secondary insertion into the narrative, etc., would equally render it unlikely that these hymns were composed by the individuals to whom they are attributed in the narrative.[3] At this point let us turn to the theory that the hymns were composed by Luke himself.

The Theory of Lucan Composition

The next simplest solution to the problem of the origin of the hymns is the theory that Luke himself composed these hymns. This is not a widely held position but it remains, nevertheless, one which ought to be examined, particularly since the theory has been revived in recent years in Great Britain.

The theory that Luke himself composed the hymns of the infancy narratives is of German rather than British manufacture, however. It was, to the best of my knowledge, first advanced by Harnack in 1900.[4] Harnack's theory appears to have met with little acceptance in his native land;[5] his conclusions were most vigorously disputed by H. Gunkel, ironically, in a Festschrift dedicated to Harnack[6] and it is this latter article which has been widely influential in Germany.

In England, however, the theory sprang into new life. Creed, Sparks, Goulder and Sanderson, Tinsley, Drury and possibly Turner have all held this position.[7] It is through Creed who explicitly credits Harnack with this insight[8] that the theory appears to have taken root in English soil. On the other side of the Atlantic, H.J. Cadbury, the great American expert on Luke, came down rather tentatively in favour of the Lucan composition theory as, more recently, has R.C. Tannehill.[9] As one might expect, these scholars do not use precisely the same arguments to prove their common point. These more detailed arguments will be discussed in the course of the chapter. They share, however, the same general viewpoint, that the hymns are heavily influenced by the LXX and that Luke was a man who loved and knew well his Greek Old Testament.

Although the number of adherents of this position is not large, names like Harnack and Cadbury are weighty ones indeed, so their theory must be examined carefully. I believe, however, that in the end it must be rejected.

Speaking of the problem of discerning sources in Luke–Acts in general Cadbury wrote,[10]

> The third Evangelist's personal style is never so totally wanting as to prove alien origins for a passage, and is never so pervasive as to exclude the possibility that a written source existed, although the source be no longer capable of detection by any residual difference of style.

It is indeed difficult to determine what part of the Gospel and its sequel come from the evangelist himself without the aid of written sources and what parts were, in fact, drawn from such sources. Nevertheless, while it may not be possible to determine the extent to which Luke used sources in general it may well be possible to determine whether or not Luke himself composed the hymns of his infancy narrative.

Luke was without doubt an author of considerable literary dexterity. I shall suggest in this chapter, however, that no evidence shows him to have been the accomplished poet who composed these hymns, weaving numerous Old Testament allusions into theologically and poetically coherent wholes. On the contrary, I shall argue that Luke did not compose the hymns of the infancy narratives but took hymns which already existed and placed them in his narrative, making slight alterations to suit them to their new literary contexts. I shall draw evidence from two general areas, the 'external' and the 'internal'. The 'external' area involves evidence from a consideration of Luke–Acts as a whole. The 'internal' area concerns evidence drawn from a study of the hymns themselves.

There are, however, several sorts of evidence which will be considered in later chapters rather than in this one. First, I shall not consider at this point the question of the original language of the hymns. This question is not the same as the question concerning Lucan authorship. It is quite possible to believe that the hymns were composed in Greek by someone other than Luke.[11] On the other hand, if the existence of Semitic originals for these hymns could be proved, it would be almost conclusive evidence that Luke did not compose them. In a later chapter I shall present evidence to suggest that these psalms were, in fact, translated from one of the Semitic languages, probably Hebrew.[12]

Furthermore, I shall not consider here the form of the hymns. Gunkel inferred from his observation of the fact that the hymns conform to the patterns of late Jewish poetry that they could not have been composed by the Gentile Luke.[13] The form of the hymns will be considered at length in a later chapter.[14] It does appear abundantly clear that Luke's hymns adhere closely to the canons of Jewish poetry. Although form as well as content can be imitated it seems reasonable to suppose that the more closely the poems adhere to Jewish patterns the less likely it is that they are the evangelist's free compositions. Finally, there will be no attempt here to contrast the theology expressed in the hymns with the theology of Luke–Acts as a whole. One presumes that there must be a certain congruence between the two or Luke would never have included the hymns in his Gospel. The extent of this congruence will be discussed in the concluding section of this work. To use the presence or absence of such congruence as a criterion for authorship is a highly dubious procedure, however. Consider the following two deductions from the mention of the Gentiles in the Nunc Dimittis.

> This is the only passage in the canticles that directly concerns the Gentiles, so that conversion of the Gentiles was not a major motif in the Jewish Christian community that composed them. This is another argument against composition by Luke himself.[15]

On the other hand, Drury can speak of the 'glimpse of the revelation to the Gentiles which foreshadows the Acts' among a list of phenomena by which Luke's 'claim to authorship is vindicated'.[16]

Those who argue that Luke was the author of the infancy hymns usually declare that the hymns are centos or mosaics of Septuagintal allusions. Therefore, they argue, they could have been composed by anybody familiar with the LXX. Luke was just such a man, it is said, for he displays an impressive familiarity with his Greek Bible. 'To find a man with a head full of the Septuagint we need look no further than Luke himself.'[17] But this argument, if true, only indicates that Luke might have had the capacity to compose the hymns, not that he actually did compose them himself.[18] To prove the latter point one would need further evidence. Is there evidence other than the mere presence of the hymns in the infancy narratives to show that Luke did compose hymns?

There are many points in the Gospel and Acts at which characters in the narrative praise God or are filled with joy that might reasonably express itself in praise. For example, we have the description of the response of the witnesses to the raising of the son of the widow of Nain: 'Fear seized them all; and they glorified God, saying, "A great prophet has risen among us" and "God has visited his people"' (Lk. 7.16). The latter saying of the people is reminiscent of the first line of the Benedictus in which God is praised as the one who has visited his people, ἐπεσκέψατο in both cases. And yet there is no hymn here. Or could not the woman healed of infirmity have spoken words similar to those of the Magnificat at Luke 13.13? Would not a hymn similar in some ways to the Nunc Dimittis have expressed the joy of the church at Acts 11.18? There the church, on hearing of the gift of the Spirit to Gentiles 'glorified God saying, "Then to the Gentiles also God has granted repentance unto life?"' There are hymns at neither of these points. What we do have are short prosaic accounts of the content of the praise of the people,

accounts which are very different from the developed poetry of the
hymns of the infancy narrative.

There is one passage in the rest of Luke–Acts, however, which
does bear some similarity to one particular point in the poetry of the
birth narrative. Just as Jesus' birth is praised by a heavenly host (Lk.
2.14), so his entry into Jerusalem is praised by an earthly host:

> Blessed be the King
> who comes in the name of the Lord,
> Peace in heaven
> and glory in the highest! (Luke 19.37)

And yet, despite the similarity of the last two lines of this quatrain to
what may well be the fragment of a hymn in the infancy narrative the
main point still stands: the hymns of the infancy narrative are
without parallel in the rest of Luke–Acts.[19] Why is this so if Luke
could, and in fact did, compose hymns?

It is, of course, puzzling that Luke did not continue to quote
hymns even if he did not compose them himself. However, it is easier
to explain the absence of quotations than of compositions by the
evangelist himself. Several explanations might be given: 1. the hymns
may have been part of a connected source or sources which Luke
used in the composition of the infancy narrative; 2. the evangelist
may have known only a few hymns which he considered suitable for
inclusion in the gospel; 3. placing important quotations at the
beginning of the work may have been a characteristic of the
evangelist. The first possibility seems not to be the case. There is
strong evidence that the hymns were secondarily inserted into the
narrative.[20] The second is speculative. Investigating the third
possibility may, however, be helpful at this point.

It is certain that Luke does use quotations from at least one source.
That source is the Old Testament. Significantly these quotations
cluster at the beginning of the gospel. There are brief quotations later
in the book but to find longer, poetic quotations one must look to the
very beginning of the story. In ch. 3 we find a quotation which
describes the role of John the Baptist, a quotation which is significantly
longer than its parallel in Matthew. In the following chapter there is
the famous reading from Isaiah 61 with which the ministry of Jesus is
inaugurated. In Acts the picture is somewhat different. Here there
are many more scriptural quotations than in the gospel, all but one of
which are contained in the sermons or speeches. The quotations are

spread more evenly through the work than is the case in the gospel, perhaps because quotation from scripture was seen to be an integral part of the sermons which are so prominent a part of Acts. Even in this book, however, more of the quotations come relatively early. All but three Old Testament quotations can be found in chs. 1–15. Several very significant Old Testament citations come very early indeed. One thinks particularly of the quotation from Joel in Peter's sermon at Pentecost. An important exception to this general tendency is the quotation of Isaiah 6:9-10 in the final verses of Acts. This quotation seems to have a corresponding but opposite function to some of the earlier citations. The reading at Nazareth and the quotation from Joel at Pentecost introduce and encapsulate the true theological significance of the story narrated by the author. Like the hymns of the infancy narrative they are poetic and of great theological import. They lay bare the true nature of events. This last is also the function of the concluding, summary quotation in Acts. Just as the passage read from Isaiah 61 shows the nature of the gift of the proclamation of Jesus and the quotation from Joel explains the amazing gift of speech to the disciples at Pentecost so the hymns explain the true significance for the people of the coming of Christ. Bultmann once called the whole story of the reading at Nazareth a 'programmatic entrance'.[21] In a sense these hymns are also 'programmatic entrances'.

The hymns thus function in a manner similar to the quotations from the Old Testament. This is not surprising when we consider that Luke must have known what is so obvious to modern commentators: the hymns are a mosaic of Old Testament allusions. They are, in effect, distillations of Old Testament scripture. It is interesting to note that these mosaics of scripture function in a manner similar to material clearly not composed by Luke himself, that is, quotations from the Old Testament.

The hymns of the infancy narrative also function in a manner similar to the psalms included in the narrative of various Old Testament books. As J. Drury wrote:

> A further observation argues for Lucan authorship.
>
> In the Old Testament psalms are by no means confined to the book of that name . . . the books of history, Luke's models and tutors, are punctuated by bursts of song which serve, as in these chapters of his, to make explicit the theology latent in the narrative.[22]

However, this argument by no means indicates that Luke did compose the hymns. It only suggests a motive for the inclusion of psalm-like pieces and says nothing whatever about the origin of such pieces. Ironically, most of the Old Testament songs mentioned by Drury in this connection were not composed by the authors of the various narratives in which the songs are presently found. In fact two, the song of the sea in Exodus 15 and Deborah's song in Judges 5, are widely considered to be, at least in their kernels, among the oldest pieces of literature in the Bible. But all this is almost irrelevant, for we need to know not what modern scholars think of these Old Testament pieces but rather what Luke thought of them. Did he suppose, influenced perhaps by the practice of Greek historians, that the authors of the Old Testament histories had composed these songs? There is no way of knowing for sure. However, it must be said that Luke could hardly have thought this of, for example, the psalms in 2 Samuel 22 or 1 Chronicles 17. With his 'head full of the Septuagint' he must have known that these are both direct quotations from the Psalter! Thus, if anything, the process of comparison of the hymns of the infancy narrative with the songs of the Old Testament history books argues against, rather than for, Luke's authorship of the former.

All these arguements fall short of proof that Luke did not compose the hymns of the birth narrative, although they make it seem probable that he did not do so. As H.J. Cadbury, who rather thought that Luke had indeed composed them himself, wrote of other views of their origin: 'The relative merits of such alternative explanations can be settled, if at all, only by a detailed study of the text'.[23] It is time, therefore, to turn to the evidence of the hymns themselves.

The Internal Evidence

Earlier in this chapter it was suggested that hymns very much like the hymns of the infancy narrative would have been appropriate at various junctures in Luke–Acts. There, the point was that it is somewhat surprising that Luke included no more hymns if he were in the habit of composing them. The other side of that observation is that the hymns are of a rather general character, containing very little that ties them to their present literary contexts. The hymns praise God in a non-specific, general manner. If they were removed from their present settings and a few words excised from each we should hardly suppose that they have anything to do with the birth of a child. Indeed the tone of the Magnificat and the Benedictus is so martial that it has been seriously suggested that both are hymns of victory from the Maccabaean wars![24] Furthermore, with respect to the Magnificat Brown wrote: 'The fact that there could be the debate . . . as to whether Mary or Elizabeth spoke the Magnificat is eloquent proof of the non-specific nature of the canticle'.[25] One would have expected that had Luke composed these hymns himself they would have been more obviously à propos.

Moreover, if the Lucan hymns were removed from their present positions the narrative would flow just as smoothly as at present. In fact, the story would move more smoothly without the Magnificat. As the text stands it is rather surprising that v. 56 reads, 'And *Mary* remained with *her*', for it is Mary who has just been speaking, not Elizabeth. Many scholars have argued that the Magnificat should be attributed to Elizabeth rather than Mary, partly because of this very problem. However, the vast majority of witnesses support the reading 'Mary' in v. 46, and there are strong theological grounds for supposing that Luke did, in fact, intend to attribute the hymn to Mary.[26] If this is so there is reason to suspect that the Magnificat was not an original part of the narrative. The least one can say is that the intelligibility of the narrative would not suffer from the absence of either hymn. The looseness of connection with the surrounding narrative suggests the possibility that the hymns were secondarily inserted into the narrative. Only a few words attach either the Magnificat or the Benedictus to the infancy narrative. In the Magnificat v. 48 is the connecting verse. Here the speaker calls herself 'handmaiden' just as Mary does in 1.38. In v. 45 Elizabeth blesses Mary, and in the hymn the apparent response to that blessing is 'henceforth all generations will call me blessed'. It appears, therefore, that this verse (v. 48) may well have been inserted by Luke in order to adapt the hymn to its present use. If it can be proved that this verse is, in fact, a Lucan insertion it would be very strong evidence that he did not compose the hymn as a whole, at least for the purpose of inclusion in the infancy narrative, and there is no evidence that would lead one to suppose that he wrote hymns for any other purpose. The great Adolf von Harnack used an ingenious method of analysis to attempt to prove that Luke *did* compose the Magnificat.[27] Here, this same method will be used to attempt to prove that v. 48 is a Lucan insertion and, therefore, that Luke did *not* compose the hymn.

Harnack based his belief that Luke was the composer of the hymn on a careful comparison of the Magnificat with some of its apparent sources of Septuagintal allusions. He subtracted from the hymn all words or expressions present in the Septuagintal sources and found that fourteen expressions remained. Some of these were typical Lucanisms, he believed. In short, what is not from the Septuagint is Lucan. Therefore, he reasoned, 'der Verfasser des Lucas-Evangeliums hat auch das Magnificat verfasst'.[28]

At this point we come face to face with the problem of just what is 'Lucan' or a 'Lucanism'. The problem is made more difficult here because, assuming for the moment that the hymns were composed in Greek, most of the vocabulary of the hymns is drawn from the Septuagint and it is Luke of all the synoptic evangelists whose language is most Septuagintal.[29] Harnack's method of subtraction clears away much of the material to be considered, but how shall we judge whether or not what remains is Lucan?

There are those who suggest that in fact nothing remains when the Septuagintal material is subtracted. Spitta[30] and Machen[31] attempted to show that all the vocabulary of the Magnificat and the Benedictus is drawn from the Septuagint. They argued that Harnack's study is flawed in one vital respect: it does not carry the process of subtraction far enough.[32] 'Subtract the Septuagint words and phrases and really nothing remains to indicate Lucan authorship.'[33] It is certainly true that the list of LXX passages which Harnack used as the basis for his method of subtraction was arbitrarily limited, as we shall see when we turn to a more detailed study of the fourteen expressions in question. On the other hand, one cannot simply dismiss a word or phrase as possible evidence for Lucan authorship merely because it occurs at some point in the Septuagint. (This is, in essence, what Spitta and Machen do.) As Hawkins's study shows, most of Luke's vocabulary comes from the Septuagint. One might say that Septuagintal language is characteristic of Luke. I suggest that we may consider as possible evidence of Luke's hand those words and phrases which, although they may occur at some point in the Septuagint, do not appear in those verses which seem to supply direct inspiration for the thought and vocabulary of the hymns in question.

But is what remains after the process of subtraction 'Lucan'? One cannot determine this simply by consulting Hawkins's list of characteristic words and phrases. This would be a misleading process, for these lists were prepared by a process of comparison with the other synoptic evangelists. Hawkins takes as 'characteristic' the words and phrases which occur at least four times in this Gospel, and which either (a) are not found at all in Matthew and Mark, or (b) are found in Luke at least twice as often as in Matthew and Mark together'.[34] One finds in his lists the preposition ἐνώπιον, for example, which appears in the Benedictus and which Harnack points to as a Lucanism. Nevertheless, the use of this word is not peculiar to Luke. The word appears frequently in the Septuagint 'especially in Samuel–Kings and the Psalms',[35] the very books from which most of the allusions of Luke's hymns are drawn, and furthermore appears no less than thirty-three times in Revelation. Thus the presence of the word in the Benedictus proves no more than that it is highly unlikely that the hymn was composed by Matthew or Mark. This is hardly a useful conclusion!

One would be on safer ground considering only those words and phrases as characteristically Lucan 'which appear at least four times in the gospel' and not at all or at least infrequently in the Septuagint and the rest of the New Testament. Thanks to the studies of Spitta and Machen one can safely say that there are no such characteristic words or phrases in the hymn. However, it is doubtful that one should expect many such words or phrases in hymns which, if composed by Luke, were deliberate imitations of Old Testament forms.

It might be better to relax the standards slightly and consider as characteristically Lucan those words or phrases which occur with some regularity in Luke–Acts and only rarely elsewhere in the New Testament which is, after all, a work of some literary variety. I shall adopt this as my criterion of judgment. Let us now turn to the fourteen 'left-overs' which remain after Harnack's method of subtraction has been applied.

1. μεγαλύνω (v. 46) appears three times in Acts and once elsewhere in Luke, but only once in the other gospels (Mt. 23.58), and there in a different sense, and twice in Paul. However, this is hardly enough evidence to call this word a Lucanism. Furthermore, the verb does appear in the LXX, in Ps. 69.21, for example, in a situation of praise like this one and three times in parallel with ἀγαλλιάω (Ps. 35.27; 40.16; 70.4).

2. ἀγαλλιᾶν and ἀγαλλιάσις (v. 47). A form of the verb used here can be found in the passages which are more likely sources for this verse than Hannah's song, Ps. 34.9 and Hab. 3.18.

3. σωτήρ used of God. This also appears in Hab. 3.18 which reads: ἐγὼ δὲ ἐν τῷ κυρίῳ ἀγαλλιάσομαι χαρήσομαι ἐπὶ τῷ θεῷ τῷ σωτῆρί μου.

4. ἐπιβλέπειν ἐπί (v. 48). This construction appears only at Lk. 9.38 and Jas 2.3. This is not a frequent enough usage to be significant by itself. Furthermore it appears in 1 Sam. 1.11 to which this verse alludes.

5. ἰδοὺ γάρ (v. 48). This expression appears six times in Luke–Acts and once elsewhere in the NT. It is found at 1.44 and 2.10 in the infancy narrative.

6. ἀπὸ τοῦ νῦν (v. 48). Similarly, this phrase occurs six times in Luke–Acts and once elsewhere. 'In most of the Lucan instances there is a reference to the salvific moment (12.52; 22.18; 22.69; Acts 18.6).'[36]

7. γενεαί (v. 48). Harnack thought this word worthy of no particular observation. The use of this word is neither evidence for or against the theory of Lucan composition.

8. μεγαλεία or μεγάλα (v.49). μεγαλεία is found in the NT only at Acts 2.11, as Harnack notes. However, μεγάλα which seems the preferable reading is in Deut. 10.20 of which this verse seems to be an echo.

9. δυνατός (v. 49) used substantively is found only here in the NT. Harnack called attention to the use of the word at Lk. 24.19 where Jesus is described as δυνατὸς ἐν ἔργῳ καὶ λόγῳ. However, the word appears at Zeph. 3.17, a passage of which this verse is somewhat reminiscent.

10. κράτος (v. 51). Since this word appears only here and at Acts 19.20 it can hardly be considered a Lucanism.

11. διανοίᾳ καρδίας (v. 51). Harnack considered this expression not worthy of any particular observation. It certainly cannot be called a Lucanism.

12. καθεῖλεν (v. 52). This word appears, as Harnack notes, five times in Luke–Acts but only three times in the rest of NT. However, the word is found in the very similar Ecclus 10.14 θρόνους ἀρχόντων καθεῖλεν ὁ κύριος.

13. ἐξαπέστειλεν κένους (v. 53). The verb is used ten times in Luke but only once elsewhere in the NT. The whole expression appears only twice, at Lk. 20.10, 11.[37] However, the chief word in question appears in a Septuagintal passage which is echoed by the Magnificat, Job 12.19: ἐξαποστέλλων ἱερεῖς αἰχμαλώτους, δυνάστας δὲ γῆς κατέστρεψεν.

14. λαλεῖν πρός (v. 55). This expression occurs fifteen times in Luke–Acts but not in the other gospels. At first sight this does look like a Lucanism but a glance at a chart prepared by Machen which compares the use of πρός with accusative and, on the other hand, the dative after verbs of saying is more frequent in Luke–Acts than in the other NT books, with the possible exception of Hebrews, even in Luke–Acts verbs of saying are more often than not completed by the dative.[38] The same charts demonstrate that the use of πρός with the accusative after verbs of saying is quite common in the LXX. If the use of such an expression is considered a Lucanism one must still reckon with the possibility that Luke altered very slightly the text in the process of transmission. Such an alteration may well have been unintentional. At any rate, this phrase, isolated as it is after a reconsideration of the other instances advanced by Harnack as evidence of Luke's hand, can hardly be considered compelling evidence that Luke composed the whole hymn.

An application of Harnack's own method shows that very little remains once the language drawn from the Septuagint is removed from the hymn. There is, however, a cluster of three expressions, numbers 5 through 7 of the analysis on the preceding pages, which all occur in one verse, v. 48. One of these expressions would, by itself, be of little significance, but considered together the three as a group strongly suggest the possibility that Luke composed this verse. Likewise, the concentration of evidence of Luke's hand in this verse and the absence of such evidence from the rest of the hymn suggests that this verse is the ony part of the hymn that Luke did compose.

I wrote earlier that v. 48 serves to connect the hymn to the surrounding narrative. The scriptural allusions in this verse are particularly appropriate for that task. At other points in the hymn where there are apparent allusions to Hannah's hymn the wording is actually closer to other Old Testament passages.[39] The first half of v. 48 does point to Hannah, however, for it echoes her prayer in 1 Samuel 1.11: ἐὰν ἐπιβλέπων ἐπιβλέψῃς ἐπὶ τὴν ταπείνωσιν τῆς δούλης σου. Hannah is quite possibly the ideal mother of the Old Testament and is therefore a fit model for Mary.[40] There are also echoes of another Old Testament mother, Leah. Leah is also an appropriate model for Mary for she is the mother of Judah. It is from Judah, the tribe, that the Messiah is to come. In Genesis 30.13 Leah rejoices: μακαρία ἐγὼ ὅτι μακαρίζουσίν με πᾶσαι αἱ γυναῖκες. The resemblances to Luke 1.48 are clear.

As we have seen, the praise of God in the Magnificat is general rather than specific in its content, making very little reference to its narrative context. If the hymn is removed from its present position the narrative reads slightly more smoothly than is presently the case. Only one verse serves to connect the hymn to the surrounding narrative. In that verse and in that verse alone are several Lucanisms. What is the most likely explanation for all this? The most plausible answer seems to be that Luke formed his own addition to a hymn which already existed.[41] His was not a creation 'ex nihilo', however. His raw material was drawn from the words of two Old Testament mothers, both of whom were particularly suitable as models for Mary. Upon this insertion he left several characteristic marks. In short, Luke did not compose the hymn as a whole.

When we turn to the Benedictus we see a picture that is at once simpler and more complicated. The complexity stems from the fact that 'here the material from the Greek Bible has been more severely edited than in the case of the Magnificat'.[42] It is, therefore, more difficult to disentangle by a simple process of subtraction any elements which may have been inserted by Luke.

On the other hand, the Benedictus does not display the same internal consistency and regularity that the Magnificat does. There is an obvious and abrupt change in the character of the song at the end of v. 75. Up to this point the finite verbs are aorist, after it, future. Before the break the Benedictus is a hymn, very similar in character to the Magnificat. In vv. 76ff. it becomes a prophetic oracle or perhaps a genthliakon, a birthday hymn. In its first section the hymn speaks of God in the third person singular. In its final section it addresses the infant John in the second person singular.

As was the case with the Magnificat this song could be omitted without disrupting the flow of the narrative. One could simply read v. 80 after v. 66. Indeed, the placement of the hymn here is slightly odd. There appear in v. 64 the words καὶ ἐλάλει εὐλόγων τὸν θεόν but no hymn follows. In v. 67 a completely different introduction appears which serves to lead on the Benedictus. In the narrative as it stands there are, therefore, two introductions but only one hymn.[43] Furthermore the hymnic section of the Benedictus consists of general non-specific praise of God. Only vv. 76ff. connect the hymn as a whole to its present literary setting. On the surface there seems to be a strong case for considering vv. 68-75 the original hymn and vv. 76ff. a separate composition. Many scholars believe that this is, in fact, the case.[44]

There are various other estimates of the extent of the additions to the original hymn. All of these are incompatible with the view that Luke composed the Benedictus as it stands. These theories will be treated in greater detail in the exegesis of the Benedictus. I shall discuss here only that theory which I find most convincing, the analysis advanced by P. Benoit and subsequently by R. Brown.[45] In their opinion vv. 76 and 77 are later additions to the original hymn inserted by Luke to connect the Benedictus to the narrative. One of the more appealing aspects of this solution is that it pictures Luke adapting this hymn in a manner very similar to the way I have suggested he adapted the Magnificat.

The elements from which Luke constructed this insertion can be easily identified. In the first part of v. 76 the infant John is called 'prophet of the Most High' (1.32). The second part of this verse is made up of echoes of two Old Testament passages which, as was the case with the allusions in v. 48 of the Magnificat, point clearly to the significance of the person in question. The wording of this verse reminds us of the two famous passages which the church had already applied to John the Baptist, Isaiah 40.3 and Malachi 3.1. From John's birth it is recognized that he is to be:

A voice crying in the wilderness,
'Prepare the way of the Lord'.

This prophecy at John's birth gives a true understanding of his vocation.

Verse 77 is not reminiscent of any Old Testament passage in particular, but it does remind us of the description of John 'preaching a baptism of repentance for the forgiveness of sins' (Lk. 3.3). The phrase ἄφεσις ἁμαρτιῶν is quite characteristic of Luke as eight of eleven New Testament occurrences of the phrase are in his writings. As even Machen admitted: 'The argument for Lucan authorship is stronger here than in the cases which have been discussed before'.[46] Furthermore, this is the one expression in the hymns which does not appear in the Septuagint (although Machen quotes a similar expression in the Psalms of Solomon). The use of the word salvation, σωτηρία, is not, by itself, evidence for Lucan composition either here or earlier in the hymn.

This kind of direct evidence of Luke's hand ceases at the conclusion of v. 77. A glance at Brown's chart of parallels to the Benedictus shows that once again the language of the hymn is reminiscent of various Old Testament and extra-canonical works.[47] Furthermore, the people of Israel are again referred to in the first person plural as in vv. 68-75. Thus we read:

> through the tender mercy of *our* God . . .
> when the day shall dawn upon *us* . . .
> to guide *our* feet into the way of peace.

In other words, there is a considerable change in character in the middle of the Benedictus. In vv. 68-75, 78-79 there is general, non-specific praise of God. The verbs are aorist[48] and the people of Israel are referred to in the first person plural. Verses 76-77 alone connect the poem to the narrative. These verses are composed of material drawn from the common Christian tradition about John, rather than directly from the Old Testament, and in them one apparent Lucanism may be recognized. The most plausible explanation of all this appears to be that Luke followed the same procedure here as he did with respect to the Magnificat. That is, he adapted a hymn which already existed, by creating out of appropriate literary references an insertion which fitted the hymn as a whole to its present literary setting.

If vv. 76 and 77 are indeed an addition by Luke the phrase διὰ σπλάγχνα . . . would have followed immediately after v. 75 in the original hymn. Thus, all the benefits spoken of in the preceding verses are accomplished 'through the tender mercy of God'. This is certainly an intelligible progression of thought. The connection of v. 78 to v. 75 may be somewhat awkward syntactically but no more so than the present connection to v. 77. The internal links of the hymn are generally rather loose. If this reconstruction is correct the verb in v. 78 probably was originally an aorist ἐπεσκέψατο, rather than a future. There is also considerable textual support for reading an aorist here.

When one removes the possible Lucan insertions there is very little left which might indicate that Luke did compose the Benedictus. Harnack listed several instances of what he considers to be evidence of Luke's hand.[49] Perhaps only three such instances need be mentioned here. The first, the use of σωτηρία in vv. 69 and 71 can hardly be considered very strong evidence since the cognate verb appears in Psalm 105.10 which supplies most of the vocabulary for v. 71. With the interconnected nature of the thought of the hymn it is not surprising to see σωτηρία in another verse as well. The expression ποιῆσαι ἔλεος μετά has a rather close parallel in Luke 10.37. Finally, one ought to mention the use of the preposition ἐνώπιον which Harnack considered Lucan but which, as was argued earlier, need not be considered to be so. Perhaps only the second expression, ποιῆσαι ἔλεος μετά could actually be considered possible evidence of Luke's hand. However, this expression may well be the literal translation of the Hebrew expression עשה חסר עם[50].

Harnack also argued that the Benedictus only masquerades as a Semitic hymn. In fact, vv. 68-75 'present the form of a single, complicated, correctly constructed Greek period . . . the hands are Esau's hands but the voice is the voice of Jacob'.[51] Even if this is true it proves no more than that the hymn was composed in Greek perhaps by a reasonably skilled writer. In fact, as Machen points out, this sentence is quite different from Luke 1.1-4 which certainly is 'a single, complicated, correctly constructed Greek period'.[52] Unlike that sentence the Benedictus is a loosely connected series of phrases which could be broken off at almost any point and still make good sense. One suspects that Harnack would never have advanced this arguement if he had known of the Qumran writings. In the so-called 'Hymn of the Return' (1QM XIV. 4ff.) we find a Hebrew poem with a structure identical to that of the Benedictus even down to the series of infinitives.[53] The voice of the Benedictus is indeed the voice of Jacob, that is to say, the voice of Israel not Hellas.

If v. 48 is removed from the Magnificat and vv. 76-77 from the Benedictus, the two hymns can be seen to share a simple structure. Each begins with an introductory word of praise which is followed by a single clause introduced by ὅτι which expresses the motive for praise. This, in turn, is followed by a series of statements concerning God's gracious acts, statements which serve to amplify the motive clause.

	Magnificat	*Benedictus*
Introductory praise	46-47	68a
Motive clause	49a	68b
Amplifying statements	49b-55	69-75, 78-79

This similarity in structure seems appropriate in hymns which are so similar in other respects.[54] It may be slight confirmatory evidence for the positions affirmed earlier in the chapter.

It seems reasonable to suppose, considering the evidence, that neither the Magnificat nor the Benedictus was composed by Luke. They appear to have been inserted by Luke into their present

narrative position in order to enrich the story. With the Nunc
Dimittis the picture is somewhat different. This hymn fits smoothly
into its present context (no one would ever call this a Maccabean war
song) and no part of the hymn can be considered an addition; the
structure of three distichs indicates that the hymn is a coherent
literary whole. For these reasons A. George argued that, although
Luke did not compose the other hymns, he did compose this one in
order to produce a hymn for Jesus' birth parallel to the Benedictus.[55]

This seems unlikely, however. The Nunc Dimittis, like the other
two hymns, is a mosaic of allusions to a number of Old Testament
passages.[56] That the allusions in this hymn are mainly to Deutero-
Isaiah rather than to the Psalms was considered by George to be a
sign that Luke composed the hymn.[57] But that the poem refers
exclusively to Deutero-Isaiah is hardly evidence that it was composed
by an author whose interest in the LXX was by no means confined to
that book. Luke's head was full of more than Deutero-Isaiah alone.
More important must be the fact that even Harnack could find no
Lucanisms in this hymn. Jeremias put it quite bluntly, the Nunc
Dimittis is 'fast ganz frei von Lukanismen'.[58] George claimed that
there were Lucanisms in the Nunc Dimittis but his definition of a
Lucanism was rather easy. For example, σωτήριον, which appears
only here, in the Old Testament citation in Luke 3.6 and in Acts
28.28, is called a Lucanism.[59] Moreover, the hymn is structurally
very similar to the other hymns of Luke 1–2.[60] Finally, all the
general objections to the Lucan composition theory apply with even
more force once it is decided that Luke did not compose the
Magnificat and Benedictus. It seems best to suppose that this hymn
too was not composed by Luke himself.

If Luke did not compose these hymns himself, two important
questions immediately arise. In what language were they composed
and in what circles did they originate? To the first of these questions
we now turn.

THE ORIGINAL LANGUAGE OF THE HYMNS

I. *A Survey of Scholarly Opinion*

'An orgy of Hebraic Greek.' So W.L. Knox described the first two chapters of Luke's Gospel.[1] Almost all scholars would agree that the Greek of Luke 1-2 differs considerably from the language of the rest of Luke–Acts but there is no such agreement as to the explanation of this phenomenon, this Hebraic 'orgy'. Some scholars argue forcefully that the Hebraic Greek of these chapters results from the translation of a Semitic source or sources. Others argue, equally forcefully, that Luke is here writing 'Bibilical Greek', imitating the LXX, the sacred book of early Christianity. The difficulty of the problem can be more clearly appreciated when one remembers that the LXX itself is 'translation Greek'. Those who hold that the linguistic character of the first two chapters of Luke is the result of deliberate imitation of the LXX are saying, therefore, that these chapters are 'imitation translation Greek'. Translation Greek or imitation translation Greek? This is the choice that faces those who investigate the literary origins of Luke 1-2.

Furthermore, if the hymns were originally independent of the narrative of Luke 1-2 a conclusion with respect to one need not, in itself, lead to the same conclusion with respect to the other. In these chapters we could have Greek narrative and Hebrew hymns, or Hebrew narrative and Greek hymns. Or both hymns and narrative could have been composed in the same language. One cannot, therefore, assume that the original language of the hymns was the same as the narrative. One cannot even assume, it should be added, that all the hymns must have been composed in the same language,[2] although the general probability that all come from the same source seems rather strong. Finally, the narrative itself may not be of one provenance[3] so that proof, for example, that Luke 1 is translation Greek would not constitute proof that ch. 2 is also such.

There is only one statement which can be made with considerable certainty; the hand of 'Luke' can be seen in these two chapters. The first two chapters of Luke were not simply appended to the Gospel by an unknown redactor. Rather, the author of Luke–Acts had some hand, whether as composer, translator, or redactor, in the formation of the infancy narratives of his Gospel. This can be demonstrated by vocabulary, syntax and characteristic themes.[4] The first two chapters of the Gospel may indeed be 'an orgy of Hebraic Greek' but they are also characteristically Lucan.

René Laurentin outlined four different sorts of solutions to the problem of the original language of these chapters.[5] These are: 1. the Septuagintal pastiche, 2. the use of a Greek source, 3. translation from Aramaic, 4. translation from Hebrew. Of these, only the first and the last are widely held today. As Laurentin has shown, option 2, the use of a Greek source tends to resolve itself into one of the other options in order to explain the Hebraic nature of the text.[6] That these chapters were translated from an Aramaic source was formerly a widely held opinion.[7] Laurentin suggested that this former popularity was due to the assumption that Hebrew was a dead language in the first century AD. Those who wished to attribute the peculiar linguistic character of Luke 1–2 to the use of a Semitic source were therefore compelled to suppose that this source was an Aramaic one.[8] That Hebrew was not, in fact, a dead language at that period has been proved by the discoveries at Qumran and Murabba'at.[9] Certainly, when one reads statements in the older commentators such as, 'frequent Hebraisms indicate that a great deal of Luke's material was originally in Aramaic',[10] one could be easily persuaded that Laurentin was quite correct in his explanation of the former popularity of this position. The abandonment of this theory is due to the fact that it is now widely agreed that the Semitisms of Luke 1–2 are Hebraic rather than Aramaic.[11]

There are, then, two widely held explanations of the Semitic character of Luke 1–2; that it represents the translation of a Hebrew source, and secondly, that it is a pastiche of Septuagintalisms, the result of a deliberate imitation of the style and vocabulary of the LXX. Luke himself, it is claimed, is the author of this pastiche.

The latter theory goes back to Gustaf Dalman's important work, *Die Worte Jesu*.[12] While not absolutely denying the possibility of a

Hebrew original, he wrote:

> It might even be maintained that the strongly marked Hebrew style of those chapters (Luke 1–2), is on the whole due not to the use of any primary source, but to Luke himself. For here, as in the beginning of Acts, in keeping with the marvellous contents of the narrative, Luke has written with greater consistency than usual in biblical style, intending so to do and, further, affected by the 'liturgic frame of mind'.[13]

The various Hebraisms of these chapters Dalman ascribed to the influence of the LXX. He even created an epigram-like summary: 'the more numerous the Hebraisms in any passage the greater the interference of Hellenistic redactors'.[14] This epigram would be correct if the spoken and written language of the people was universally Aramaic and if that Aramaic was relatively free of Hebraisms, as Dalman claimed.[15] Under those circumstances the presence of Hebraisms in a Greek document would indeed probably constitute proof that the text did not derive from an Aramaic original but rather had been influenced by another Greek text containing frequent Hebraisms, i.e. the LXX. The premise is not, however, correct. At the very least, 'pockets of Palestinian Jews also used Hebrew, even though its use was not widespread',[16] and there was considerable literature in that language as the Qumran discoveries prove.

The epigram cannot now be considered correct, for the presence of Hebraisms can be no argument that a text is not translated from Hebrew. There are, after all, a considerable number of Hebraisms in the LXX. One can hardly credit these to the interference of Hellenistic redactors! Certainly the epigram contradicts Dalman's earlier reasoning with respect to Luke: 'If Luke had worked in dependence upon a Hebrew original, then such idioms [Hebraisms] would have occurred much more frequently than they do'.[17] Furthermore, Dalman does not reason in accord with his own epigram when he discusses 1 Maccabees: 'There can be no doubt that the First Book of Maccabees goes back to a Hebrew original . . . Its phraseology is that of historical narrative in the Bible, which the author has imitated of set purpose.'[18] 1 Maccabees, it seems, is not to be explained as a pastiche of Septuagintalisms. In short, Dalman's arguments greatly diminish the possibility of an Aramaic source but do not do so with respect to a Hebrew source, a possibility the likelihood of which seems much greater in light of the many discoveries made between Dalman's day and our own.

Dalman did present one very ingenious argument against a Semitic original for these chapters. For the 'rising light' to be able to 'visit' the people (Lk. 1.78), he must be a person, Dalman reasoned. This means that the rising light, ἀνατολή, is likely the messianic figure of the LXX of Jeremiah 23.5, Zechariah 3.8, and 6.12, where the 'sprout' or 'branch' is translated by ἀνατολή.

> For Luke, therefore, ἀνατολή ἐξ ὕψους is simply God's Messiah, משיחא דיי with which the Targum renders צמח, Is. 4.3. As the Hebrew צמח excludes the allusion to light which follows in v. 79, it is clear that in Luke chap. 1 an original in Greek lies before us.[19]

The statement, 'in *Luke chap. 1* an original in Greek lies before us', goes beyond the evidence. Even if Dalman's argument with respect to the 'rising light' is correct the most that can be said is that the latter half of the Benedictus was originally composed in Greek. There are many scholars, most notably Gunkel and Winter, who hold that vv. 76-79 were a later addition to the hymn.[20] However, not only the application but also the force of the argument has been challenged. P. Winter denied that ἀνατολή referred to the Messiah; rather, as the subject of the verb ἐπισκέψεται, it must refer to God,[21] he argued, thus removing any allusion to צמח at all. Not content with that argument he followed G. Box[22] in suggesting the idea of light was already present in the Hebrew צמח. There is a certain amount of evidence to support this latter contention. First, the Syriac cognates of צמח are used of light, splendour, and related ideas.[23] Secondly, the LXX gives a somewhat surprising translation of Isaiah 4.2. There, the words 'the branch, צמח, shall be' are translated as, ἐπιλάμψει ὁ θεός, showing that these radicals were already associated with the idea of light.[24] Furthermore, Box found instances in the Midrashim in which the cognate verb צמח occurs with the meaning 'shine' or 'grow bright'.[25]

Dalman himself pointed out that the targum to Isaiah 4.2 identified צמח as the Messiah, משיחא דיי,[26] and it is certain that the Messiah was connected with light. The star which rises (ἀνατέλλω) from Jacob was interpreted messianically at Qumran (CD 7.18; 1QM 11.6; 4QTest 12), and the Testaments of the Twelve Patriarchs (T. Levi 18.3; T. Judah 24.1) and by Justin Martyr (*Apol.* 1.32).[27] It may be, therefore, that ἀνατολή could be explained as a reference to the Messiah without recourse to the LXX translation of צמח. Whether or

not that is the case a combination of the Messianic images can be
found in Revelation 22.16:

> 'I am the root and offspring of David, the bright morning star'.

It appears not unlikely that the idea of light may have already been
associated with the word צמח in Hebrew both from its own range of
meanings and from its use as an appellation for the Messiah. If this is
so Dalman's argument may be mistaken.

The most significant proponent of the Septuagintal pastiche
theory was Adolf von Harnack. His work is particularly important
for our purposes for two reasons. First, he was certain that the hymns
in particular were free compositions in Greek by Luke. Secondly, he
advanced positive arguments to prove that such was the case. Most of
the arguments of the proponents of the Septuagintal pastiche theory
are essentially negative. They content themselves with countering
the arguments of the Hebrew source theorists by explaining any
phenomena that appear particularly Hebraic by reference to the LXX.
Harnack did not confine himself to this procedure. His method was
the ingenious one discussed in the previous chapter, the 'subtraction'
method.[28]

For the remainder of the infancy narratives Harnack contented
himself with pointing out 'Lucanisms'.[29] However, since those who
hold that a Hebrew source, or sources, lies behind these chapters
generally credit Luke with some hand in the final shape of the
narrative, the presence of Lucanisms does not serve to diminish the
possibility of a Hebrew source. Similarly, it may be added, the mere
piling up of Hebraisms does not serve to diminish the possibility of
deliberate imitation of the LXX.[30]

An important English discussion of the subject was the treatment
of Luke's Semitisms in J.H. Moulton's *A Grammar of New Testament
Greek*.[31] That treatment shows the influence of Dalman and Harnack
at several points, so it is no surprise to read that Moulton considered
Luke capable of 'a very limited imitation of the LXX idiom, as
specially appropriate while the story moves in the Jewish world'.[32]
One presumes that Moulton would include the setting of Luke 1–2 in
that Jewish world. He quotes at considerable length both Harnack
and C.C. Torrey, the Semitist who advocated the theory that great
stretches of the New Testament are translation Greek.[33] It is clear
that Moulton sides with Harnack for he takes issue with Torrey's
assertion that Luke 1.51 cannot be explained by reference to LXX

parallels. 'The Hebraic phraseology is beyond question, but there is nothing that lies beyond the range of composition by one who was steeped in the diction of the Greek version of the Psalter.'[34] The appeal to the LXX for usages which could have served as models for Luke has become the chief, indeed almost the only, argument advanced by those who hold the Septuagintal pastiche theory. Most later arguments have, like Moulton's, been essentially defensive, responding to points made by the Hebrew source theorists.

As we have seen, later English-speaking scholars such as Creed, Sparks, Turner, Goulder, and Sanderson also believed that these chapters were composed in an imitation of Biblical style, but added little that was new to the discussion.[35] On the other side of the Atlantic the leading American Lucan scholar, H.J. Cadbury, also judged, although somewhat tentatively, that the nativity hymns were composed by Luke after Septuagintal models.[36]

An exception to the rule that proponents of the Septuagintal pastiche theory are content with negative arguments can be found in the recent, spectacularly audacious, work of Michael Goulder, *The Evangelist's Calendar*.[37] This book attempts to explain the development of the Gospel of Luke and much of the rest of Scripture by means of a lectionary cycle theory. Thus, the Gospel of Luke is the result of an ordered series of midrashic homilies on the Old Testament lectionary cycle of Luke's church. He appears to believe that the evidence particularly favours his theory with respect to the first few chapters of Luke.[38] Therefore, no Semitic sources are to be expected for any part of Luke; his only sources are Matthew, Mark, and the Greek Bible. There is no space here for a detailed discussion of Goulder's theories. That would require a book almost as long as Goulder's own.[39] However, one point ought to be made. Goulder assumes rather than proves that there are no Semitic sources, indeed, no sources of any sort, behind Luke 1–2. His book is not in itself a detailed examination of the text of the Gospel; it is an alternative explanation of the way it might have come into existence. Acceptance of that alternative explanation would inevitably lead one to deny the existence of sources behind Luke 1–2 but, equally, proof of the existence of such sources would cause grave damage to Goulder's theory.

The chief weakness of the Septuagintal pastiche theory lies in its failure adequately to explain why Luke saw fit to indulge in so much more 'Biblical' a style in chs. 1–2 than in the rest of Luke–Acts. That these chapters 'move in a Jewish world' is quite true. However, almost all the events of the rest of Luke and the first half of Acts also take place in Palestine among Jews, often in Jerusalem and even in the Temple itself. The more highly 'Jewish' and 'Old Testament' atmosphere of these first chapters of Luke is largely caused by the language itself rather than by peculiarity of setting or subject-matter. Why was that sort of strongly 'Biblical' language particularly appropriate in these chapters?[40] Those who believe that Luke composed these chapters in an imitation of Biblical style must explain more clearly his purpose in doing so.

There has always been a considerable number of scholars who have maintained that, to a greater or lesser degree, the Greek narrative of Luke 1–2 rests on a Hebrew foundation.[41] These scholars have no difficulty explaining the peculiarity of the language of the infancy narratives; in these chapters Luke's language is influenced by that of his source or sources. From this influence spring the many Hebraisms. It is time to consider the arguments with which these scholars have attempted to prove the existence of a Hebrew source or sources behind Luke 1–2.

> The most weighty form of evidence in proof that a document is a translation from another language is the existence of difficulties or peculiarities of language which can be shown to find their solution in the theory of mistranslation from the assumed original language.[42]

Many scholars have sought this form of evidence, these 'mistranslations', in the New Testament texts. Among them are Julius Wellhausen, C.C. Torrey, T.W. Manson, and C.F. Burney.[43] Torrey thought several mistranslations can be found in Luke 1–2, proving that these chapters were translated from Hebrew.[44] Most of these may be passed over quickly but one, Luke 1.39, must shortly be considered in more detail.

Luke 2.1. In this verse we read that 'all the world' was taxed. Torrey considers this a mistranslation of the familiar כל הארץ, 'all the land', which a Gentile could understand as 'all the world'.[45] This phrase could be explained as the result of either misinformation or exaggeration on the part of a Greek author, however.

Luke 2.11. In this verse 'Christ the Lord' may have been an attempt to translate משיח אדני, that is, 'the Lord's anointed'.[46] Torrey does not blame this error, if it be one, on Luke himself but on an early copyist. Strictly speaking, this means that in Torrey's opinion this expression is not actually a mistranslation. A scribe could just as easily have corrupted a text originally composed in Greek. However, the expression Χριστὸς κύριος does appear at Psalms of Solomon 17.36, where it may also be a mistranslation, of course, and the expression is consistent enough with Luke's thought to have been chosen as title for a recent study of Lucan theology.[47] κύριος could be understood as a parenthetical explanation of the title Χριστός.

Luke 1.66. Torrey objects to the tense of the verb 'to be' in the last clause of this verse, 'for the hand of the Lord *was* with him'.[48] He supposes that in the original Hebrew text these words were the continuation of the outcry of the people, containing no verb at all, ויד ארני עמו. Luke mistakenly supplied a past rather than a present tense. However, it is not necessary to suppose that these words are part of the crowd's acclamation. They could represent the evangelist's summary statement concerning the whole life of John which, from Luke's perspective, was in the past.

Luke 2.21, 27. Torrey found a redundant 'and' in each of these verses. One wonders why Torrey bothered to include these instances since, as he himself wrote, 'Such cases could not be classed as mistranslations, nor are they quite impossible Greek. The use of the conjunction to introduce the apodosis, after a temporal protasis, has its examples in Homer, for instance.'[49]

A more significant possible mistranslation can be found in Luke 1.39. In that verse we read the strange expression, εἰς πόλιν Ἰούδα, the usual translation of which is 'into a city of Judah'. In view of the fact that Ἰούδα or Ἰουδαία is normally declined in Luke as at Luke 1.5, 65 and 2.4, Torrey argued that the best rendering of these Greek words would be 'into the city, namely Judah'. Behind our Greek text, he asserted, stood a Hebrew original reading, מדינת יהודה.[50] In an article written about this one verse,[51] Torrey argued persuasively that in Gentile Aramaic מדינה meant 'city' but in Jewish Aramaic, 'region' or 'province'. Under the influence of the former interpretation of the word Luke misunderstood a Hebrew original which really meant 'into the region, namely, Judah'.[52]

Many scholars have found this argument persuasive and their number has not been confined to the circle of those having a special interest in the origins of Luke 1–2.[53] However, I believe the argument rests on an incorrect assumption—that Luke did not know that Judah was a province rather than a city. An error about the meaning of מדינה is perfectly possible; an error about the meaning of 'Judah' is not. Luke shows his knowledge of the correct meaning of Judah in 1.65 and 2.4 Torrey's statement to the contrary is, I believe, completely mistaken.[54]

Let us suppose, for the sake of argument, that Luke had before him a Hebrew original reading מדינת יהודה and also that he misunderstood the meaning of מדינה. But he could not have made a similar error with respect to the meaning of the word Judah unless we suppose him to have been completely ignorant at 1.39 and well informed at 1.65 and 2.4. If all this is true Luke would have translated the phrase in question as into 'a city *of* Judah' not 'namely, Judah' and we should still be left asking why Ἰούδα is left undeclined, contrary to Luke's normal usage. We must seek some entirely different solution for that problem. In other words, the supposition that Luke had before him a Hebrew original reading מדינת יהודה throws no light on the unusual form πόλιν Ἰούδα, the observation of which was the starting point for Torrey's reasoning.

This argument does not eliminate the possibility that Luke had a Hebrew original reading מדינת יהודה or even that he misunderstood מדינה; it only suggests that there is no positive reason to suppose that such was the case. After all, עיר, not מדינה, is the most common Old Testament word for city. Furthermore, there is no particular evidence in the Greek text that points to a translation from Hebrew at all. In fact, it can be argued that this unusual form is evidence of composition in Greek since a very similar phrase occurs in the LXX at 2 Samuel 2.1, in which Ἰούδα is undeclined.[55]

There are several other possible explanations of εἰς πόλιν Ἰούδα. The simplest is to blame an early copyist's carelessness. Secondly, it seems possible that Ἰούδα is here the name of the person rather than the territory,[56] which might well have been undeclined as at Luke 3.33, in the geneology, which reads ... τοῦ Φάρες τοῦ Ἰούδα. A more likely explanation is that Luke sometimes left Hebrew proper nouns undeclined as he did at 1.5, ἐφημερίας Ἀβιά and 2.4 εἰς πόλιν Δαυίδ. The former, at least, could easily have been declined. He may well have been influenced at this point by the example of his Greek Bible at 2 Samuel 2.1 and Isaiah 40.9.[57]

It appears that none of these mistranslations offers convincing evidence that these chapters were, in fact, translated. If it could be established by other means that Luke 1–2 are translation Greek several of Torrey's suggestions would need careful reconsideration.[58] They themselves cannot establish that point.

The presence of non-Septuagintal Hebraisms would be convincing evidence of translation in these chapters. Old Testament allusions which more closely resemble the Masoretic Text than the LXX would clearly be Hebraisms of this sort, and several scholars have approached the problem by searching for them.[59]

This approach to the problem is most clearly illustrated by the exchange between P. Winter and N. Turner.[60] Winter described his intention in his first article: 'we shall have to comb the two chapters for Hebrew idioms which are at the same time non-Septuagintal'.[61] Winter thought he had found several such cases and I shall describe three of them in order to make clear the sort of evidence involved.

In Luke 1.7 appears the phrase προβεβηκότες ἐν ταῖς ἡμέραις, 'advanced in their years'. This appears to correspond to באים בימים (Gen. 18.11), and בא בימים (Gen. 24.1; Josh. 13.1; 23.1; 1 Kings 1.1). In the LXX of Genesis 18.1 we read προβεβηκότες ἡμερῶν. Winter pointed out that in this translation and in that of the other similar passages cited there are no occurrences of ἐν to represent the Hebrew ב. The preposition does occur in Luke 1.7. This, he suggested, indicates that Luke or Luke's source was translated from a Hebrew text directly rather than depending on the LXX.[62]

Turner was forced to concede that ἐν is indeed present, 'against our present LXX evidence', but argued that the not inevitable choice of προβεβηκότες for באים and ἡμέραις for ימים, which he interpreted as 'years', shows dependence on the LXX.[63] Winter, in turn, replied that 'προβεβηκότες might not be an inevitable choice when the word is rendered into Greek, but it is the obvious choice'.[64] Furthermore, he contended that ימים does not mean 'years', as Turner implied, but rather 'days', so that 'ἡμέραις is not the Septuagintal translation of ימים, but the translation'.[65]

In Luke 1.37 we read οὐκ ἀδυνατήσει παρὰ τοῦ θεοῦ πᾶν ῥῆμα, 'Nothing that comes from God is impossible'. Winter suggested that these words are closer to the Hebrew of the obvious Old Testament parallel (Gen. 18.14) היפלא מיהוה דבר than to the LXX, μὴ ἀδυνατεῖ παρὰ τῷ θεῷ ῥῆμα. Luke's παρὰ τοῦ θεοῦ, 'from God', represents the Hebrew מיהוה better than does the LXX, παρὰ τῷ θεῷ, 'Nothing done *by God* is impossible'. Turner, on the other hand, argued that Luke and the LXX share θεός for יהוה and the use of παρά (although with a different case). Furthermore he asked rhetorically whether ἀδυνατεῖν is a natural enough translation of פלא to have occurred to two independent translators.[66]

In rebuttal Winter claimed, rather significantly, that 'the passage in Luke is not a direct quotation of the words in Gen. 18.14 but it is couched in Hebraistic idiom reminiscent of the Genesis passage'.[67] Therefore, Luke's Hebrew original may have read מאלהים. On the other hand, the LXX used θεός and κύριος 'interchangeably' as equivalents for יהוה. Luke could well have rendered יהוה as θεοῦ. Winter then observed that it is the case of that which follows the preposition παρά which determines its meaning. Luke differs from the LXX and agrees with the MT with respect to *meaning*. Lastly, Winter disposed of Turner's last objection by listing three instances in the LXX, presumably the work of independent translators, in which פלא is translated by ἀδυνατεῖν (Dt. 17.8; Zech. 8.6; Prov. 25.18 [LXX 24.53]).[68]

Finally, let us consider Luke 1.51a, a part of the Magnificat. That verse reads: ἐποίησεν κράτος ἐν βραχίονι αὐτοῦ, 'He has shown strength with his arm'. The related OT texts are Psalms 89.10(11) and 118.16. The latter is the more significant: ימין יהוה עשה חיל, 'the right hand of the Lord does strength'. The LXX translates חיל not by κράτος but by δύναμις. Similarly, in Psalm 89.10 the Hebrew עז is rendered by the LXX δύναμις. Winter claimed that κράτος is not only an independent translation of the two Hebrew words for strength but actually a more vigorous, more exact one.[69]

Turner responded by pointing to several occurrences of κράτος in the LXX which may have influenced Luke's language at this point.[70] This response is not entirely relevant since Winter's point is that the LXX passages which are usually considered to have provided the content of Luke 1.51 do not explain the presence of κράτος in that verse. The MT version of those texts does explain it. That κράτος occurs from time to time at other points in the LXX is beside the point. Winter's response to this objection was equally irrelevant. He merely pointed out that in none of the texts Turner adduced does κράτος translate חיל. This argument assumes what he is trying to prove, that there was a Hebrew original behind Luke 1.51 which probably read עשה חיל. If there was no such Vorlage it does not matter in the least that the LXX does not use κράτος as an equivalent for חיל.

I should judge that Winter had slightly the better of the scholarly duel, partly because he had the last word, and partly because Turner

certainly blundered with respect to the translation of the verb פלא.
However, I should also judge that neither scholar has proved his case
very convincingly because of two problems, one of which both
acknowledge. First, the texts to which both scholars appeal are
uncertain. Turner, when pressed by the force of Winter's arguments,
wrote, 'The LXX tradition certainly developed. St. Luke's Greek
Bible cannot have been quite the same as ours.'[72] This insight is
probably correct and, furthermore, is one with which Winter agreed
in principle.[73] However, Turner is quite inconsistent in his application of the insight. He applies it when Luke's Greek seems to differ
from that of the LXX but not when there appears to be a resemblance
between the two. That uncertainty about the exact shape of the first-
century Bible renders some of the more precise arguments of both
Winter and Turner rather dubious.[74] There is yet another problem,
one to which Winter alluded when he, in turn, was pressed by the
force of Turner's arguments. With respect to Luke 1.37 he wrote, in
italics, '*The passage is not a quotation*'.[75] This is true for most of the
passages in Luke 1–2 for which Old Testament parallels have been
proposed. They are not quotations but simply allusions. Here Winter
was inconsistent in his application of his own correct insight. He
used it to explain variations from the Hebrew text but did not apply
the same reasoning to variations from the Greek text of the OT. As
allusions rather than quotations Luke's words must not be expected
to reflect precisely the wording of either the Greek or Hebrew OT.
But such precision would be necessary if the arguments of Winter
and Turner are to have validity.[76]

It has also been suggested that translation of Luke 1–2 into
Hebrew reveals certain literary devices, the presence of which cannot
be accidental. Among these literary devices are etymological allusions,
assonance, alliteration and metre.

Several scholars have seen allusions to the names of characters of
these chapters in the narrative and hymns of Luke 1–2, but the most
systematic and thorough discussion of the question is undoubtedly
that of R. Laurentin. In two successive numbers of *Biblica* Laurentin
considered carefully the possibility that such allusions exist.[77] He
concluded that there were indeed allusions to the names of the
following characters:

1. Jesus, Lk. 2.11; 1.69; 2.30; 1.47, 71.
2. John, Lk. 1.13, 58, 72,54,78.

3. Gabriel, Lk. 1.17, 35, 49, 59.
4. Zechariah, Lk. 1.72, 54.
5. Elizabeth, Lk. 1.73, 54.
6. Mary, Lk. 1.69, 78, 46, 54.[78]

If there are as many etymological allusions as this list would suggest one might well be forced to conclude that Luke 1–2 depends on a Hebrew source. However, there are several serious problems with Laurentin's approach.

First, there is the problem of uncertainty in translation, a problem which affects several of the possible etymological allusions. One usually cannot be sure that the Hebrew with which Laurentin translated the Greek of Luke 1–2 is necessarily that of the putative original. Occasionally, his translation is quite unlikely. When one consults a concordance of the LXX one sometimes finds that there are in the Hebrew OT equivalents for Luke's words far more common than the Hebrew which Laurentin proposes.[79]

For example, Laurentin found an allusion to Mary in the first verse of the Magnificat: 'My soul magnifies the Lord'. This he did by translating the verb μεγαλύνει by the hiphil participle מרימה, 'raises up'. However, the LXX never uses μεγαλύνω to translate רום. The most common equivalent for the Greek verb is some form of גדל.[80] He detected another allusion to Mary in the Benedictus (Lk. 1.69), by translating the verb ἤγειρεν by the same hiphil participle. He claimed, 'Le mot ἤγειρεν répond de façon aussi certaine que possible, selon l'usage des Septante au hiph'il de רום'.[81] In fact, the LXX only once uses ἐγείρω as a translation of רום. Behind that Greek verb usually lies some form of the verb קום. Laurentin here clearly assumed that Luke 1.69 is an allusion to 1 Samuel 2.10. That part of Hannah's song reads in the LXX: ὑψώσει κέρας Χριστοῦ αὐτοῦ. Behind ὑψώσει lies the Hebrew וירם (not, we may note, a hiphil participle). Given the fact that the verb in Luke 1.69 is ἐγείρω, not ὑψόω, and that the Hebrew original of the latter verb is not a hiphil participle in 1 Samuel 2.10, Laurentin's proposal seems less than persuasive.

Laurentin also found an allusion to Elizabeth, a name derived from the verb שבע, 'to swear', in Luke 1.55: 'as he spoke to our fathers'. The Greek verb ἐλάλησεν he translated by שבע although the LXX never renders שבע by λαλέω. The usual equivalent of λαλέω is דבר. Furthermore, he saw allusions to John wherever the word ἔλεος occurs in Luke 1–2, as in 1.54, 58, 72, 78. He suggested that behind those occurences of ἔλεος is a Hebrew word derived from the verb חנן. That verb, 'to show favour' or 'to be gracious', is also the root of the Hebrew name John. There are, in fact, ten instances in the LXX in which ἔλεος translates a word derived from חנן. Furthermore, Laurentin argued that the expression ποιεῖν ἔλεος of Luke 1.72 is used to translate the verb חנן at Judges 21.22.[82] However, there are well over one hundred cases in the LXX in which ἔλεος renders חסד, which is therefore the far more likely candidate for a Hebrew original. Furthermore, in Luke 1.72 the expression is not stimply ποιῆσαι ἔλεος but ποιῆσαι ἔλεος μετά. That phrase translates עשה חסד עם at Judges 1.24; 8.35; 2 Samuel 2.6; 9.1, 37; 10.2. In Judges 21.22 the preposition μετά / עם does not appear.

In all these cases Laurentin's identification of the Hebrew *Vorlage* is rather unlikely. For the remaining possible allusions there are varying degrees of probability but I should judge that in few cases is Laurentin's proposal certain.

There remains, after the removal of Laurentin's more unlikely proposals, a certain number of potential allusions. Unfortunately for Laurentin's case, the supposed allusions involve the use of some of the more common words of the Hebrew Bible. These are the Hebrew roots of the names of the characters of Luke 1–2:

Jesus	ישע	to save
John	חנן	to show favour
Gabriel	גבור	a mighty man
Zechariah	זכר	to remember
Elizabeth	שבע	to swear
Mary	רום	to lift up[83]

Of these Hebrew words only חנן occurs less than 150 times in the OT (74 occurrences). It might be added here that the noun חסד, which usually lies behind ἔλεος, occurs more than 200 times. Moreover, the concordance shows that these words appear frequently in the psalms, the source of so much of the vocabulary of Luke's hymns.

Nor is it at all surprising that these concepts cluster together in Luke's hymns for they also do so in other parts of the Bible where there can be no question of allusions to the characters of Luke 1–2. For example, the 'Elizabeth/Zechariah' combination, that is the coincidence of שבע and זכר, can be found in Psalms 63, 89, and 132. The second of these psalms is particularly interesting. We find in the last few verses of Psalm 89 the following words:

v. 48	זכר		Zechariah
v. 49	גדר		Gabriel
v. 50	חסד	= ἔλεος	which could, according to Laurentin's arguments, be a translation of חנן. Therefore, we can find here an allusion to John.
v. 50	נשבעת		Elizabeth
v. 51	זכר		Zechariah

To make matters even more complete the psalm also contains four occurrences of רום and one of salvation, ישע (v. 27), in other words, potential allusions to Mary and Jesus. If one were to apply Laurentin's methods one might conclude that this psalm too appears to contain allusions to all the chief characters of Luke 1–2.[84] In short, even if Laurentin were correct in his identification of the specific Hebrew words behind our Greek text, the mere occurrence of those common words does not prove that there was intent to create etymological allusions.

That there may be such an allusion at Luke 1.13, the annunciation to Zechariah, seems not unlikely. There the angel says to him, 'you prayer has been answered', although no prayer has previously been mentioned in the narrative. The word 'prayer', δέησις, corresponds most frequently in the LXX to one of two words derived from חנן. The answer to Zechariah's prayer is the gift of a son, John.[85] Similarly, in the annunciation to the shepherds, the birth of Jesus, the Saviour, is proclaimed: 'Unto you is born this day a *saviour*, which is Christ the Lord'. However, at Matthew 1.21 there is an undoubted etymological allusion and very few suggest that the first chapters of Matthew were translated from a Semitic source.[86] We may deduce from that reference that there was in the early church teaching concerning the significance of the name 'Jesus'. Perhaps there was similar teaching concerning other prominent figures in the history of salvation.[87] If this is true, we should not necessarily have to assume the existence of a Hebrew source to account for the apparent presence of etymological allusions in Luke 1–2. It appears, therefore, that Laurentin's research does not constitute proof that there was such a Hebrew source.[88]

Laurentin also believed that he had found assonance at several points in the reconstructed Hebrew text of these chapters. John is to go before the face (*lipnê*) of the Lord to prepare (*lipnût*) his ways (Lk. 1.17, 76). Mary stayed (*wattēšēb*) and then returned (*wattāšob*) to her home (Lk. 1.56). The one announced in Lk. 2.11 is a saviour (*môšîaʻ*), who is the Christ (*māšîaḥ*). But once again we are faced with the problem of uncertainty in the process of retranslation. One cannot be absolutely sure of the shape of the original Hebrew text. Once again the words Laurentin chooses as Hebrew equivalents for the Greek of Luke 1–2 are by no means the only possible ones. To give but one example, σωτήρ does not always translate the hiphil participle of ישע, the form required for an assonance in Luke 2.11. Moreover, it is quite possible that Luke, if he did in fact use Semitic sources in these chapters, added and subtracted material in the course of translation. 'Christ the Lord', for example, could easily be an explanatory gloss added at some point in the history of the text. Where then would be the intentional assonance?

There may also be examples of assonance in the Greek text of Luke's infancy narratives. R.C. Tannehill found both assonance (ταπεινούς, πεινῶντας) and rhyme (θρόνων/ἀγαθῶν, ταπεινούς/κενούς in the Magnificat and implied that this language is evidence that the hymn was composed in Greek.[89]

Matthew Black held that retroversion of the Magnificat into Aramaic showed certain word-plays in the poem and even ventured to rearrange the hymn because of them. He suggested that v. 49 originally followed immediately on v. 46.

> My soul doth magnify (*mᵉrabbya*) the Lord,
> for He hath done to me great things (*rabhrᵉbhatha*).[90]

The two words in question are, in the Greek text, μεγαλύνει and μεγάλα which are rather more similar, I suggest, than the Aramaic pair. Once again, the evidence concerning assonance and similar forms of word-play does not seem sufficient to prove the existence of a Semitic source.

Yet another literary device is revealed by translation into Hebrew, it is argued, namely the use of characteristic forms of Hebrew metre. This has been proposed by F.X. Zorell, R.A. Aytoun, and G.H. Box.[91] Zorell dealt only with the Magnificat, and Box with the first few verses of ch. 2, but Aytoun dealt not only with the recognized hymns but also with the direct discourse of the infancy narratives. He concluded: 'practically everything which is spoken is in verse and in regular metre'.[92] This, it is argued, can hardly be accidental. It must be, therefore, that our present Greek text represents the translation of a Hebrew original.

This is a fascinating argument and one which has not been adequately countered by proponents of the Septuagintal pastiche theory. If one could on other grounds prove the existence of Hebrew sources behind the first two chapters of Luke, one might well expect metre in some of the poetic passages of those chapters. That is, if there were a Hebrew source or sources there may have been metre in various parts of it. The presence of metre in a reconstruction of a hypothetical source does not, however, prove that the source existed in reality. There are simply too many uncertainties in the process for one to accept this sort of reasoning as proof of the existence of an underlying Hebrew source.

First, there is uncertainty in the process of retranslation itself.[93] It is not a question primarily of the choice of Hebrew words here but of the possibility of glosses, interpolations and Lucan additions. That there may have been such alterations was recognized by Aytoun. Indeed, he attempted to turn this insight to his advantage, using it as a justification for removing inconvenient bits of the hymns in order to make their metre more regular.[94] Most of these so-called glosses do not deserve this fate for their only offence appears to be that they spoil the hypothetical metre. In other respects most of them appear to be integral and original parts of the poems. On the other hand, those verses which many scholars have been inclined to regard as interpolations, 1.48 in the Magnificat and 1.76ff. in the Benedictus, fit nicely into Aytoun's metric patterns.[95] One might well question the translator's choice of glosses and interpolations. A different choice might entirely spoil the metrical scheme. One can only say that these emendations made on the basis of metre, the existence of which the critic is trying to prove, are of dubious worth.

It is also surprising that those hymns which most conspicuously display that characteristic of Hebrew poetry of which we are most certain, parallelism, do not possess the regular metre of the speeches, which may not be poetry at all. With respect to the Magnificat Aytoun wrote, 'there are more irregularities of metre and structure in this poem, in its present form, than in those we have previously examined'.[96] For the Benedictus he accepted Plummer's contention that 'the poet here modelled himself on the Prophets rather than on the Psalmists', writing that 'The prophets certainly took more liberties with the artificialities of structure than did the Psalmists'.[97] In other words, where poetry is most certainly present, regular metre is least certainly present.

Another observation stems from the neat way in which Aytoun laid out the Greek and Hebrew texts in parallel columns. Quite simply, the Greek text displays metrical regularity to almost the same degree as the Hebrew. Where, for example, there are trimeter couplets in the Hebrew translation of the Nunc Dimittis, there are also trimeter couplets in the Greek.

There is a much more serious problem, however, which has to do with the nature of Hebrew poetry itself. The problem can be illustrated by a comparison of the analyses of Zorell and Aytoun.[98] The two analyses are somewhat similar in that they are both obliged more or less to order their material after the sense units of the poem. However, there are a number of internal differences between the two units. In Aytoun's analysis of the Magnificat the first four lines arrange themselves into two tetrameter couplets while the concluding seven lines are pentameter. Aytoun considered dropping one of these lines in order to make three couplets but had difficulty choosing among three candidates for excision. Zorell, on the other hand, found in that hymn five distinct sections, each of which has the metrical form $3 + 2 + 2 + 3$. It is not my concern to judge the merits of the two analyses but to show that translation into Hebrew does not produce a text of which the metre is obvious and unmistakable. This uncertainty springs from the fact that we cannot find in Hebrew poetry the sort of regularly ordered metre we see in Greek and Latin literature.[99] Either there were no precise rules concerning the number of stresses and syllables, or we have not yet discovered them.[100] To apply imprecise rules to a hypothetical text is not the sort of procedure which is likely to yield unassailable evidence.

This uncertainty about the question of metre in Hebrew poetry may be illustrated by the following statements:

> The metric hypotheses rest upon a combination of inference from parallelism and application of the Masoretic accents, rather than on any intrinsic evidence from biblical Hebrew ... Meter, insofar as it exists in Hebrew poetry, is actually the rhythmical counterpart of parallelism of thought. Rhythm is not due to syllabic quantities but to the less definable instinct of balancing parts whose exact accentual values are not measurable and probably never were ... In Hebrew poetry regularity of stress is subordinated to regularity of balanced ideas. Thus the tendency to fill out lines with incomplete parallelisms by means of compensation is not metrical (i.e., the necessity of having two three-stress stichs) but rather is

due to the desire to oppose word-masses of about the same weight
while varying and emphasizing the thought. The concept is closer
to a temporal concern with 'mass' than to a temporal concern with
'stress'. . . . Parallelism of thought, and corresponding word-mass,
is the substance and mode of Hebrew poetic expression.[101]

'The parallelism of thought and of corresponding word-mass' is
certainly present in the hymns of Luke's infancy narratives.[102] It is
present in the Greek text as well as the Hebrew, however, so its
presence does not exclude the possibility that the hymns were
composed in Greek after Hebrew models. Nevertheless the studies of
Zorell, Aytoun, Box, and others, if they do not prove the existence of
Hebrew sources, do show how close the author or authors of these
hymns must have been to the thought-world of the Old Testament
and subsequent Judaism. The canons of Hebrew poetry, or our
knowledge of those canons, may be inexact, but judged by those
canons the hymns of Luke 1–2 are genuinely 'Hebraic', whatever
their original language.

In this connection it may be well briefly to mention the contribution
of H. Gunkel. Because the hymns so nearly conform to the patterns
of late Jewish poetry he too supposed that the hymns had been
composed in Hebrew.[103] There will be occasion in a later chapter
more thoroughly to discuss possible parallels to the Lucan hymns.
Although we must respect the critical acumen of the great Semitist
(and that of the other great expert on the Psalms, S. Mowinckel),[104]
I should not judge that Gunkel has entirely excluded the possibility
that the hymns were composed as deliberate imitations of the sort of
poems which he adduced as parallels to the hymns. This is the great
difficulty with many of the arguments about the original language of
these chapters. Anything in the Old Testament or later Judaism
brought forward as evidence of the hymns' Hebraic nature can
equally be explained as the subject of deliberate imitation in Greek.

These, then, are some of the main arguments which have been
used by scholars in the discussion concerning the original language of
Luke 1–2. Many are ingenious; more are learned; but none completely
convincing. The question remains, therefore, finely balanced. In a
boxing match the judges are instructed to favour the boxer who has
been more consistently the aggressor. If this were a boxing match one
would have to award the decision to those who have argued for a
Hebrew source theory for they have consistently been the 'aggressors'
in this match. However, scholarly discussion is not pugilism, so one

cannot apply that principle. Failing that means of resolving the issue
one might well be forced to agree with Raymond Brown's conclusion,
'The linguistic opponents have fought themselves to a draw'.[105]

II. *Raymond Martin's Method*

One can hardly be surprised at Brown's verdict on the scholarly
battle over the original language of Luke 1–2. But in coming to that
conclusion Brown seems to have overlooked the works of Raymond
A. Martin. In two articles[1] and a book[2] Martin developed a method
which purports to enable the user to determine whether or not
Semitic sources lie behind a Greek document. If Martin's method
actually works, the linguistic draw may have been broken. Scholars
no longer need play Mr Micawber, 'waiting for something to turn
up'. Something has not turned up. But will it work?

Raymond Martin informs us in the preface to his book, *Syntactical
Evidence*,[3] that he first took an interest in the question of translation
Greek when a student at Princeton Seminary. He maintained that
interest while a missionary in India, publishing at that time the two
articles mentioned earlier. One might imagine that Dr Martin
absorbed some of the legendary patience of the Orient, for the
development of his method must have involved the most tedious and
painstaking of studies. The method was then fully described in
Syntactical Evidence. There, Martin declares that he has isolated
seventeen criteria which enable one to discover the presence of
Semitic sources beneath Greek documents. A description of those
criteria will display not only the nature of the method but also
Martin's industry and thoroughness.[4]

Martin had, as do all investigators, a considerable sample of
translation Greek, the LXX. The observation of the relative frequency
or infrequency there of certain syntactical features, when compared
with works composed in Greek, lies at the basis of his method.

Criteria 1–8. *The Relative Infrequency of Certain Prepositions
compared to the Frequency of* ἐν. The first eight criteria have to do
with the relative infrequency of appearance of certain prepositions
compared to the frequency of appearance of ἐν. The preposition ב
appears very frequently in Hebrew or Aramaic and is usually
represented in translation by ἐν. Certain other prepositions which
are relatively common in original Greek do not have common

Semitic equivalents. Table 1 in the appendix to this chapter lists the eight prepositions which Martin uses as criteria. With each criterion stands a numeral: the numeral is the number of occurrences of the relevant preposition per occurrence of ἐν which Martin considers the dividing line between original and translation Greek. Thus, for example, if διά with the genitive occurs more than .06 times for each occurence of ἐν, then we are on the original Greek side of the line; if it occurs less than .06 times per ἐν, then we are on the translation Greek side of the line. Since ἐν is usually more frequent in appearance than the other prepositions, the numeral each time has a decimal point.

The dividing line is sometimes an artificial one.[5] For example, the frequency of κατά in Numbers or of πρός with the dative case in Joshua is actually well on the original Greek side of the dividing line. However, Martin's figures show that the bulk of translation Greek is clearly differentiated from original Greek with respect to these criteria.

In isolating these criteria Martin consulted a very large body of literature. On the translated Greek side he was able to use the LXX version of the entire Hebrew Old Testament. For original Greek he used writings of considerable variety, both highly literary texts and the papyri, as well as Josephus and 2–3–4 Maccabees.[6]

For the final nine criteria Martin was not able to take such a wide sample since the process of counting was more difficult than merely looking up the appropriate entry in a concordance. He did, however, analyze more than 3400 lines of translation Greek and 1500 lines of original Greek. The texts studied are listed in Table 2 in the appendix to this chapter.

Criterion 9. *The Frequency of* καί *Coordinating Independent Clauses in Relation to the Frequency of* δέ. The criterion involves the relative frequency of the use of καί copulative.[7] Semitic conjunctions are never postpositive and are, of course, very common indeed. There is a considerable difference in the handling of this feature in translation Greek between the literalness of Theodotion on the one hand and the relative freedom of the LXX version of Genesis on the other. However, original Greek, according to Martin's figures, always has less than two occurrences of καί copulative for every occurrence of δέ.

Criterion 10. *Separation of the Greek Article from its Substantive.* Nothing can be inserted between a Hebrew article or its equivalent in

Aramaic, the emphatic state, and its substantive. This is not the case in Greek. As one might, therefore, expect, Martin found that a relatively small percentage of articles are separated from their substantives in translation Greek, 5% or less.[8]

Criterion 11. *The Infrequency in Translation Greek of Dependent Genitives Preceding the Word on which they Depend.* The genitive is expressed in Hebrew and Aramaic by constructions which follow rather than precede the substantive on which they depend. This is not necessarily the case in original Greek. In Martin's sample of translation Greek there are always 22 or more dependent genitives following their substantives for every such genitive preceding its substantive.

Criterion 12. *The Greater Frequency of Dependent Genitive Personal Pronouns in Greek which is a Translation of a Semitic Language.* Pronominal suffixes are extremely common in Hebrew and Aramaic and are usually translated by dependent genitive personal pronouns. As one can see from the graph such pronouns are therefore more common in translated Greek. This is one of several criteria expressed as a number of lines of text for each occurrence of the phenomenon in question. In this case the point of division is nine lines per occurrence.

Criterion 13. *The Greater Frequency of Genitive Personal Pronouns Dependent upon Anarthrous Substantives in Translation Greek.* This criterion is closely related to the last and is based on the fact that nouns with pronominal suffixes are normally anarthrous in the Semitic languages. It appears that in translation Greek genitive personal pronouns dependent on anarthrous substantives occur every 77 lines or less.

Criterion 14. *The Infrequency in Translation Greek of Attributive Adjectives Preceding the Word they Qualify.* Criterion 14 also rests on an observation of word order. Attributive adjectives normally follow the word they qualify in the Semitic languages but may frequently precede it in Greek. Here the dividing line is at .35 attributive adjectives preceding for every one following the word it qualifies.[9]

Criterion 15. *The Relative Infrequency of Attributive Adjectives in Translation Greek.* Attributive adjectives are used relatively infrequently in Hebrew and Aramaic and one might therefore expect that Greek translated from these languages would share that characteristic. Martin's calculations show that this is, in fact, the case. One may well be puzzled by Martin's positioning of the line of demarcation, however. A considerable part of his sample of translation Greek has attributive adjectives appearing more frequently than once every 10.1 lines, the dividing line here.

Criterion 16. *Frequency of Adverbial Participles.* While Greek frequently expresses subordination by the use of an adverbial or circumstantial participle the Semitic languages do not do so. Infrequent use of such participles may therefore be a sign of translation Greek. Martin found that translated Greek possessed such participles no more frequently than one every 6 lines.

Criterion 17. *The Frequency of the Dative Case.* This criterion is closely related to the first eight in that it measures the relative frequency of ἐν. Dative, locative and instrumental ideas are often expressed with the preposition ב in Hebrew and Aramaic but need not be expressed with ἐν in Greek. According to Martin's figures one might suspect the presence of translation Greek when there are less than two instances of the use of the dative without the use of ἐν for every instance with it.[10]   After all these criteria have been applied to the texts in question, the counting done, and the appropriate calculations made in each case, Martin finds the total number of criteria which indicate the presence of original Greek and subtracts from it the number of criteria indicating translation Greek. The result can be either a positive or a negative number depending on whether the criteria showing original Greek (positive result), or translation Greek (negative result), predominate. For example, when one applies the criteria to Genesis 39 one finds 4 original Greek frequencies, 10 translation Greek frequencies and 3 for which there is insufficient evidence to make a determination. One subtracts 10 (translation Greek frequencies) from 4 (original Greek frequencies) and comes up with a net score of -6.

In the texts studied by Martin, the values for original Greek ranged from +15 to +17 while the values for translation Greek were consistently negative, from -4 to -14.[11] Clearly there is a considerable difference with respect to these criteria between original and translation Greek in *the sample which Martin studied.*

Martin also considered the possibility that Semitic sources might be embedded in documents that, as a whole, had been originally composed in Greek. This sort of Semitic source might very likely be quite short and, as a result, more difficult to identify. He therefore divided his material into smaller units of text and subjected these units to the analysis described earlier in this Chapter. Predictably he found that 'as the unit of text which is being analysed become smaller, syntactical variations due to content and style becomes more pronounced'.[12] To this point all the text units with which Martin had worked were 58 lines or longer. He divided these texts into smaller units of 50-31 lines or 30-16 lines or 15-4 lines in length.

With units of 31-50 lines there is no overlap between the results for original and translation Greek.[13] With units of 16-30 lines there is some overlap although the bulk of the material is still separated. There is a rather considerable overlap when one considers units of 4-15 lines in length. This overlap is caused primarily, however, not by the more frequent appearance of translation Greek frequencies in original Greek texts but by less frequent appearances of such frequencies in translation Greek. Never, even in the shortest units, did translation Greek frequencies predominate in an original Greek text. Martin concluded: 'the differences between the original Greek and the translated Greek is [*sic*] sufficient in all units of 31-50 lines in length, in most units of 16-30 lines in length, and in many units of 4-15 lines to indicate that they are indeed translation rather than original Greek'.[14] Nevertheless, he must admit that, in this last case, at least a third of the translation Greek appeared on the 'wrong' side of the dividing line and thus could not certainly be detected by means of this method.[15]

The most adequate summary of the results of this study is Martin's own:

a. For units of 31 to 50 lines in length, 'these criteria clearly indicate translation Greek if *in such a section one or fewer net original Greek frequencies or one or more translation Greek frequencies occur*'.

b. For units of 16 to 30 lines of length: '*if one or fewer net original Greek frequencies or one or more translation Greek frequencies occur this indicates translation of a Hebrew or Aramaic document. If 2 to 4 net original Greek frequencies occur this probably indicates translation of a Semitic document*'.[16]

c. For units of 4 to 15 lines in length: '*only if one or more net translation Greek frequencies appear is translation from Hebrew or Aramaic definitely indicated*'.[17]

Martin then applied his method to the Acts of the Apostles. This, he argued, is an ideal test case since the book has two halves of more or less equal length but of quite different character. The second half of the book, 15.35–28.31, can hardly be drawn from Semitic sources but 'it is quite generally conceded that at least in some parts of the first half of Acts the writer does use Aramaic sources'.[18] (One might quarrel with the adverb 'generally'). Martin found that the second half of the book displayed 16 net original Greek frequencies, the same, in fact, as Plutarch. Even the smallest units studied were safely above the lowest limit for original Greek frequencies. The first half of Acts, on the other hand, displayed only 8 net original Greek frequencies, a figure which falls in the gap between the frequencies displayed by the original and translation Greek frequencies analysed earlier in the book. Furthermore, the figures for every indicator except one, διά + genitive, are closer to translation Greek frequencies than the comparable second half figures. When one turns to the smaller units of text one finds that a number of these units display translation Greek frequencies. No smaller units in any of the original Greek which Martin had studied previously had displayed such frequencies. Similarly, none of the smaller units of translation Greek had displayed the original Greek frequencies one finds in many of the other units and in Acts 1–15.35 as a whole. 'The explanation for this non-conformity to either original or translation Greek is clear. Acts 1–15.35 contains some material which was originally composed in Greek and also some which has been translated from Semitic sources.'[19]

It is not my intention to dwell longer on the Acts of the Apostles than is absolutely necessary. Let it only be said that the results of the study of the second half of Acts where there can hardly be a question of Semitic sources may be useful for purposes of comparison with the Infancy Narratives where there may be such sources.[20]

To apply this method to Luke 1–2 is an obvious step at this point. The method has one great advantage for this purpose; it is almost inconceivable that an author would consciously imitate the syntactical features analysed by it. It has been argued that Luke here has adopted a 'Septuagintalizing' style, imitating the vocabulary, the concerns and rhythms of the LXX. It would, I suggest, take an extremely hardy proponent of this theory to argue that Luke discovered and reproduced the correct frequencies of the various syntactical features discussed earlier in this chapter. It is one thing to imitate the vocabulary of the Old Testament and give a writing some of its atmosphere by inserting characteristic expressions like καί ἐγένετο; any moderately literate modern could imitate the Authorised Version in a similar fashion. It is quite another consistently to reproduce some of its more obscure characteristics which do not depend on subject matter or vocabulary. Conscious imitation of these phenomena appears unthinkable. One cannot totally discount the possibility that a writer extremely senstive to literary nuances, 'a first-century James Joyce',[21] might, in the course of his imitation of the LXX, unconsciously reproduce as a by-product of that imitation some of these characteristics, some of the time. One could hardly expect him to do so consistently. These criteria do not concern themselves with idiom, with vocabulary, or theology, which are the natural subjects of imitation; they consist of the obscure unconsidered building blocks of language.

Furthermore, we know that Luke, where certainly uninfluenced by Semitic sources, as in Acts 15.36ff., wrote Greek that displays frequencies characteristic of original Greek. Martin's study shows that Acts 15.36ff. exhibits the same net number of original Greek frequencies as Plutarch and that not one of the smaller units displays translation Greek frequencies. It is not the case, therefore, that Luke's own style was necessarily Semitic.

When we turn to the infancy narratives and apply Martin's method we find that Luke 1–2 as a whole and also in its various parts consistently displays translation Greek frequencies. The 'score' for Luke 1–2 as a whole was -16. That is to say, every criterion that could be applied (one, the frequency of πρός with the dative, was inapplicable) pointed to the conclusion that these chapters are translation Greek. All the smaller units, including the hymns, were also safely on the translation Greek side of the dividing line.[22]

A standard test of statistical significance was applied to the results gained by the application of each of the 16 criteria to Luke 1–2 as a whole. (It is a weakness in Martin's study that he nowhere mentions the application of such tests to his results.) To do this one forms a 'null hypothesis' to be falsified, in this case, that the data for Luke 1–2 belongs to the normal distribution of values for original Greek. In all 16 cases the results were 'significant at the 1% level' or better. This means that the results for Luke 1–2 were more extreme than 99% of the values one might expect for original Greek. Such a level of significance is considered 'fairly conclusive' evidence that the null hypothesis is untrue.[23] In fact most of the 16 results were significant at well beyond this level even when the values of the writer nearest to translation Greek were taken as the mean value for original Greek rather than the actual mean. The Greek of Luke 1–2 differs significantly from the original Greek *in the sample which Martin studied.*

Several points ought to be made before proceeding. The score for Luke 1–2 as a whole, -16, shows a higher number of translation Greek frequencies than even the samples of the LXX which Martin examined. This makes a striking contrast with the +16 of the second half of Acts. Of the two chapters it is clear that the first is more Semitic in style than the second both in total score and with respect to the data for each individual criterion.[24] However, it would be inaccurate to suggest in a similar fashion that the hymns, on the basis of this data, must be considered less Semitic than the narrative. The lower score, -4, for the hymns as a whole, is a reflection of the lesser number of lines. In a shorter unit a single expression such as διὰ στόματος τῶν ἁγίων ἀπ' αἰῶνος προφητῶν αὐτοῦ (Lk. 1.70), can have a much greater statistical effect than in a larger unit of text. Furthermore, there is always bound to be a greater number of criteria for which there is not enough data to come to a conclusion. In fact, with respect to many of the criteria, the hymns appear more Semitic than does the narrative.

Considering the results one can hardly escape the conclusion that Luke 1–2 is translated from a Semitic source or sources. But is the method reliable? This is the question which must be considered in the rest of this chapter.

Martin's method certainly appears to be impressive; the graphs with which he illustrated his work create a strong visual impression in its favour and there is a persuasive explanation of the significance of each of the criteria. Furthermore, the method gives the impression of being 'scientific' and 'objective'. The method is, however, by no means easy to apply. The eye skips a line; the finger presses the wrong button on the calculator; the same word is counted twice. More importantly, the user could wish at times for slightly more specific directions concerning what 'counts' and what does not under some of the criteria.

There are, however, certain problems and difficulties which are of a more serious nature and which may point to flaws in the method itself. One difficulty has to do with the number of criteria. Criteria 1–8 purport to be eight separate indicators showing the relative infrequency of various prepositions. One might well suppose, however, that there is but one criterion here, the relative frequency of ἐν. Furthermore, criterion 17 which compares the number of occurrences of the dative without the use of ἐν to the number of such occurrences with it is, at least in part, a measure of the frequency of ἐν. Are there nine separate criteria here—or just one?

It seems best, however, to retain Martin's method intact in this respect. That the texts in question agree or disagree with translation Greek not only with respect to the frequency of ἐν but also with respect to the relative infrequency of seven other prepositions, each according to its proper proportion, is worthy of note. Furthermore, in order conveniently to compare the results of this study with the results of Martin's own study the retention of his system is advisable.

Another problem lies in the fact that one can find the same phrase being counted several times under different criteria, and so having a strong, perhaps too strong, influence on the overall result. Consider, for example, the unusual expression mentioned earlier, διὰ στόματος τῶν ἁγίων ἀπ' αἰῶνος προφητῶν αὐτοῦ (Lk. 1.70), which for various reasons has sometimes been considered an insertion by Luke into the hymn. Here we have one expression which counts under six different criteria and by its singular presence makes several of them come down on the original Greek side with respect to the hymns.

There are also several more minor flaws in the system which have to do with the counting. The only one worth mentioning here is that for a particular criterion among the first eight to be counted, at least one of the relevant prepositions must be present. For example, if in a particular passage there are 10 instances of ἐν and 4 of εἰς the criterion can be considered to indicate translation Greek. If, on the other hand, there are 10 instances of ἐν but none of εἰς the criterion may not be counted at all, even though the point of the criterion is that εἰς is relatively infrequent in translation Greek compared to ἐν.

A more serious problem involves the question of the relative importance of the criteria. In Martin's system all seventeen of the criteria are of equal value numerically. One criterion, one vote. My own impression is that the last nine criteria ought to be of more significance than the relative frequency of the individual prepositions. These latter seem 'lightweight' by comparison in that one is using some of the same data, the number of occurrences of ἐν, repeatedly. Once it is admitted that the various criteria are not equal value, however, the certainty of the mathematical rules disappears. One net score of -3 might be more significant than the next -3 depending on which criteria made up the score. In fact, if the criteria are of unequal significance it is hard to imagine reducing the data to a numerical score at all. After considering all the data one might merely be left with an impression of translation Greek or original Greek, hardly a completely objective process.

There remains a still more serious problem. In a review of *Syntactical Evidence* John J. Collins wrote, 'M's criteria make no allowance for the possibility of a poor quality Greek influenced by Semitic idiom'.[25] If Martin's method cannot distinguish between Greek translated from a Semitic language and Greek written by one influenced by Semitic idiom its usefulness for application to the New Testament, mainly written as it is by Semites, will be limited. I have chosen several texts for analysis in an effort to determine whether or not this is the case.

The first text chosen is Luke 5.12–6.11 and the second is its parallel in Mark, Mark 1.40–3.6. The third text is Luke 12.13–13.9 of which the central portion appears to be drawn from Q.[26] The other two sections of the text, Luke 12.13-21 and 13.1-9, contain material peculiar to Luke. There are some who claim that the Synoptic Gospels are translated from Aramaic.[27] Furthermore, if there is any historical root in the life of Jesus, or even in the situation of the early Aramaic-speaking church, to the sayings and stories recounted in these texts, there must certainly have been a Semitic substratum in their tradition history. One cannot, therefore, predict with confidence the result of an analysis of these texts. It will be useful, however, to have data from the Lukan texts for purposes of comparison with Luke 1–2 and with Acts. The passage from Mark was chosen in order to discover whether the characteristic studied in Martin's method could be passed from one Greek document to another dependent on it.

I know of no scholar who suggests that Romans and Galatians were composed in Hebrew or Aramaic. From these books I have chosen a passage of doctrinal exposition, Romans 5, and a passage which contains biographical narrative, Galatians 1.1–2.5.[28] Finally, there are two texts of somewhat different character, Revelation 3 and 4.1–5.10. The former is the concluding section of the letter to the seven churches while the latter forms the beginning of the apocalyptic vision itself. This latter section contains narrative, direct discourse, and hymnic materials, as do the infancy narratives of Luke. Of the author of Revelation R.H. Charles wrote, 'while he writes in Greek, he thinks in Hebrew'.[29] Revelation, it appears, may serve as our example of 'poor quality Greek influenced by Semitic idiom'. The results of the analysis of these texts may be found in Table 6 in the appendix to this chapter.

The bulk of this material displays frequencies which fall into the gap between the results for translation Greek and those of original Greek in Martin's study.[33] Revelation with a net score of -5 is the only exception, having a score similar to that of the Genesis selections, -4, and 1 Kings 17, -6. The passages from Paul, which display the most original Greek frequencies in this sample, do not approach the scores of the original Greek examined by Martin. The exact significance of this data may not immediately be clear but it does appear that the method may not always be able to differentiate between translation Greek and Greek composed by one who thinks in a Semitic language.

With respect to the relative frequency of prepositions the concordances enable one to accumulate data for the entire New Testament. In more than half the cases for which a determination is possible, 98 out of 184, the frequencies are typical of 'translation Greek'. In fact, it appears that Acts is one of the few books in the New Testament in which original Greek frequencies predominate. However, these figures do not prove that the frequencies Martin has isolated are not characteristic of translation Greek but only suggest that such frequencies may also be characteristic of Greek written by one influenced by Semitic idiom.

All these considerations must throw doubt on the ability of this method reliably to distinguish between translation Greek and much of the rather Semitized Greek of the New Testament.[31] I suggest, however, that the use of Martin's method might well help us come to a conclusion about Semitic sources in Luke 1-2. It is important to remember that none of the passages from the rest of the New Testament shows the consistent translation Greek frequencies of Luke 1-2. Not even Revelation 4.1-5.10 comes close to doing so. In the case of every available criterion the former chapters exhibit frequencies characteristic of translation Greek. (It may be worth mentioning in passing that if all the criteria point in the same direction the objection that these criteria are of differing significance loses its force.)

Secondly, the results of the wider application of the method throw doubt primarily on the ability of the method to distinguish between Greek translated from a Semitic language and Greek written by a person heavily influenced by Semitic idiom, in fact, a person with a limited command of Greek. But Luke was not necessarily the latter as the testimony of Acts 15.35ff. shows. He was quite capable of writing Greek free from the sort of Semitic characteristics we have been studying, when not influenced by Semitic sources, or by sources written in the kind of Semitic-like Greek of much of the New Testament. Consider the different 'scores' of the various parts of Luke–Acts. Acts 15.35ff. shows a score of +16, the selections from the body of the Gospel a score of 0, and the infancy narratives a score of -16. What can be the explanation of these variations?

Luke had no Semitic sources for the latter half of Acts and he wrote a text which consistently shows the characteristics of original Greek. In other words, it appears that Luke's normal Greek, that is, the Greek which he wrote when certainly not influenced by Semitic sources, is similar to the sample of original Greek which Martin studied. In the selections from the Gospel, on the other hand, he appears to have been dependent on Semitic-like sources. In these chapters Luke displayed translation and original Greek frequencies about equally. It appears that Luke's Greek may here be rather similar to that of his source when judged by Martin's criteria.

With respect to Luke 5.12–6.11 and its source in Mark, it appears that in every case except criterion 9, the ratio of καί to δέ, there is a marked similarity between the figures for the two gospels. The ratio is 6.75 to 1 in Mark but only 1.77 to 1 for Luke. Luke is considerably less Semitic here than is Mark and it rather looks as if Luke has 'improved' on the language of his source at this point. Even in the case of the two criteria in which Mark falls on the original Greek side of the divide and Luke on the other, the figures are remarkably similar. In criterion 11 the figures for dependent genitives are:

	Post-	Pre-
Luke	29	0
Mark	27	2

In criterion 17 the numbers of datives without ἐν are almost identical, 17 for Mark, 16 for Luke. The difference in the result of the calculations derives from the fact that Luke uses ἐν slightly more frequently than does Mark, for example in the characteristic construction ἐν τῷ + infinitive. In some cases Mark appears the more Semitic, in other cases, Luke, but the similarity between the two is obvious. In fact, Luke 5.12–6.11 is usually closer to Mark in its frequencies than it is to Luke 12. The most plausible explanation for all this is that

Luke's style with respect to these seventeen criteria absorbs some of the characteristics of his source. The fact that Luke altered the language of his source with respect to the καί/δέ ratio, which is probably the most immediately noticeable of the Semitisms discerned by Martin's method, but did not alter Mark's language with respect to the other criteria, may well indicate that the use of the syntactical features discerned by them is below the level of conscious control. The absorption of these Semitic characteristics may not therefore be related to any desire to imitate Semitic style but rather to the level of Semitism of his source. That is to say, Luke's language is not conditioned here by his own literary strategy but by the character of his source.

What then of Luke 1–2 with its 'score' of -16? This is radically different even from that of the Greek of Luke 5.12–6.11. What can be the explanation of this? With respect to Martin's criteria it appears that:

1. *Luke 1–2 is dissimilar to original Greek.*
2. *Luke 1–2 is similar to translation Greek.*
3. *Luke could absorb characteristics discovered by Martin's method from a source.*

Given these three observations, the most plausible explanation for the Hebraic colouring of Luke 1–2 must surely be that Luke has once again absorbed some of the style of a source. Furthermore, if even Revelation, written in Greek by an author thinking in Hebrew, does not display the consistently Semitic frequencies of Luke 1–2, it seems reasonable to suppose that the source was not simply Semitic Greek but rather had actually been composed in one of the Semitic languages. The application of Raymond Martin's method produces evidence which appears to break the draw, of which Raymond Brown wrote, in favour of the advocates of Hebrew source theory.

The use of Martin's method does not provide all the information an investigator of these chapters might desire. One cannot tell, for example, whether there is one source behind Luke 1–2 or several, nor whether the source or sources were oral or written. These questions need not concern us, however, for the hymns, not the narrative, are the focus of interest of this study. It does appear that these hymns may depend upon Semitic, probably Hebrew, originals.

APPENDIX
Tables Illustrative of Raymond Martin's Syntactical Studies
and of Their Application to Luke 1–2.

Table 1

Raymond Martin determined that the frequency of appearance of the following eight prepositions relative to the frequency of appearance of ἐν could function as criteria for determining the presence or absence of translation Greek. Translation Greek frequencies are *less than* the numeral that appears in the right-hand column.

1. διά with the genitive case   .06
2. διά in all occurrences   .18
3. εἰς   .49
4. κατά with the accusative case   .18
5. κατά in all occurrences   .19
6. περί   .27
7. πρός with the dative case   .024
8. ὑπό with the genitive case   .07

Table 2

Translated Greek	Lines of Greek Text
Genesis 1–4, 6, 39	382
1 Samuel 3, 4, 22	194
1 Kings 17	58
2 Kings 13	71
Daniel—Hebrew Sections—LXX	482
Daniel—Hebrew Sections—Theodotion	460
Daniel—Aramaic Section—LXX	595
Daniel—Aramaic Section—Theodotion	634
Ezra—Hebrew Sections	328
Ezra—Aramaic Sections	211
Total Lines of Translated Greek	3418

Original Greek	
Plutarch's *Lives*	325
Demosthenes I, II, III, XXI	
Cicero I, II, XXX, XLIX	
Alexander L, LI, LII	
Polybius—*The Histories*	192
Book I, 1-4	
Book II, 7	
Epictetus—*The Discourses*	138
Book III, Chapter II	
Book IV, Chapters II and III	
Josephus	215
Contra Apionem, Book I, 1-4	
Antiquities, Book XIV, 1	
Papyri (Numbers 1, 2, 3, 16, 18-115, 117, 121, 127)	630
Total Lines of Original Greek	1500

[See page 10 of R.A. Martin's *Syntactical Evidence*]

Table 3
Texts Studied by Raymond Martin

Text	Net Result
Genesis 1–4, 6, 39	-4
1 Samuel 3, 4, 22	-11
1 Kings 17	-6
2 Kings 13	-12
Daniel Hebrew LXX	-10
Hebrew Theodotion	-12
Aramaic LXX	-12
Aramaic Theodotion	-13
Ezra Hebrew	-14
Ezra Aramaic	-12
Plutarch, Selections	+16
Polybius, Books I, II	+15
Epictetus, Books III, IV	+17
Josephus, Selections	+16
Papyri, Selections	+17

The original of this table is found on page 39 of Raymond Martin's *Syntactical Evidence.*

Table 4
Frequencies in Shorter Units

Unit Length	Original Greek	Translation Greek
31-50 lines	+13 to +7	+1 to -8
16-30 lines	+12 to +3	+4 to -9
4-15 lines	+12 to 0	+7 to -6

[See R.A. Martin's *Syntactical Evidence*, pp. 49-53]

Table 5
Results for Luke 1-2

Section	Lines	Net
Chapter 1 without hymns	107	-12
Hymns of Chapter 1	30	-4
Chapter 2.1-40 without hymns	57	-5
Hymns of Chapter 2	5	-2
Chapter 2.41ff.	23	-2
Chapter 1 total	137	-14
Chapter 2 total	80	-5
Hymns total	35	-4
Grand total	217	-16

Note: Luke 1.1-4, Luke's introduction to the Gospel, was not counted.

Table 6
Results for Other New Testament
Texts

Text	Lines	Net
Luke 5.12–6.11	91	0
Mark 1.40–3.6	89	+2
Luke 12.13–13.9	109	-2
Lukan passages (total)	200	0
Romans 5	50.5	+2
Galatians 1.1–2.5	56	+3
Paul (total)	106.5	+3
Revelation 3	59	-2
Revelation 4.1–5.10	61	-5
Revelation (total)	120	-5

THE FORM OF THE HYMNS

It might seem superfluous to argue at length that hymns which speak of 'our fathers' and mean by that expression Abraham and the patriarchs, that bless the God of Israel, and that call Israel 'his' people, are in some sense Jewish. It might seem especially superfluous after presenting evidence that these hymns were composed in Hebrew. That they were composed, used, and transmitted by those who were, after the flesh, Jewish seems self-evident. These Jews may have belonged to a sect which believed that the Messiah had come, the early church or perhaps an hypothetical baptist sect, or they may have been among those who still longed for his advent, but Jews they were. If one were compelled to prove what seems so self-evident, however, one would search for parallels to the hymns, parallels in vocabulary and form, in the poetry of late Judaism. And in so doing one might well be able more precisely to identify the particular background of Luke's hymns.

It is a point of some interest that when three of this century's greatest experts on the Psalms, H. Gunkel, S. Mowinckel, and C. Westermann, came to deal with the hymns of Luke 1–2 they greeted these poems as old friends. From their study of the Psalter and other Jewish poetry they were already familiar with much of the vocabulary, the patterns of thought, and even the form of the New Testament hymns. Of these similarities, the similarity in form is the most significant. The use of Biblical phraseology indicates only that the Old Testament was honoured by the circle in which Luke's hymns originated, but similarities in form may indicate that they were part of a living tradition of prayer and praise.[1]

By a comparison of the hymns of Luke 1–2 with other Jewish hymns of the period it may be possible more exactly to determine the nature of that tradition, whether Jewish, on the one hand, or some special sort of Jewish on the other, that is, Jewish-Christian or baptist. This possibility exists because the strongest argument that the hymns are unqualifiedly Jewish rather than baptist or Christian appears to be that of Hermann Gunkel. He identified these poems as 'eschatologische Hymnen, und zwar solche von völliger Stilreinheit'.[2] For this reason Gunkel considered it unnecessary and indeed mistaken to search for any particular historical event against which to interpret the aorists of Luke's hymns. These merely reflect the 'prophetic perfect' of the Semitic original. This position renders irrelevant Brown's otherwise crucial point that 'one would have to find a Jewish situation in the two centuries before Christ which would explain the canticles' tone of salvation accomplished'.[3] Salvation had not been accomplished in the time of the composer of the hymns; they could have been written by anyone who longed for the fulfillment of God's purposes.

On the other hand, C. Westermann believed that these hymns are 'declarative psalms of praise':

> The declarative psalm of praise is found also in the NT. The examples, Luke 1.68-75 (declarative praise of the people) and 2.29-32 (1.46-55) (of the individual) show that declarative praise was again awakened when God performed the decisive, final deed of salvation for his people in the sending of his Son.[4]

Here the aorists are interpreted as referring back to a particular event, in Westermann's view the coming of Jesus Christ. The precise identification of the particular event, however, is a matter of content rather than form. A declarative psalm of praise could refer back to any event which had been perceived to be an instance of God's saving power at work. At this point Brown's demand quoted above becomes relevant. What event in Jewish history could be so interpreted and be described in the sort of language we find in the hymns of Luke 1–2? This is a question which must be taken up at greater length in another chapter.

Sigmund Mowinckel also considered the hymns in Luke 1–2 to be Jewish-Christian:

> Finally we must refer to the lingerings of psalmography to be found among the first community of Jewish Christians ... the hymns of praise by Zacharias and Mary in the gospel of Luke. Here the rejoicing over the deliverance already experienced through the actual coming of Jesus-Messiah find expression in the ancient

epiphany psalm style; the hope for the future is actualized through the new experience that, in Christ, God has again come to his people and has created salvation and established his kingdom for all time.[5]

For our purposes, however, Mowinckel's analysis of these psalms, tied up as it is with his conception of the great festivals of Temple worship, is less useful than that of Westermann. For the latter declarative praise 'has its location 'out there', in the midst of history, yes, while still on the battlefield—in the hour and place where God has acted'.[6] Psalmody does not originate in the cult; it springs from life at the point at which God touches human affairs. 'The Sitz-im-Leben of the hymn is: the experience of God's intervention in history. God has acted; he has helped his people, now praise must be sung to him.'[7] The difference here is slight but important. Both Mowinckel and Westermann believe that the praise of God in Luke's hymns responds to the saving act of God, the sending of Jesus Christ, but for the former the shape of the praise is determined by the ritual of an ancient festival; it is imitative and archaic, the 'lingering' of a form of speech. For the latter scholar the praise springs afresh from the nature of the contact between God and humanity; it takes its shape because God has once again acted. It seems less useful to categorize the hymns of Luke 1–2 according to their similarity to the hypothetical liturgies of an ancient feast than to do so by means of the way they speak of the God who acts.

These then are the two options that present themselves to the investigator of the form of the hymns; the poems are eschatological hymns or they are declarative psalms of praise. If they are the former they are almost certainly unqualifiedly Jewish. If they are the latter we may examine the content of the hymns to determine against which event in history it is best to interpret them. If this can be done with any degree of certainty we shall have discovered the community in which the hymns of Luke 1–2 probably originated.

It must be emphasized that this investigation is at this point purely a form-critical one. It may well be that the hymns and in particular the Magnificat speak of events which have occurred and yet have consequences for the future. The hymns' perspective on salvation history is a complicated one and it will not do unduly to flatten it into one temporal viewpoint.[8] The present investigation is merely an attempt to decide which of the identifications proposed by Gunkel and Westermann is the more correct.

It is appropriate to begin with Gunkel, the father of form-criticism of the Psalms, and, more specifically, with his description of the eschatological hymn.

> Solche Dictungen [eschatological hymns] haben etwa die Form der Hymnen. Durchweg findet sich der bekannte Hymnenstil, die imperativische Einführung mit folgendem *ki* oder dem hymnischen Partizipium, das erzählende Hauptstück mit dem Perfekt oder dem historischen Imperfekt usw.... Was diese Hymnen zu eschatologische Hymnen macht, ist ihr Stoff.[9]

The clearest examples of the eschatological hymn are found not in the Psalter but in the prophets.[10] Such hymns are especially frequent in Deutero-Isaiah.

> Break forth together into singing, you waste places of Jerusalem;
> For the Lord has comforted his people, he has redeemed Jerusalem.
> The Lord has bared his holy arm before the eyes of all the nations;
> And all the ends of the earth shall see the salvation of our God (Is.
>   52.9-10).

Here we see the structure characteristic of the hymn in a poem which speaks of events which, from the perspective of the poet, were yet to come as if they had already happened. There is no need to seek here for an historical event which had prompted such praise; the praise had sprung forth from the certainty of God's future salvation.[11]

As was mentioned earlier, Gunkel saw in these poems the characteristic structure of the hymn. There are, of course, many departures from the basic structure but the distinguishing elements of the hymn may be described as follows:

1. Introductory word of praise, often second person imperative plural.[12]
2. A transition or motive clause often beginning with the word 'for'.[13]
3. A series of statements of praise to God expanding the motive clause.
4. A concluding formula (optional).

There are several other sorts of psalms in Gunkel's system of classification the burden of which is the praise of God, the songs of thanksgiving (*Danklieder*) of Israel and the individual being the most important. These psalms have a structure similar to that of the hymns. The difference between these *Gattungen* is not a matter of form. 'Die Unterschied ist, dass die Danklieder über die besondere Tat jauchzen, die Gott soeben an dem Dankenden getan hat, während die Hymnen die grossen Taten und herrlichen Eigenschaften im allgemeinem besingen.'[14]

For Westermann, however, there are but 'two basic modes of speaking to God, praise and petition'.[15] Within these two modes of speaking of God are further subdivisions; within petition one finds laments of the people and laments of the individual and within praise are declarative psalms of praise, again of the people and of the individual, and descriptive songs of praise. The distinction between the two sorts of praise, the declarative on the one hand and the descriptive on the other, is more or less the same as Gunkel's distinction between hymns and songs of thanksgiving. 'The difference between the two groups lies in the fact that the so-called hymn praises God for his actions and his being as a whole (descriptive praise), while the so-called song of thanks praises God for a specific deed, which the one who has been delivered recounts or reports in his song (declarative praise; it could also be called confessional praise).'[16] As we shall see, however, there is also a structural difference between the two kinds of praise for Westermann. It may seem odd or even somewhat pedantic that Westermann did not rest content with the names of categories used by Gunkel. It is important to understand that Westermann believed that the word hymn describes a phenomenon of literary or cultic origins while the psalms rest on the experience of God acting and are a direct reaction to that experience. The origin of the psalms lies in simple one-sentence exclamations of praise. 'Song of Thanksgiving' is also a misleading term because the Hebrews had no separate concept of 'thanks' as we do. This concept was bound up in the broader and more lively concept of 'praise' compared to which our modern concept of thanks is narrow and inadequate.[17] For these reasons he believed the old names of the categories were misleading and ought to be dropped.

Within the psalms of petition there is already praise, the vow of praise near the conclusion of both sorts of lament and the words of praise towards the end of the 'heard' lament of the individual. (Laments of the individual can be either 'open' or 'heard'; the latter are those in which the psalmist declares his confidence that his petition has been heard by God.) A particularly fine example is Psalm 28.6ff. of which the first line is: 'Blessed be the Lord for he has heard the voice of my supplications'.[18]

This sort of language is already declarative praise and indeed Psalm 28.6 contains the exact form of the central sentence of the declarative psalm of praise of the people.[19] There are 'three elements which are in general determinative for declarative praise.

1. The praise of Yahweh for a deed he has done.
2. The nature of these sentences as immediate response to God's intervention.
3. The essentially joyful nature of this praise.

In their structure (shout of praise and the reason for it: God has acted) as well as in these three elements the *baruk* sentences in the historical books correspond to the declarative Psalms of praise.'[20] Similarly in the declarative psalm of praise of the individual there is an introductory summary which has this same structure, word of praise and reason for it.[21]

The classic declarative psalm of praise is the Song of the Sea, Exodus 15.21: 'Sing to the Lord for he has triumphed gloriously; the horse and his rider he has thrown into the sea'.[22] Here we have the cry of praise and the reason for it all in one sentence. This is an important point for Westermann who believed that all true confession or praise of God can be concentrated into one sentence.[23]

The introductory word of praise of the one sentence confessional praise is almost never a second person plural imperative. That is, it is not a summons to praise; it is praise itself. Only in a declarative psalm of praise which has become a liturgy, Psalm 118, do we find the imperative. (Westermann follows the LXX in reading 'Let us sing' in Ex. 15.21.)

We are now able to summarize Westermann's description of the declarative psalm of praise.

1. It is an immediate joyful response to God's act.
2. It can be comprehended in one sentence.
3. The structure of the psalm is typically: word of praise plus reason for it (God has acted).
4. The word of praise is not second person imperative plural.

Just as declarative praise developed out of the lament so descriptive praise developed out of declarative. The development can be seen in two places.[24] First, it can be seen in Solomon's prayer at the dedication of the Temple. 'Blessed be the Lord who has given rest to his people Israel, according to all that he promised' (1 Kings 8.56).

This word of praise is no longer an immediate response to a specific act but rather looks back to God's favour over a long period. Secondly, there appear late in the declarative psalms of the individual statements which look beyond the particular deed of God to his wider activity. Psalm 18.27: 'Thou dost deliver . . . and thou dost bring down'; 34.22 'The Lord redeems the life of his servants; none of those who take refuge in him will be condemned'. Another example is Psalm 30.45 in which declarative praise not only employs some characteristic motifs of descriptive praise but assumes its characteristic form, the call to praise in the imperative: 'Sing praises to the Lord, O you his saints, for his anger is but for a moment and his favour is for a lifetime'. The imperative call to praise is an essential part of descriptive psalms of praise; all such psalms have it. Most give the reason for praise (motive clause) which, as in declarative praise, is developed and expanded. These psalms praise God for both his majesty and his grace although in late examples there is a tendency for one of the two aspects of descriptive praise to swallow up the other.[25]

Westermann does not forget to discuss the eschatological song of praise.[26] He noticed that Gunkel had classified these hymns as eschatological because of their content but claimed that Gunkel had correctly identified their form as well. They all possess an imperative introduction and a narrative main body. The verbs in this narrative body are, in the examples which concern us most, in the prophetic perfect. In other words, the narrative main body of the declarative psalm of praise has been joined to the introduction of descriptive praise thus creating an entirely new form. The large number of these songs in Deutero-Isaiah lead Westermann to suppose that the form was created by that prophet.[27]

None of the hymns in Luke 1–2 begins with an imperative call to praise.

> My soul magnifies the Lord . . .
> Blessed be the Lord the God of Israel . . .
> Now lettest thou thy servant depart in peace . . .

When one examines the poems which either Gunkel or Westermann considered eschatological hymns one finds an impressive consistency in structure. One finds the structure of imperative plus 'for' plus prophetic perfect in Isaiah 12.4-6; 44.23; 48.20; 49.13; 52.9; Jeremiah 20.13; 31.7-9; Joel 2.21ff.; Zechariah 2.14. Zephaniah 3.14-15 lacks only the word 'for'. In the psalter Psalm 98 has precisely this structure as does Psalm 9.12-13 (if this is to be considered eschatological). The following poems have the structure of imperative plus 'for' plus imperfect: Deuteronomy 32.43; Zechariah 9.9; Isaiah 40.9-11. Very similar are Isaiah 54.1, imperative plus 'for' plus nominal sentence and Psalm 148, imperative plus 'for' plus participles. The poems which concern us most are those which use the prophetic perfect to speak of future events. Other psalms speak from time to time of the future but their orientation is made clear by the use of the Hebrew imperfect. Among such psalms are Psalms 9, 68, 75, and 148 and Tobit 13. Such psalms are not at all similar to the hymns of Luke 1–2 and therefore need not concern us greatly.

There remain a few psalms to consider. In Isaiah 12.1-6 there are two short psalms, vv. 1-2 and 4-6, each preceded by the rubric, 'you will say in that day'. The first psalm is a perfect miniature psalm of declarative praise, the second a perfect miniature descriptive psalm of praise. As one might expect, the first psalm (declarative praise) does not begin with an imperative but rather with a voluntative. Like the so-called Hymn of the Return, 1QM XIV. 4ff., it is not in itself an eschatological hymn but a psalm which by means of its literary context is made to speak of future events. That is to say, the rubric rather than the poem itself is eschatological. The setting, not the verbs, is prophetic.

Isaiah 25.1-5 appears to be a declarative psalm of praise set in the midst of Isaiah's little apocalypse. It is only loosely connected to its context; the first words of 25.6, 'on this mountain', seem to refer back to Mt Zion which is last mentioned in 24.23 (there is no mountain in 25.1-5). Nevertheless, the psalm may be 'a prophetic psalm of thanksgiving composed specifically for its present place'.[28] It may be that the song is governed by the unexpressed rubric 'on that day', a rubric which appears at 25.9, 26.1, and 27.2.[29] Nevertheless, it is entirely possible that we have here an eschatological hymn which does not begin with an imperative but contains verbs in the prophetic perfect.

It seems almost certain that Isaiah 61.10 is an eschatological hymn.[30] This poem does not begin with an imperative call to praise. Indeed, its introduction is somewhat reminiscent of the Magnificat's, 'I will greatly rejoice in the Lord; my soul shall exult in my God (LXX καὶ εὐφροσύνῃ εὐφρανθήσονται ἐπὶ κύριον, ἀγαλλιάσθω ἡ ψυχή μου ἐπὶ τῷ κυρίῳ), for he has clothed me with the garments of salvation'.

The example of Isaiah 61.10 indicates clearly that the imperative call to praise is not an absolutely essential feature of the eschatological hymn. Nevertheless, it would be fair to call the imperative introduction a regular feature of these hymns. Indeed, the eschatological hymns are structurally more consistent than many other form-critical types identified by Westermann and Gunkel.

Another feature recurs in a number of these hymns. Consider once again Isaiah 52.9-10.

> Break forth together into singing . . .
> for the Lord has comforted his people . . .
> And all the ends of the earth shall see the salvation of our God.

Westermann considered this last line a 'variation' or 'expansion' but very similar variations occur in a number of eschatological hymns.[31] Many of them conclude, as does this poem, by shifting into the imperfect tense. There is a shift of perspective so that the prophet no longer speaks from the vantage point of the eschaton but from his own proper time. This shift in perspective may also be found in Isaiah 61.10ff.; Jeremiah 31.7-9; Joel 2.21ff.; and Psalm 98. The 'proper' vantage point of the poet is made clear in another way as well, by the literary context in which the hymns are found. In Deutero-Isaiah, for example, the eschatological songs tend to conclude extensive blocks of material which show that the prophet is speaking of future events. One could observe much the same with respect to the other examples, except, of course, for Psalm 98.

We are now in a position to summarize the characteristic structure of the eschatological hymn.

1. An imperative call to praise (almost always).
2. A motive clause frequently using the prophetic perfect.
3. A perspective shift (optional).

This sort of hymn looks forward to a saving act of God.

Although the key sentence of a declarative psalm of praise may be expanded in a variety of ways its essential structure is:

1. Word of praise (imperative).
2. Reason for praise: God has acted (motive clause).

This sort of hymn look back with joy to a saving act of God.

All the evidence brought forward to this point has been drawn from the OT. It must be asked whether the forms described above survived into the intertestamental and early Christian era. Fortunately, a large sample of hymnic material from that era has survived. In the apocryphal and pseudepigraphical literature and in several of the Qumran scrolls there are many references to praise and some fine hymns can be found embedded in that material. Furthermore, several collections of psalms have survived, the Psalms of Solomon, the Hodayoth, and the apocryphal psalms of caves 4 and 11 of Qumran.

It seems reasonable to suppose that the hymnic material in the apocrypha and pseudepigrapha reflects the form of praise actually used in worship because many of the prayers found in that literature are structurally identical to the Shemoneh Esreh, the most ancient of Jewish prayers. I quote here from the Babylonian recension of the prayer and include the fifteenth of the eighteen benedictions because of its similarity to the language of the Benedictus.

> Blessed art thou Lord our God and God of our fathers, God of Abraham, God of Isaac, God of Jacob, great, mighty and fearful God, most high God who bestowest grace ... Cause the shoot of David to shoot forth quickly, and raise up his horn by thy salvation. For we wait on thy salvation all the day. Blessed art thou, Lord, who causes the horn of salvation to shoot forth.[32]

The prayer of Azariah (Additions to Daniel 1.3, 19) reads: 'Blessed art thou, O Lord, God of our fathers and worthy of praise ... Do not put us to shame but deal with us in thy forbearance and in thy abundant mercy.' The same structure, benediction, ascription of praise and petition, can be found at a number of other points in this literature.[33]

If then the apocryphal and pseudepigraphical literature can accurately reflect the structure of Jewish prayer it seems reasonable to suppose that it can also do so with respect to Jewish praise.

There are three sorts of occurrence of praise in the apocryphal and pseudepigraphical literature: 1. the bare report of praise, 2. a brief prose summary of praise, 3. the inclusion of relatively lengthy psalms. I shall not pursue the question of whether these poems were composed for their present literary contexts. The question is not an important one for even psalms composed to enrich a story must be modelled on psalms actually in use.

As one might expect there are very many reports of praise. These reports appear with impressive consistency immediately after and in response to some event which is interpreted as a gracious act of God. After victory the army of Judas 'sang hymns and praises to heaven, for he is good, for his steadfast love endures forever'. So Baruch 'gave glory to God who counted me worthy of such honour'.[34] In the same manner Abram says in the Genesis Apocryphon, 'and there I called upon the name of the Lord of ages and I praised the name of God, and I blessed God and I gave thanks there for all the flocks and the good things which he had given me; because he had done good to me; because he had brought me back'.[35]

One could go on piling up such examples indefinitely.[36] The pattern is clear, however; praise in this literature almost without exception looks back to a saving event. As was typical of declarative praise in the OT this sort of praise reports God's goodness to the speaker or to the people. One can even see in the examples given above traces of the typical structure of the declarative psalm of praise, word of praise + reason for it: God has acted.

Slightly more elaborate than the reports of praise are brief summaries of praise which also appear very frequently in the literature. As Gunkel noted, these summaries commonly employ the formula 'Blessed art thou' or 'Blessed be' (ברוך).[37] As was the case with the reports of praise, the summaries follow an act of God and thank him for it. So Tobit says, upon seeing his son before him, 'Blessed art thou O God, and blessed is thy name forever, and blessed are all thy holy angels. For thou hast afflicted me, but thou hast had mercy on me; here I see my son Tobias' (Tob. 11.14-15). Similarly after the favourable decree of Artaxexes, Ezra praises God saying, 'Blessed be the Lord alone who put this into the heart of the king, to glorify his house which is in Jerusalem' (1 Esd. 4.60). An interesting passage reminiscent of the Nunc Dimittis is found in Jubilees 45.3-5. Jacob, Israel, speaks these words upon seeing Joseph:[38]

> Now let me die since I have seen thee, and now may the Lord God of Israel be blessed, the God of Abraham and the God of Isaac who hath not withheld his mercy and his grace from his servant Jacob . . . It is true enough for me that I have seen thy face whilst I am yet alive; yes, true is the vision I saw at Bethel. Blessed be the Lord my God forever and ever. Blessed be his name.

The structure of the declarative psalm of praise can be seen clearly in these examples. The reason for praise is explicitly given. The word of praise is not necessarily 'Blessed' despite the examples given above. Various other introductory words appear; sometimes the introductory word of praise is absent.[39]

Rather lengthy hymns may also be found in the same literature. Magnificent psalms appear at the conclusion of Tobit, Judith and Sirach and another hymn, the song of the three children, may be found in the Additions to Daniel 1.29ff.[40] A commentary on these hymns is well beyond the scope of this chapter but the following observations may be made.

Sirach 51.1-12 is a particularly fine example of the song of thanksgiving of the individual (Gunkel) or declarative psalm of praise of the individual (Westermann).[41] As such the psalm responds to an act of grace experienced by the psalmist.

By virtue of their positions the psalms in Tobit, Judith, and the Additions to Daniel all refer to a specific deed of God. Much of the content of the song of Judith likewise refers to the central act of the book. The structure of the hymn is very similar to that of the song of Deborah in Judges 5 on which Judith's song may be modelled. Like that ancient psalm the song begins with an imperative call to praise. 'Begin a new song to my God ... For God is the Lord who crushes wars.' The account of the death of Holofernes forms the expansion of the motive clause. It is worthy of note that the motive clause itself describes a repeated or regular action of God and thus is closer to descriptive than to declarative praise.

The psalm in Tobit 13, on the other hand, has little to do with the surrounding narrative and is an unusual mixture of motifs. The introductory word of praise is a benediction but the motive clause introduces a motif typical of descriptive praise. Subsequently, however, there are numerous instances of the imperative call to praise. The latter half of the psalm is shot through with eschatological predictions, expressed in the future tense.

Although the Song of the Three Children comes from the heart of the flames it too is a response to a saving act of God for the angel of the Lord has joined the three Hebrews and has preserved their lives. This poem contains one verse of declarative praise inserted to adapt the rather general hymn to its literary context.[42] In this verse we find the motive clause reporting the action of God which is the reason for praise, 'for he ... has delivered us from the midst of the burning fiery furnace' (Add. Dan. 1.66). The introductory word of praise is imperative, 'Bless the Lord', but this is a clear case of imitation of the style of the remainder of the hymn.

The Qumran Hodayoth form a considerable body of late-Jewish hymns. Repeatedly one finds in them the familiar structure of declarative praise, word of praise + reason for it: God has acted. 'I praise thee, O Lord, for thou hast placed my soul in the bundle of the living.'[43] At several points this formula is replaced by a benediction, 'Blessed art thou, O Lord',[44] which functions in exactly the same way. One notices immediately that the saving act for which the psalmist praises God is spiritual and personal rather than physical or historical. The poet thanks God for the nature of his relationship to God, for election, illumination, knowledge, forgiveness, etc. As is the case with Luke's hymns, the Hodayoth are full of Old Testament terminology. 'They imitate biblical psalms to such an extent that most Essene hymns are patchworks of phrases from the Psalter, and, notably, from the prophets.'[45]

The Hodayoth are not the only psalms from Qumran. Apocryphal psalms have been discovered in Cave 11 and Cave 4.[46] Of these psalms only 11QPs[a] plea shows any of the characteristics of declarative praise. The central portion of that psalm contains 'an individual Danklied for deliverance from death'.[47] The familiar structure of declarative praise is clearly visible. 'Blessed be the Lord who executes righteous deeds . . . Near death was I for my sins . . . but thou didst save me, O Lord.' Several other psalms from these caves will be considered under the category of eschatological hymns.

In 1930 M. Noth published five apocryphal Syriac psalms and argued that they had originally been composed in Hebrew.[48] Later it was suggested by M. Delcor and M. Philonenko that these psalms were connected with the Essenes.[49] These suppositions were strikingly borne out when the first three of these compositions were discovered at Qumran in the psalm scroll from Cave 11. The remaining two Syriac psalms have not been discovered there but it is reasonable to suppose that they too go back to Hebrew originals. Of these two psalms the second, or fifth overall, is also a hymn. This psalm represents a slight departure from the familiar structural pattern. The psalm begins with the imperative call to praise of the descriptive psalms, 'Praise the Lord, all ye peoples', but eventually becomes declarative praise, 'He delivered me from the snare of Sheol . . . '[50]

Hymns can also be found in two of the longer non-poetic scrolls from Qumran. The concluding portion of the Manual of Discipline is a rather lengthy hymn-like poem. It is marked by a great expansion of the expression of intention to praise God. As was the case with the

Hodayoth the poet speaks primarily of the nature of his relationship with God.

For the purposes of this chapter a far more important psalm is the so-called hymn of the return in 1QM XIV. 4ff. This is the hymn to be sung on the battlefield the morning after the great victory over the Kittim. The exact extent of this hymn is in dispute. Yadin appeared to find its conclusion in 1QM XIV. 15. Osten-Sacken found a two-strophe hymn culminating in line 12a, and P.R. Davies saw three originally independent hymns in 1QM XIV. 4-16.[51] It is not necessary to resolve this difficulty in order to compare the structure of the hymn to the patterns we have already seen. Here is Yadin's translation of parts of 1QM XIV. 4ff.:

4   Blessed be the God of Israel who preserves mercy for his covenant,
5   and times ordained for salvation for the people to be redeemed by Him.
     He hath called them that stumble into wondrous (mighty deeds) . . .
6   so as to raise up by judgment them whose heart had melted,
     to open the mouth of the dumb ones
     to sing God's mighty deeds,
     and to teach weak (hands) warfare . . .
8   and all their mighty men shall not be able to resist.[52]

The familiar structure of declarative praise is clearly present: word of praise + reason for it (God has acted). It is especially to be noted that the act of God for which the people praise him is the final eschatological victory over the heathen. It is not, therefore, an eschatological hymn in the same sense as the songs in Deutero-Isaiah, for, unlike those poems, this hymn looks back on the eschaton and therefore uses the language and form of declarative praise. It is the kind of song pious Jews could imagine themselves singing in response to the ultimate triumph of God. At present the hymn has no setting in life; its only setting is in fantasy. What cannot be ignored, however, is that it looks back to the triumph of God and so has the typical structure of psalms which do the same in real life.

The hymn of the return is very similar to the Benedictus in its introductory benediction and in its use of several key words, covenant, salvation, redeemed, etc. Another similarity lies in the series of infinitives in line 6 which function in much the manner as the infinitives in the Benedictus. In lines 7 and 8 we do have a slight shift in perspective, however. If the hymn was composed for its present literary setting this doubtless represents a slip back into the poet's proper time somewhat analogous to the perspective shift sometimes found in the eschatological hymn proper. If the poem existed separate from its present context it may have celebrated the establishment of the community of which so much was expected.

No survey of intertestamental poetry, even one as brief as this, would be complete without reference to the Psalms of Solomon. There are marked similarities between these psalms and the hymns of Luke 1–2 but these are chiefly similarities in vocabulary. The parallels are verbal rather than formal.[53] In form there is little similarity between these psalms and Luke's hymns. Compare, for instance, the structure of the messianic psalm 17 with that of the Benedictus or Magnificat. However much the language of the former psalm might remind one of the NT hymns, the structure is still completely different. Indeed it is very difficult to classify these psalms using the categories developed from the study of the canonical psalms. One does find from time to time, however, various motifs typical of descriptive praise.[54] One also finds certain reminiscences of declarative praise and once even its usual structure.[55] 'I will give thanks unto thee, O God, for thou hast helped me to my salvation' (Ps. Sol. 16.5). That the Psalms of Solomon resemble Luke's hymns in vocabulary but not in form is an interesting contradiction, one that deserves more attention in the next chapter.

It is apparent that the concept of declarative praise had not died out in intertestamental Judaism. Constantly one finds in the apocrypha and pseudepigrapha evidence that praise was understood to be a joyful response to a saving act of God. One also finds regularly in this literature and in the surviving psalms of the period the typical structure of declarative praise, word of praise + reason for it. The most common introductory word of praise is 'Blessed be' or 'Blessed art thou'. Occasionally the second person plural imperative call to praise occurs, perhaps in the imitation of the style of the very numerous descriptive psalms of praise of the psalter. In general, however, it seems fair to state that declarative praise is present in the literature and that its characteristic structure is readily recognizable.

That declarative praise is also present in the NT is equally clear. James M. Robinson traced the influence of the Hodayoth formula in particular through the NT and early Christianity.[56] Its influence can be seen in the opening thanksgivings in Paul's letters. 'I thank my God through Jesus Christ for all of you because your faith is proclaimed in all the world' (Rom. 1.8). Similar formulae appear in 1 Corinthians 1.4-5, 1 Thessalonians 1.2ff., 2.13, 2 Thessalonians 1.3, 2.13, and also in 1 Timothy 1.12. Only two hymns show this structure, Matthew 11.25-27, Luke 10.21-22 and Revelation 11.17-18. The latter begins: 'We give thanks to thee, Lord God Almighty . . . that (ὅτι) thou hast taken thy great power and begun to reign'. Robinson notes that in Christian praise, and perhaps already in that of Hellenistic Judaism, there is a tendency to replace the use of words of benediction with words of thanks. This change is epitomized by the fact that the Jewish tractate on prayer is called Berakoth but the central Christian rite is the eucharist.[57] Apart from OT citations, benedictions appear in the NT only in the Benedictus and in the opening verses of 2 Corinthians, Ephesians, and 1 Peter.[58] On the other hand, the use of formulae of blessing remained common in Judaism. Indeed, some rabbis apparently took a dim view of the proliferation of books of berakoth.[59] 'Books of benedictions, even though they may contains words and quotations from the Torah, do not defile the hands' (Tosephta Yadaim, 1). 'Books of benedictions containing quotations from the Torah must not be rescued from a fire (on the Sabbath)' (jShabbath XVI, 1).

There are fewer examples of the eschatological hymn in inter-testamental literature. Two certain examples are Baruch 4.36ff. and Psalms of Solomon 11. These two poems are not unrelated; indeed, it is clear that one is dependent on the other. The question of priority is not an important one for our purposes and may safely be left aside. Since both passages are ultimately dependent on Deutero-Isaiah it is no surprise to meet in them the familiar structure of the eschato-logical hymns, imperative + reason for praise. The imperatives are not directly exhortations to praise God but otherwise the hymns are identical in form to the earlier eschatological hymns. One notices especially the use of the 'prophetic perfect' (aorists as in Luke's hymns): 'The woods and every fragrant tree have shaded Israel at God's command' (Bar. 5.9), 'for God hath had pity on Israel in visiting them' (Ps. Sol. 11.1). The perspective shift is also present, 'For God will lead Israel with joy in the light of his glory' (Bar. 5.9). 'Let the Lord do what he hath spoken concerning Israel and Jerusalem' (Ps. Sol. 11.9). There is no major change here in the structure of the eschatological hymn.

The concluding portion of 11QPs^a 154 may also be an eschato-logical hymn. Unfortunately the lines in question have all but disappeared in the decay of the psalm scroll from Qumran. Here is Sanders's translation of the verses in question, lines 18-20:

> Bless the Lord who redeems the humble from the hand of strangers and delivers the pure from the hand of the wicked, who establishes a horn out of Jacob and a judge of peoples out of Israel. He will spread his tent in Zion and abide forever in Jerusalem.[60]

Sanders is here following Noth's reconstruction from the Syriac of the underlying Hebrew text. If this reconstruction is correct the usual structure of the eschatological hymn is present although in this case participles replace the use of the prophetic perfect. However, the key word ברכו is read as ברוך by various scholars.[61] If this reconstruction is correct this psalm may be an eschatological hymn beginning with the formula 'Blessed be'. D. Lührmann, one of the scholars who follows this reading, denies that the hymn is eschatological or messianic, however.[62] It is rather a poem which describes the descent of Wisdom and her dwelling with the people. On the other hand, J. Magne suggests that the present psalm is a result of the combination of a sapiential poem and an invitation to a cult of praise equivalent in value to Temple worship.[63] The verses in question form the conclusion of the latter psalm. It does seem probable that line 18 should be related to the imperative call to praise which forms the first three lines of the psalm. However, the text and its interpret-ation are too uncertain for use as evidence in the present study.

Two poems discovered in Qumran Cave 4, apocryphal psalms B and C, may also be eschatological hymns.[64] Unfortunately the first three lines of Psalm B are missing. The remaining portion of the psalm begins: 'et qu'ils louent le nom de Yahweh car il vient juger tout oeuvre', and concludes: 'Que mangent les pauvres (ענוים) et que soient rassasies ceux qui craignent Yahweh'. This hymn clearly speaks of the future and may begin with an introduction other than an imperatve.

Psalm C begins: 'Sois plein de joie, Juda... Célèbre tes fêtes, accomplis tes voeux, car il n'y a pas de Belial au milieu de toi.' I have adopted here Starcky's somewhat tentative suggestion that the head of the column in which Psalm C occurs contains the conclusion of another psalm, 'que toutes les étoiles du soir jubilent donc'. There is a blank in the manuscript at the conclusion of this line[65] and, I suggest, no clear connection in thought or structure between it and what follows. Once again there is a shift in perspective late in the psalm, 'Voici que les ennemis vont périr et que seront dispersés tous les artisans de mal'. This psalm certainly seems to show the characteristics of the eschatological hymn.

Although it is possible that some eschatological hymns have lost the imperative call to praise, it appears that the characteristic structure of the form survived. The literature of the intertestamental period, especially the apocalyptic writings, contain various descriptions of the future, but the eschatological hymn is the only sort of description of the future which bears even a passing resemblance to the hymns of Luke 1–2.

When one turns to the hymns of Luke 1–2 one finds a consistent structure: word of praise + reason for it (God has acted).[66] The word of praise is not an imperative in any of the three hymns.

> My soul magnifies the Lord . . . for he who is mighty has done great things for me.
> Blessed be the Lord the God of Israel for he has visited and redeemed his people.

The structure is also present, admittedly in an unusual form, in the Nunc Dimittis. The example of Jubilees 45.3 in which Israel's statement that he is willing to die now that he has seen Joseph is parallel to a berakah shows that the opening words of the Nunc Dimittis can be considered an unusual and extravagant form of praise.[67]

> Lord, now lettest thou thy servant depart in peace according to thy word, for mine eyes have seen thy salvation which thou hast prepared in the presence of all the peoples.

If these poems were eschatological hymns one might well expect in them an introductory call to praise in the imperative plural. That not one of the three has this distinguishing mark of the eschatological hymn seems strong evidence that they do not belong to that category. Furthermore, none of them possesses the same kind of perspective shift which often appears in such hymns.[69] Since these hymns are similar in structure to the many examples of declarative psalms of praise and dissimilar to the structure of the much less common eschatological hymn, it seems reasonable to consider the hymns in Luke 1–2 declarative psalms of praise. Such an identification does not in itself preclude the possibility that the hymns were unqualifiedly Jewish or proved that they were Jewish-Christian. It does allow the investigator to proceed to a study of the content of the hymns to determine, if possible, which event in the history of the period could justifiably be described by the language used in them.

THE COMMUNITY OF ORIGIN

At this point I suggest we may regard as proven the theory that the hymns of Luke 1–2 are, in some sense, Jewish. Their conformity to the patterns of late Jewish poetry and their many similarities in vocabulary to that poetry are, I believe, conclusive evidence of this.[1] Now we may consider more specifically whether the hymns are unqualifiedly Jewish, or some special sort of Jewish, i.e. baptist or Jewish-Christian.

If, as seems probable, the hymns of Luke 1–2 are declarative psalms of praise it is right to seek an event in Jewish history against which to interpret them. In doing so one is seeking 'a Jewish situation ... which would explain the canticles' tone of salvation accomplished'.[2] Paul Winter thought he had discovered such a situation in the triumphs of the Maccabaean wars.[3] In 1 Maccabees 4.24 it is said that the triumphant Jewish warriors sang on their return from battle, 'hymns and praises to Heaven, for he is good for his mercies endure forever'. 1QM XIV. 3 also speaks of a 'hymn of return' after victory.[4] The Magnificat, Winter argued, is also a psalm of thanksgiving sung after success in battle while the first part of the Benedictus was a prayer said before the struggle.[5] That Winter has chosen in the victories of the Maccabaean era the only purely Jewish setting which might plausibly account for such triumphant psalms appears indubitable. In demonstrating the extent of post-canonical Jewish poetry Winter could give only exceedingly mournful examples. 'It is one of the rare moments in the history of Jewish thought when despair prevails over hope.'[6] Here Winter referred primarily to the reaction to Titus's destruction of Jerusalem, but the statement is not entirely inapplicable to the period as a whole.[7] If Winter's identification of the hymns is incorrect it may therefore be necessary to seek something other than a purely Jewish setting for the hymns of Luke 1–2.

For several reasons I should judge that Winter's argument is, in fact, incorrect. First, there is the general implausibility of his theory. In what form and in what setting did victory songs from the Maccabaean wars survive the two centuries that must have elapsed before the composition of the infancy stories? What community preserved the hymns and to what use were they put? There may be adequate answers to these questions but Winter does not provide them. Secondly, Winter's argument is flawed in several key details. For example, he suggested that the method of composition of the hymns in Luke was identical with that of the psalm in 1 Chronicles 16 and that the composition of the three psalms must therefore have occurred in the same period.[8] (Winter offered no proof that 1 Chr. 16 was composed in the Maccabaean period.) In fact, there is little similarity with respect to the method of composition of the three hymns. The Lucan psalms are mosaics of loose allusions to many parts of scripture; 1 Chronicles 16 is a nearly exact rendering of Psalm 105.1-15 and 96.1b-13 with a small concluding addition from Psalm 106.1, 47-8.[9] Furthermore, Winter's identification of the Benedictus as 'a prayer incanted before battle'[10] is certainly incorrect. He compared the Benedictus to 1 Maccabees 4.30 which genuinely is such a prayer. That comparison shows clearly that the Benedictus is not the same sort of prayer; it is not addressed to God in the second person singular and makes no petition to him. The Benedictus is, as has been shown, form-critically identical to the Magnificat. Both are responses to God's saving acts and must be differentiated from prayers for deliverance such as 1 Maccabees 4.30ff.

Most importantly, Winter's theory ignored the fact that the Benedictus, at least, speaks of a Davidic Messiah, 'a horn of salvation in the house of David his servant'.[11] This kind of language could hardy be applied to the levitical Hasmonaeans.[12] Certainly, by the time of the composition of the Psalms of Solomon those who hoped for the advent of the Davidic Messiah stood in sharpest opposition to the Hasmonaeans who 'set a worldly monarchy in place of (that which was) their excellency; they laid waste to the throne of David in tumultuous arrogance' (Ps. Sol. 17.7-8).[13] As was mentioned earlier, there are many verbal parallels between the Psalms of Solomon and the Lucan hymns.[14] If the two sets of psalms come from circles with similar mentalities and with similar devotion to a Davidic redeemer it seems hardly likely that the latter hymns are to be connected with Hasmonaean victories. Admittedly, the Magnificat lacks such clear

Davidic overtones, but the great similarity between the two Lucan hymns makes it more than probable that both stem from the same circle if not the same person.

There are also numerous verbal parallels between the two hymns. F. Gryglewicz found that 17 of the 46 'Grundwörter' in the Magnificat and 24 of the 56 in the Benedictus are used in common.[15] (Some of these Grundwörter occur more than once in each hymn. This accounts for the difference of the number of occurrences in each hymn.) Gryglewicz's reasoning is not always entirely convincing but his demonstration of the common use of key terms is significant and persuasive.[16] The use of the OT in the two hymns is also remarkably similar.[17] Furthermore, the Nunc Dimittis displays 'the same cento technique we have seen in the Magnificat and the Benedictus'[18] and there are certain verbal links between it and the Benedictus.[19] One could hardly call the Nunc Dimittis a Maccabaean war song. Indeed Winter himself conceded that this was part of a Christian adaptation of the Infancy narratives.

It seems, therefore, that Winter was probably incorrect in supposing that the hymns of Luke 1 were originally hymns of victory from the era of the Maccabaean wars. Indeed, Winter's theory has met with little acceptance; to the best of my knowledge only two scholars have publicly endorsed it.[20] If Winter's hypothesis is adjudged incorrect it will be necessary to seek something other than a purely Jewish origin for these hymns.

It will be remembered that Gunkel identified these poems as eschatological hymns because of their content.[21] Gunkel was not mistaken in asserting that the content of the hymns is eschatological; a comparison of Luke's hymns with the illustrative material from late Jewish poetry adduced earlier in the chapter will show their eschatological nature. He only erred, I believe, in his explanation of that eschatological content. The poet was not gazing forward to the great victory of God; he could now look back to it. I suggest that the only event which could spark such triumphant 'eschatological' praise would be one that might be interpreted as the sign of the advent of the last days, the coming of the Messiah. We know that one Jewish sect of the period, the early church, claimed that the Messiah had come. It is possible that another group, the disciples of John the Baptist, also venerated its master as Messiah. From one of these two groups the hymns in Luke 1–2 may well have come.

It has been suggested by many scholars that a source emanating from baptist circles might lie behind parts of Luke 1–2.[22] At least the account of the events surrounding John's infancy, Lk. 1.5-25, 57-66, may have originated in a baptist community. Questions concerning the origin of the narrative sections of Luke 1–2 are outside the scope of this study; I shall only deal with such matters indirectly. More important for my purposes are suggestions that either or both of the hymns of Luke 1 are baptist. (I have not discovered any scholar who supposes that the Nunc Dimittis is baptist.)

Not every scholar who finds a baptist source in the narrative sections of Luke 1 believes that the hymns are also baptist. Dibelius, for example, explicitly denied that they were baptist, preferring Gunkel's explanation of their origin.[23] Erdmann believed that only the Magnificat had been part of the Baptist legend while the Benedictus was composed by Luke himself using the former hymn as a model.[24] It will therefore be necessary to examine the two hymns separately. Of the two the Benedictus will require the closer examination since it may well contain direct and explicit references to both John and Jesus.

The Magnificat, on the other hand, is claimed for baptist circles only on the basis of a wider baptist source theory. The supporters of this theory usually argue that the hymn ought to be attributed to Elizabeth rather than to Mary. She may have sung the hymn at Luke 1.25 (Bultmann), at 1.42 (Völter, Erdmann), or in its present location (Kraeling).[25] Aside from questioning the baptist source theory itself, which is outside the scope of the present work, one can only make two points. First, there is nothing in the psalm itself which is peculiarly baptist aside from the rather doubtful interpretation of ταπείνωσις as barrenness. This is more probably a reference to Mary's humble rank.[26] Furthermore, the reference occurs in a verse which Luke may well have added in order to adapt the hymn to its present context.[27] This leads on to the second and vital point. The hymns very probably were once independently circulating compositions, a fact which is widely admitted even by proponents of the baptist source theory.[28] If the Magnificat circulated independently there is no positive reason to assume a baptist origin for it. The possibility of a baptist origin becomes very small indeed if one agrees that v. 48, the verse which adapts the hymn to its context, was the work of Luke himself.

There would be, in my opinion, but one good reason for attributing the composition of the Magnificat to baptist circles, evidence that the closely related Benedictus came from such circles. It is almost beyond argument that the 'child' of v. 76 is John the Baptist.[29] That verse and at least the following one attribute to John an exalted role in the history of salvation. It is therefore reasonable to consider the possibility that the hymn originated among those who venerated John as Messiah.

Proponents of this theory face one major problem; the hymn appears to celebrate the arrival of a Davidic Messiah. 'He has raised up a horn of salvation in the house of David his servant' (Lk. 1.69). That this verse, as it stands, refers to a Davidic Messiah has not been challenged by those who hold the baptist source theory. Therefore I shall not expand on this important point until later in this chapter.[30] We read in Luke 1.5 that both parents of John were of priestly families so it would seem unlikely that references to a Davidic Messiah would appear in a hymn honouring the Baptist.

Proponents of the baptist origin theory have attempted to avoid this difficulty in three ways.

First, it has been claimed by C. Bowen that John was a Davidide.[31] He argued that the genealogy of Luke 3.23ff., which mentions King David, was originally the genealogy not of Jesus but of John. (This explains why it differs so drastically from the Matthaean version.[32]) Bowen also inferred from the account of the threat to John's life in the Protevangelium of James that traditions were circulating which placed John's birth in Bethlehem.[33] Leaving aside the fact that placing a birth in Bethlehem and claiming Davidic descent are not exactly the same, we need only note that the Protevangelium of James does not specify the birthplace of John. More importantly, in what, according to Bowen and other supporters of the baptist source theory, is a baptist document, Luke 1, Davidic descent is not claimed for John and his priestly descent is affirmed. It appears safe, therefore, to lay aside Bowen's theory.

The second means of dealing with the Davidic reference of Luke 1.69 is to strike it from the hymn. This is the option chosen by Völter, the originator of the baptist source theory, and, more recently, by H. Schonfield and C. Scobie.[34] Only Völter's position requires close examination. That scholar deleted both Luke 1.69 and 70, arguing that they were the work of the Christian redactor who created the story of the annunciation to Mary. One could hardly be more emphatic than Völter in asserting that these verses speak of the long awaited Davidic Messiah. 'Hier ist die Rede vom Horn "des Heils" das Gott bereits im Hause Davids aufgerichtet hat . . . Das kann nur auf ein Messias aus des Stamm Davids gehen.'[35] These verses, he argued, can easily be excised and the hymn would then proceed smoothly from 1.68b to 1.71. σωτηρίαν (v. 71) would more naturally complete the verb ἐποίησεν (v. 69).[36] Moreover, argued Völter, to refer at the time of the birth of one's own son to salvation wrought through an entirely different personage would be 'etwas unnatürliches'.[37]

It is true that the Benedictus is so loosely constructed that various bits and pieces can be excised without fatal damage to the sense of the poem. (I have proposed the deletion of vv. 76 and 77.[38]) There is nothing outside v. 68, the one-sentence kernel of the poem, which is absolutely essential to its coherence. But to suggest that such excisions are possible is not to say that they are justified. Moreover, there may well be an allusion in the berakah itself to the words of David at 1 Kings 1.48 who greets the elevation of Solomon to his father's throne with the identical blessing.[39] The Davidic language of v. 69 follows this blessing very naturally. Furthermore, the accusative noun σωτηρίαν does not actually complete either the verb ἐποίησεν or ἤγειρεν. Rather, it sums up the whole event described in vv. 68 and 69 as 'salvation'. It stands in loose apposition to both λυτρῶσιν and κέρας σωτηρίας.

The argument that it would be 'unnatural' for Zechariah to praise God for the advent of another person, the Messiah, on the occasion of the naming of his own son is equally suspect. First, such an argument presupposes that the hymn had been at all times an integral part of the narrative. The Benedictus may have been an independently circulating poem and as such may well have referred to a person other than John. Such references would have been entirely 'natural' in an independent messianic poem. Secondly, it must not be forgotten that we are not considering first of all what a father might say at the birth of his child in 'real life'; we must consider the role of the father in the story. In this story with its parallelism which subordinates John to Jesus the really important event is precisely the coming of a Davidic Messiah. In this context the reference to the Davidic Messiah is once again entirely 'natural'. It would only be 'unnatural' if one assumed that the Benedictus is a hymn which formed an integral part of a self-contained baptist source and *this is precisely what Völter is trying to prove*. It can be seen, therefore, that this argument requires its own conclusion as its presupposition. Völter's argument is indubitably correct in only one respect; such Davidic allusions would be 'unnatural' in a strictly baptist hymn. Two entirely different inferences may be drawn from this, however, on the one hand that the Davidic references should be excised, or on the other hand, that the hymn is not baptist. The latter seems the more reasonable deduction.

Most modern advocates of the baptist composition theory opt for a third method of dealing with the problem of the Davidic references. Scholars such as Bultmann, Vielhauer, Kraeling and Thyen make use of Gunkel's theory that the first part of the Benedictus was originally a Jewish eschatological hymn.[40] They suggest that a disciple of the Baptist adapted a traditional hymn to his own purposes by inserting the words about John in vv. 76ff.[41] This is a brilliant solution to the problem, for it allowed these scholars to concede the original independence of the poems if they so desired,[42] and to explain the Davidic references as part of the general Jewish expectation of the period. There was, therefore, no need to excise slices of the text or to transform John into a Davidide. By making use of Gunkel's theory they were able to avoid the objections I have adduced with respect to other statements of the baptist origin theory.

The reader who casts his mind back to the last chapter will notice, however, that there may be a serious flaw in this brilliant solution, namely its dependence on Gunkel's estimate of the psalms as eschatological hymns. Before considering this flaw more thoroughly it would only be fair to describe the details of the solution more thoroughly. Of the scholars listed above it is Vielhauer who presents by far the most thorough case. Where the others used at most a page to state their case Vielhauer devoted an entire essay to the question of the Benedictus. This essay has been the most widely influential statement of the position. 'Dass auch der Benedictus aus Täufer kreisen stammt, kann nach der erhellenden Untersuchung von P. Vielhauer als sicher gelten.'[43]

Vielhauer assumed that at least Luke 1.5-25, 57-66 was dependent on a more or less unaltered baptist source. He did not also assume, however, that the two hymns were part of this source, but affirmed with Dibelius their independence.[44] This means that the ultimate origin of the psalms can be determined only by appeal to internal indications rather than by consideration of the setting in which they find themselves. As was mentioned above, Vielhauer accepted Gunkel's identification of the poems as eschatological hymns. He did not accept, however, Gunkel's further statement that the additions to the original hymns which fitted them to their narrative contexts, Luke 1.48 and 76-9, were Christian.[45] In the second part of the Benedictus, he asserted, there is a messianology which is congruent with the teaching of the baptist community concerning its master which can presently be found in Luke 1.5-25. As is the case in that scene John is pictured as the forerunner, whether of God or the Messiah, using the imagery of Malachi 3.1ff. Vielhauer admitted that the hymn subordinates John to the κύριος of v. 76, who, in the psalm's present setting, can only be interpreted as Jesus.[46] But separated from this literary context, he affirmed, the identity of the κύριος becomes problematic. It could well be God rather than Jesus.

Another problem lies in the identification of the ἀνατολὴ ἐξ ὕψους of v. 78. This figure, who is at once star and representative of the Messiah, is not to be identified with the κύριος (v. 76), but with the προφήτης ὑψίστου, i.e. John.[47] This description of John as the dayspring derives from Malachi's description of the final days καὶ ἀνατελεῖ ὑμῖν ἥλιος δικαιοσύνης (Mal. 3.20). Against this specifically Messianic estimate of the Baptist John 1.8 affirms, 'He was not the light'.[48] The description of John in this part of the Benedictus tallies with that found in Luke 1.13ff. in that both treat John as Messiah. The correspondences between the two may be outlined as follows:

Prophet of the Most High (1.76)	Great (1.17a)
Forgiveness of Sins (1.77)	The 'turning' of Israel (1.16, 17b)
Preparation of God's way (1.17b)	Preparation of God's people (1.17)
Epiphany of God's mercy in the ἀνατολή	Eschatological joy 1.14

If this argument is correct the Benedictus must be adjudged to be a baptist hymn.

It can be seen, however, that Vielhauer's argument rests on three main points, all of which may be disputed. These are: first, that vv. 68-75 were originally a Jewish eschatological hymn, secondly, that Luke 1.5ff. is a baptist document, thirdly, that the picture of John in the Benedictus corresponds to the estimate of John in Luke 1.13ff. and not to the estimate of John current in Christian circles.

First, the hymn may not be 'eschatological' in Gunkel's sense of the word. As I have attempted to show, the Benedictus and the other Lucan hymns are better described as declarative psalms of praise.[49] If this is so the references to a Davidic Messiah, the existence of which Vielhauer and others are willing to admit, cannot be interpreted as merely part of the general eschatological expectation of Judaism; rather they celebrate the arrival of one who actually was considered to be 'a horn of salvation in the house of David'. I consider this point in itself fatal to the baptist origin theory.

The second point is also open to attack. Whatever the ultimate origin of the account of John's birth in Luke 1.5ff., it can hardly be denied that it is now not baptist but Christian scripture.[50] One surely must acknowledge that in Luke's view it was or had been made 'safe for Christian consumption'. A Christian could describe John in the manner of the account of Luke 1.5ff. Therefore, parallels between the second part of the Benedictus and the 'baptist' sections of the narrative are no proof of the 'baptist' origin of the hymn; they could equally be signs of Christian composition.

Finally, it appears that the description of John in Luke 1.76-77 is not shaped solely by the language of the annunciation to Zechariah. It is sometimes more easily explained by reference to the common Christian tradition about John. For example, Vielhauer suggested that 'prophet of the Most High' in the Benedictus corresponds to 'great before the Lord' in the annunciation to Zechariah. This strikes one as a rather tenuous connection. Surely it corresponds more nearly to the language of Luke 7.26, 'A prophet? Yes, and I tell you more than a prophet.' The reader may wish to compare the following table with the table of correspondences suggested by Vielhauer which appears above.[51]

Prophet of the Most High (Lk. 1.76)	A prophet . . . and more than a prophet (Lk. 7.26)
Knowledge of the forgiveness of sins (Lk. 1.77)	Baptism for the forgiveness of sins (Lk. 3.3)
Preparation of God's way (Lk. 1.76)	Prepare ye the way of the Lord (Lk. 3.4; cf. Is. 40.3)

This table shows, I suggest, that the language of Luke 1.76-77 is actually more similar to the descriptions of John in the body of the Gospel than it is to the description of John's future activity in Luke 1.13ff.

It seems, therefore, that the arguments of those who hold that the hymns of Luke 1–2 originated among disciples of John the Baptist may be at fault. A more likely explanation of the origin of these hymns would be that they were composed in a community which believed that the Messiah of David's line had already come.

Before naming this group it might be well to identify the possible allusions to a Davidic Messiah which can be found in the Benedictus. The first such reference may lie in the blessing itself, which reproduces exactly David's words on hearing of Solomon's elevation to the throne, 'Blessed be the Lord the God of Israel who has granted one of my offspring to sit on my throne this day' (1 Kings 1.48). Not too much should be made of this similarity by itself for very similar blessings conclude four sections of the Psalter.[52] Nevertheless, one should note the fact that the blessing in the Benedictus functions in the same manner as the one in 1 Kings 1.48 whereas the four blessings in the psalms function as 'eulogies' which are liturgical conclusions to hymns.[53]

There is a much clearer allusion to David in the following verse. The redemption for which the poet praises God has been achieved through a 'horn of salvation in the house of his servant David'. This verse appears to be an allusion to 1 Samuel 2.10 where it is said that God will 'exalt the power (horn) of his messiah'. Very similar language may be found in Psalm 132.17 and Ezekiel 29.21. The 'horn of salvation in the house of David' can only be the Messiah of David's line. Even more striking is the similarity to the fifteenth benediction of the Shemoneh Esreh in the Babylonian version: 'Cause the shoot of David to shoot forth quickly and raise up his horn by thy salvation . . . Blessed art thou, Lord, who causest the horn of salvation to shoot forth.'

That the Messiah is here called not only 'horn' but 'shoot' leads on to the next Davidic allusion, for ἀνατολή is the LXX translation of צמח, shoot or sprout.[54] That pair of words is used to describe the coming scion of David's house at Jeremiah 23.5; 33.15 (40.15 Theodotion); Zechariah 3.8; 6.12. Thus, for example:

> Behold the days are coming, says the Lord, when I will raise up for David a righteous Branch, and he shall reign as king . . . (Jer. 23.5).

The next line of the Benedictus, which describes the work of the ἀνατολή, continues the Davidic motif as it is reminiscent of the language of Isaiah 9.1(2). There the light which shines on those in darkness is connected with the appearance of the prince who will rule from David's throne.

It appears, therefore, that the Benedictus may well be a hymn of those who believed that the Davidic Messiah had already come. It is almost what might be expected on the lips of a pious Jew who had become certain that the fifteenth petition of the Shemoneh Esreh had been heard, and that the prayed-for one had come to Israel. We do know of one Jewish group that believed that the Messiah had come, one 'who was descended from David after the flesh'. This is, of course, the early church.

There are certain indications beside the Davidic references in the Benedictus which may well point to a Christian origin for these hymns. I have mentioned earlier the verbal similarities between the Lucan hymns and the Psalms of Solomon.[55] Along with this verbal similarity there exists a striking dissimilarity in tone. Where the Psalms of Solomon are mournful, the Lucan hymns are triumphant. This suggests that the hymns of Luke may have originated among the same sort of people who produced the Psalms of Solomon but under changed circumstances. The circle which produced those psalms prayed and hoped for a Davidic Messiah. 'Behold, O Lord, and raise up to them their king, the son of David' (Ps. Sol. 17.21). The one who was to come was to be Χριστὸς κύριος or κυρίου (so Rahlfs) (Ps. Sol. 17.32). One reasonable explanation of the difference between the two sets of psalms might well be that those who produced the Lucan psalms were convinced that the one whom their forbears had expected had come. It must be noted here that the resemblances to the Psalms of Solomon are not confined to the explicitly Davidic Benedictus but can be found in all the Lucan hymns. Not all the parallels listed by Ryle and James[56] are entirely convincing but there remain enough impressive similarities to suggest that there may well have been a connection of the sort I have suggested between the two sets of psalms.

M. Wilcox found parallels between the Lucan hymns and the great prayer in 1 Clement.[57] He concluded that 'a possible explanation of the common elements and similar style would be that both were drawing upon language and modes of expression current in the early church'.[58] This point is an interesting one but fails to convince entirely since Wilcox presented only five parallels between 1 Clement and the Lucan psalms. Moreover, any similarity between the two, it could be argued, might stem from 1 Clement's ultimate dependence on *Jewish* liturgical language.[59]

The Nunc Dimittis contains one reference which suggests that it, too, may be Christian. This is the phrase φῶς εἰς ἀποκάλυψιν ἐθνῶν. The Nunc Dimittis reminds one strongly of certain passages in Deutero-Isaiah such as, 'I shall give you as a light to the nations (gentiles)' (Is. 49.6), or, 'I have given you as a covenant to the people, a light to the nations' (Is. 42.6). The question both with respect to Deutero-Isaiah and to the Nunc Dimittis is whether the Gentiles are to be participants in the salvation of Israel or merely witnesses of it. Whatever is the case in Isaiah, the Nunc Dimittis seems to imply that the Gentiles will share in the salvation.[60] Such a formulation would most likely be Christian.

I suggest that the hymns of Luke 1–2 can best be understood as Christian psalms. One can be even more specific: they are Jewish-Christian.

There has been a considerable scholarly debate about the meaning of the term Jewish-Christian and its equivalents such as Judaeo-Christian or Judaistic Christian.[61] Hitherto I have avoided this problem by treating the two halves of the term 'Jewish-Christian' separately. I have attempted to prove first that the hymns are Jewish by pointing to the Semitic colouring of the language and by demonstrating their similarity in form and content to late Jewish poetry. That the hymns are Jewish is, I think, beyond reasonable doubt. I have also attempted to prove that they are Christian, pointing especially to the signs in the Benedictus that the hymns thank God for the coming of the Davidic Messiah. The hymns, then, are not only Jewish but Christian, that is, Jewish-Christian.

This is a bare-bones sort of definition of Jewish-Christianity, but it is, I think, an adequate one. A more complicated definition would not significantly advance the researcher in the task of exegesis of the hymns themselves.[62] It is, in effect, the definition of the term which has been used by the many scholars who have identified these psalms as Jewish-Christian. Among these scholars are: C. Westermann, J. Gnilka, R.E. Brown, D.R. Jones, and P. Benoit.[63]

It appears, then, that the hymns of Luke 1–2 originated in Jewish-Christian circles. It may be possible to be slightly more precise about their origin. Some scholars are willing to be very precise indeed. 'A plausible argument can be constructed for the thesis that Luke got the canticles from the tradition of the Jewish-Christian community of Jerusalem.'[64] While it may not be possible to locate the origin of the hymns quite so precisely, it does seem very likely that they were composed in the Palestinian church.[65] This would be the most natural explanation for the fact that they appear to be translations of Semitic originals. Moreover, these psalms are quite different in character from hymns like Philippians 2.6-11 which were used in the diaspora church.[66]

It is likewise difficult to specify the date of composition of the hymns but again it seems reasonable to suppose that it was before AD 70. Otherwise one might have expected that the terrible events of that year would have cast a pall over the triumphant affirmation of national redemption which fills the hymns. Most of the scholars who call these hymns Jewish-Christian posit an early date for their composition.

At this point it might be well to summarize the results of the study. The evidence adduced to this point would seem to indicate that:

1. The hymns of Luke 1–2 depend on Semitic, probably Hebrew, originals.
2. They were composed by Jewish-Christians, probably in Palestine before AD 70.

More details about the community which produced the hymns may become apparent in the course of the exegesis of the hymns, a task to which we may now proceed.

PART TWO

THE MEANING OF THE HYMNS

The study of structure can be no more than a dry 'naming of the parts', but such a study can also lay bare the movement of thought in a passage. A consideration of the manner in which the three hymns fit into the structure of Luke 1–2 may therefore be useful before beginning an exegesis of the psalms. There have, of course, been many analyses of the structure of these chapters. Both A. George and R.E. Brown have performed the useful task of gathering together a representative sample of these analyses.[1]

A glance at these summaries shows that all investigators have been faced with the same problem; there is an obvious parallelism between John the Baptist scenes and Jesus scenes and yet there are elements which seriously unbalance the parallelism.[2]

With his customary succinct clarity, Brown identified seven episodes in Luke 1–2. These are:[3]

1. Annunciation about John
2. Annunciation about Jesus
3. Visitation
4. Birth/Circumcision/Naming of John
5. Birth/Circumcision/Naming of Jesus
6. Presentation in Temple
7. Finding in Temple

Clearly enough (1) and (2) are parallel scenes, as are (4) and (5). The other elements, however, spoil the neatness of the parallelism. The problems are resolved in a variety of ways as a glance at the summaries of Brown and George will show. It is worth noting that the hymns are particularly difficult to fit into these analyses. For example, Brown asserted that the Magnificat and Benedictus are parallel in almost every respect although the scenes in which they are placed, (3) and (4), are not at all parallel. Brown's own solution of the problem will be discussed in the excursus which concludes this chapter. At this point we may turn to Dibelius's analysis of the first two chapters of Luke.[4]

Dibelius's analysis is typical of the schemes drawn up by scholars. His solution is as follows:

Annunciation of John's Birth (1.5-25)	Annunciation of Jesus' Birth (1.26-38)

Parallel greeting of Mothers and Unborn Children (Magnificat) (1.39-56)

Birth, Circumcision, Naming of John (1.57-66)	Birth, Circumcision, Naming of Jesus (2.1-21)
Inspired Greeting to John (Benedictus), Growth of Child (1.67-80)	Inspired Greeting to Jesus (Nunc Dimittis) Growth of Child (2.22-40)

Evidence of Superiority of Jesus in Temple Scene (2.41-52)

This analysis displays clearly the parallelism between scenes about John and scenes about Jesus. It also identifies those elements which do not fit neatly into the parallelism, the visitation and the episode of the boy Jesus in the temple.

And yet this analysis is not complete. The concentration on parallelism which marks not only Dibelius's study but those of most other scholars as well can be dangerous, for parallelism is not the only structural feature of importance in Luke 1–2. One point, so obvious that it has not, perhaps, been sufficiently, stressed, must be made. The relationship of the parts is not merely,

Annunciation (John) ⟵⟶ Annunciation (Jesus)
Birth, etc. (John) ⟵⟶ Birth, etc. (Jesus)

but also,

The latter relationship is at least as significant as the former. The Infancy Narrative is more than a classical facade, one pillar balancing another, windows in perfect symmetry, etc. There is a movement through the narrative—a consistent flow in the story itself. A consideration of the function of the hymns in this movement shows that there is also a consistency to Luke's use of the hymns.

When one considers the movement of thought through the strands of the narrative rather than the parallelism of the individual parts one notices the following progression in the separate stories which lead up to the hymns: 1. promise, 2. fulfilment, 3. praise response. Consider the following chart:

	Promise	*Evidence of Fulfilment*
Zechariah	That his wife would bear a son	John's Birth
Mary	That she would conceive a special son	The unborn John bears witness to Jesus and Elizabeth blesses Mary
Simeon	That he would see the Messiah	He sees Jesus

	Praise Response
Zechariah	The Benedictus
Mary	The Magnificat
Simeon	The Nunc Dimittis

This pattern of promise/fulfilment is, as will be shown in the exegesis, a prominent element within the hymns themselves.[5]

Such an analysis shows that Brown was not entirely correct when he wrote, 'The canticles fit only awkwardly into the various analyses [of structure]'.[6] This awkwardness of which Brown spoke stemmed from the perception that the Benedictus and Magnificat display marked literary similarity but do not occur in parallel episodes. This analysis shows that structurally the Benedictus is neatly parallel to the Nunc Dimittis. One should not be misled by the literary similarity to the Magnificat. The structural parallel is of greater significance. Both are responses to the saving power of God manifested in the birth of a special child. Both are spoken by old men who embody the piety of Israel.

But there is yet one more structural parallel between the two hymns. It arises from more than the parallelism of episodes, as the following chart makes clear.

	Benedictus	Nunc Dimittis
Word of Praise	1.68-75, 78-79	2.29-32
Prophecy Concerning the	1.76-77	2.34-35
Child's Destiny	(Lucan additions?)	

The chief structural difference between the two hymns lies in the fact that Luke was able to interpolate the prophecy into the more loosely constructed Benedictus. The parallel prophecy had to be added at the conclusion of the Nunc Dimittis. Because of these prophecies the infancy narratives are not complete in themselves; they await their final fulfilment in the Gospel itself. There the prophecies are finally worked out.

There remains a serious problem. As we have seen, there is a consistent movement through the narrative—promise/fulfilment/praise. The problem is that there are three such progressions culminating in the three hymns but only two parallel strands to the story, the John strand and the Jesus strand.

This apparent inconsistency can be understood if one remembers that Luke consistently 'tilts' the parallelism of the narrative towards Jesus. Because he is the truly significant one the fulfilment of John's mission lies in the coming of Jesus (cf. Lk. 3.17). This relationship is anticipated in the story of the visitation. Here the promises concerning both children are first fulfilled as John hails from the womb itself the one who is to come. The Magnificat responds to the fulfilment of both sets of promises. Thus, the episode of the visitation including the Magnificat functions as a connective episode as Dibelius suggested.[7]

An expert draughtsman could doubtless design a chart of the structure of Luke 1–2 which lays out the blocks of material as Dibelius's chart does but incorporates the three promise/fulfilment/praise progressions. This chart would also indicate the tilt towards the Jesus side of the table. Such a three-dimensional creation is beyond me, but only this sort of design would, I believe, adequately display the structure of the infancy narratives and the role of the hymns in them.

Excursus
Raymond Brown's Treatment of the Structure of Luke 1–2

By a careful study of the structure of Luke 1–2 Raymond Brown hoped to lay bare the composition history of those chapters. As he wrote:

> I abandon in this commentary the thesis that by style and language one can decide the question of sources. The linguistic opponents have fought one another to a draw at the present moment of our scientific research and so I shall appeal more to arguments of content and thought pattern.[8]

The study of 'content and thought pattern' is more or less the study of structure. Only this sort of study, he believed, can reveal the existence or non-existence of sources.

Brown concluded that there were no such sources behind Luke's narrative.[9] He differed, however, from those who suppose that Luke derived his information from pious meditation on OT texts.[10] Certain items came to Luke from tradition. These items Brown identified primarily by means of a comparison with Matthew.[11] He considered it unlikely, for example, that Matthew and Luke independently hit on the same marital situation for Jesus' parents at the time of his birth, betrothed but not living together. For the purposes of this excursus the most important traditional datum was a 'tendency to compare the conception of Jesus to the conception of OT salvific figures by the use of an annunciation pattern'.[12] However, the traditional information was put into literary form by Luke and Luke alone.

As we have already seen, Brown observed that there are elements in Luke 1–2 which appear to spoil the otherwise perfect parallelism displayed in the two chapters. Brown suggested that this combination of exact parallelism and intrusive elements was due to the fact that 'Luke composed his narrative in two stages'.[13]

The first stage of composition established the parallelism:

I   Two Annunciations of Conception
   1   Annunciation about John (1.5-23)
     plus Elizabeth's pregnancy and praise of God (1.24-25)
   2   Annunciation about Jesus (1.26-38)
     plus Elizabeth's praise of Mary's pregnancy (1.39-45, 56)
II   Two narratives of Birth/Circumcision/Naming and Future Greatness
   1   Narrative about John (1.57-66)
     plus growth statement (1.80)
   2   Narrative about Jesus (2.1-27, 34-39)
     plus transitional growth statement (2.40).

Into this structure Luke inserted various other sorts of material including the hymns and the story of the discovery of the boy Jesus in the temple. These insertions unbalanced the perfect diptych outlined above. For example, the inclusion of the Magnificat made the Visitation a separate episode. Luke derived these additions, Brown affirmed, 'from sources that had come to his attention—sources that had no previous connection to infancy tradition'.[14]

The strength of Brown's approach is that it explains the present structure of the Infancy narratives. The presence of both neat parallelism and seemingly intrusive elements can be accounted for. Brown's theory seems an attractive presentation of the material. However, allowing that Brown's solution is attractive, one must still ask whether it is correct. It can, in fact, be questioned in two ways. On the one hand, one could deny that the evidence requires a two-stage composition theory. On the other, one could agree that there was, in fact, a two-stage composition but deny that Luke was responsible for the first stage. Brown's structural distinction between two layers of composition could then be used as evidence that Luke was dependent on a source. As we have seen, there is good reason to suppose that the hymns were inserted secondarily into their present narrative contexts.[15] This would seem to indicate that there actually were, at least to this degree, two stages of composition. The second approach seems, therefore, to be the one which should be pursued.

It is important to remember that Brown eschewed the use of linguistic criteria in order to appeal to arguments of content and thought pattern. This limits drastically the sort of evidence he allowed himself to adduce. Still, one cannot help observing that Brown adduced very little evidence of any sort to support his position.

The closest that Brown came to producing such evidence is an almost offhand remark in rebuttal of Conzelmann's refusal to discuss Luke 1–2. 'The artistry that Luke manifests in the parallelism between JBap and Jesus in the infancy narrative is also at work in the parallelism in Acts between the careers of Peter and Paul.'[16] It does appear that Luke loved parallelism; it has even been suggested that an emphasis on duality is a controlling theological principle for him.[17] Luke may well have deliberately established a parallelism between the careers of Peter and Paul in Acts. One must, however, consider a more important problem, whether Luke intended to establish such a parallelism between John and Jesus. There is material outside the infancy narratives which can be examined in order to answer this question, chs. 3 and 4 of the Gospel.

Those chapters again describe both John and Jesus but lack the exact parallelism that one finds in Luke 1–2. C.H. Talbert, an exceptionally ingenious seeker after parallelism, could find only the following parallels between the two figures:[18]

	John		*Jesus*
3.1-6	John's person. He is the prophet of the eschaton.	3.21-28	Jesus' person. He is the Son of God.
3.7-17	John's mission. It is eschatological, ethical and anticipatory.	4.1-13	Jesus' mission. It is the eschatological recapitulation of Adam's decisions.
3.18-20	Summary. The end of John's mission.	4.14-15	Summary. The beginning of Jesus' ministry.

We should first notice that the stories of the two figures are not intertwined as they are in Luke 1–2. More important still, the parallelism seems not at all exact, especially in comparison with Luke 1–2. There, annunciation matches annunciation, hymn matches hymn, old man (Zechariah) matches old man (Simeon), etc. The difference appears even more striking when one ignores Talbert's harmonizing titles for the various parts of Luke 3–4 and considers the content of those sections. Talbert has matched a precise dating, a description of John's preaching and an OT quotation with the account of Jesus' baptism and his genealogy, an account of John's preaching and the reaction to it with the story of the temptation, John's arrest with the transition to the Nazareth pericope! One might well question whether there is *any* parallelism here.

Secondly, Talbert has proved that parallelism was a widely used literary device in Luke's time. The third evangelist was not the only lover of parallelism in the first century AD. In short, the presence of parallelism is not, in itself, sufficient to prove that Luke was responsible for the first stage of composition of the Infancy Narrative. In fact, when one compares the way John and Jesus are described in chs. 1–2 and 3–4 one might even argue that the presence of clear parallelism in the former chapters suggests just the opposite conclusion, that Luke was *not* primarily responsible for the shape of chs. 1–2.

Furthermore, one must ask after the literary purpose of the

putative first stage of the composition. Was it the introduction to an earlier edition of Luke? In his well-known commentary on the Gospel of John, Brown advanced a theory of composition which involved several stages of redaction by the same author or circle. There may well be evidence of an earlier edition of John; there is little such evidence for Luke. If there was an earlier edition of Luke it may well have begun at 3.1. This, however, would suggest that the whole Infancy Narrative was lacking, not that there was once a 'first edition' of chs. 1–2 in Luke's Gospel.

There is also something inherently implausible about Brown's proposal. He would have us suppose that Luke spoiled his own perfectly balanced creation by adding material 'that had no previous connection to infancy tradition'.[19] The more one believes Luke to have been a lover of parallelism the more unlikely this seems. More plausible seems the possibility that Luke might have altered a composition which came to him from some source and which seemed in some respect inadequate. It seems more reasonable to suppose that Luke would have unbalanced somebody else's work than that he would have done so to his own creation.

Let us continue to suppose that Brown was correct in his identification of a first stage of composition. Simply put, that first stage consisted of two annunciation stories and two birth stories. Is it possible that this pattern could have come to Luke from the tradition? Brown has suggested, as we have seen,[20] that Jesus was already being compared to OT figures by means of an annunciation pattern in pre-Lucan tradition. A comparison of the annunciations in Luke with the annunciation in Matthew, and the annunciations before the births of Ishmael, Isaac, and Samson shows that such stories followed a stereotyped pattern.[21] All the features of the Lucan annunciations are paralleled at some point in one or more of the other annunciations. If, therefore, a story about Jesus' birth had already been told using the annunciation pattern, it would necessarily have included a large part of our present narrative. The annunciation pattern would demand that. In effect, a quarter of the 'first stage' is accounted for already.

Furthermore, an annunciation about a birth is almost meaningless without an account of the birth itself. Certainly, all three of the OT annunciation stories culminate in the description of the birth of the child. Two of the stories, those of Isaac and Ishmael, specifically mention circumcision. Another two, Isaac and Samson, have growth statements. Any annunciation story upon which Luke might have drawn would have included an account of the birth and, considering the OT antecedents, might well have mentioned circumcision and concluded with a growth statement. This is not to say that the putative annunciation/birth story would have contained all the details of our Infancy Narrative. Nevertheless, the general outline of the story of Jesus' birth may have come to Luke from the tradition. This would be half of the 'first stage' of the composition.

As we have seen, the treatment of John in Luke 1–2 differs from the treatment of him in chs. 3–4. The subordinating parallelism, such an obvious feature of Luke 1–2, is not markedly present there. It may be, therefore, that Luke himself was not the one who placed the two annunciation/birth narratives side by side.

Brown has argued that the particular shape of the Infancy Narrative is best explained as the result of two stages of composition. He also affirmed without, it appears, sufficient evidence that Luke was responsible for both stages. It appears that Brown may have failed to make his case for the latter point. By this failure he may well have allowed in a source theory by his own back door. If there were two stages of composition it seems at least possible that the 'first stage' was a source. This source could have consisted of an account of an annunciation before Jesus' birth and an account of the birth itself. A parallel story about John may well already have been attached to this narrative when it came to Luke. The use of such a source might account for the highly Semitic nature of the language of Luke 1–2 which is revealed by the use of Raymond Martin's method of syntactical analysis.

THE MAGNIFICAT

Translation

46 And Mary said:
    My soul magnifies the Lord,
47 and my spirit has rejoiced in God my Saviour,
48 for he has looked upon the low estate of his maidservant.
    For behold from now on all generations will call me happy,
49 for the Mighty One has done great things for me;
        holy is his name.
50 His mercy is from generation to generation
        on those who fear him.
51 He has shown might with his arm.
    He has scattered those who are proud in the imagination of
        their hearts.
52 He has pulled the rulers down from their thrones,
        and has lifted up those of low estate.
53 The hungry he has filled with good things,
        and the rich he has sent empty away.
54 He has helped Israel his servant,
        remembering his mercy,
55 as he said to our fathers,
        to Abraham and to his seed, forever.

Textual Note: The Attribution of the Magnificat

There is only one textual problem of significance in the Magnificat but it may be one of the best known textual difficulties in the New Testament. The entire Greek manuscript tradition and all the versions with, as we shall see, the exception of a few Latin manuscripts, attribute the Magnificat to Mary. A few Latin manuscripts and several church fathers of the West, on the other hand, read in v. 46,

'And Elizabeth said'. The controversy over which reading should be considered original has been a long and vigorous one, so vigorous, in fact, that a lengthy note by R. Laurentin[1] and an article by S. Benko[2] have been devoted to its history. Another testimony to the liveliness of the debate, especially in the early years of this century, is the fact that the Pontifical Bibilical Commission found it necessary to issue in 1912 a decree affirming the traditional attribution of the hymn to Mary.[3] The two surveys of the history of the controversy are so excellent that only the briefest outline of the discussion is necessary here. While it had been suggested earlier that the 'Elizabeth' reading was original,[4] the controversy over the proper attribution of the hymn claimed the attention of the scholarly world only with the publication in 1897 of a sermon by Niceta, the fourth-century Bishop of Remesiana (Yugoslavia) in which he twice clearly attributed the hymn to Elizabeth.[5] In quick succession appeared works by Loisy, writing under the pseudonym of F. Jacobé, and Harnack independently arguing that Elizabeth was the original reading.[6] Scholars quickly sprang to the defence of the more traditional interpretation.[7] In England too the publication in 1905 of Niceta's sermon sparked controversy over the attribution of the hymn. The most notable proponent of the Elizabeth theory was F.C. Burkitt.[8] Defenders of the traditional theory included J. Bernard, C.W. Emmet and J.G. Machen.[9] By 1912 the whole dispute had begun to take on the air of a medieval tournament; scholarly lances were broken right and left in honour of the two ladies.

The dispute has been carried on to the present day and the reader may consult Laurentin for a list of the proponents of either position up to 1957.[10] More recently the reading 'Elizabeth said' has been defended by J.G. Davies, Benko himself, F.W. Danker and J. Drury.[11] On the other hand, the hymn has been attributed to Mary by, among others, Goulder and Sanderson, Schürmann, Brown and Marshall.[12] For the most part these scholars have discussed the question more extensively than have the advocates of the Elizabeth theory. It would seem that the trend in contemporary scholarship is towards the acceptance of the more traditional reading 'And Mary said'.

Benko, however, summarized the debate as follows:

> If we examine the arguments that were brought forward on both sides, we discover that the so-called 'external evidence' is over-

whelmingly in favour of the reading 'Mary said'. But the so-called 'internal evidence' supports very strongly the opposite view.[13]

Benko is certainly correct with respect to the 'external evidence'. The reading 'Elizabeth said' is attested only in three Old Latin manuscripts a, b and the original hand of l. As we have see, it is also the reading presupposed by Niceta. There are two other witnesses to the Elizabeth reading in the Fathers, Irenaeus (*Adv. Haer.* 4.7.1) and Origen (*In Luc. Hom.* 7). However, the reading in Irenaeus is textually uncertain, two manuscripts reading Elizabeth, but the other chief witness reading Mary. Furthermore, at *Adv. Haer.* 3.10.2 the hymn is clearly attributed to Mary.[14] It is possible that the reading 'Elizabeth' in 4.7.1 can be attributed to the Latin translator's work.[15] Origen's homily on Luke exists only in Jerome's Latin translation. There the author remarks that he is not 'ignorant [of the fact] that according to other codices Elizabeth prophesies these words'.[16] It has been suggested that the one who knows of such manuscripts is not Origen but Jerome.[17] There are, therefore, no certain witnesses to the reading 'Elizabeth said' outside the Latin tradition.[18] The remainder of the manuscript tradition attributes the hymn to Mary. Such an understanding of the text is also presupposed by the second century Protevangelium of James 12.2,[19] and by most Church Fathers. The external evidence, therefore, is almost entirely in favour of the reading 'Mary said'.

Because of this near unanimity of the textual witnesses the debate has necessarily revolved around the 'internal evidence'. The chief arguments in favour of attributing the hymn to Elizabeth were clearly laid out by Loisy and Harnack and no significant addition has been made to their number. They may be listed as follows:[20]

1. In v. 41 it is said that Elizabeth is 'filled with the Holy Spirit'. Zechariah is likewise filled with the Spirit before saying the Benedictus. Of Mary, however, nothing is said which indicates that she has been inspired.

2. If the subject had been changed in v. 46 we should find εἶπεν δὲ rather than καὶ εἶπεν.

3. The words of v. 56, 'And Mary remained with *her*', imply that Elizabeth, not Mary, had just been speaking.

4. Luke treats Mary and Joseph with great reserve in Luke 1–2. It is, therefore, unlikely that he would attribute a lengthy speech to her.

5. The hymn is an imitation of Hannah's song. Elizabeth's situation is analogous to Hannah's but Mary's is not. The hymn suits

much better the one who, like Hannah, has long been childless. The ταπείνωσις (v. 48) of the speaker is barrenness.

6.   To these may be added the general observation that a change from Mary to Elizabeth is difficult to explain. The reverse is less so. In fact, Harnack supposed that neither 'Elizabeth' nor 'Mary' was original; Luke wrote simply καὶ εἶπεν. The two names were explanatory additions, Elizabeth a correct one, Mary a false.[21]

That Luke attributed the Magnificat to Elizabeth has been, as we have seen, argued with considerable learning and ingenuity. In my judgment it must, however, be rejected. The positive arguments in its favour can be countered and there remain certain important considerations which suggest that the hymn be attributed to Mary.

Taken together with the near unanimity of the textual witness, these arguments can give one considerable confidence that the hymn belongs to the one to whom it has been attributed 'from of old'.

The first task must be to refute Harnack's arguments.[22]

1.   Specific mention of inspiration does not always accompany a hymn. See, for example, the Song of the Sea (Ex. 15.1ff.) or the hymn of Tobit 13, or Judith 16. There is also no mention of inspiration before the Nunc Dimittis. Perhaps in the case of both Mary and Simeon the previous influence of the spirit (Lk. 1.35; 2.25) renders fresh inspiration unnecessary.

2.   Phrases such as καὶ εἶπεν regularly indicate a change of speaker. Schürmann found 15 such instances but only 4 in which the phrase marked the resumption of speech by the same figure.[23]

3.   The wording of v. 56, 'And Mary remained with *her*', can be explained as a sign, not that the Magnificat belonged to Elizabeth but that it was secondarily inserted into its present context.[24]

4.   Luke treats Mary with no more reserve than he treats Zechariah to whom a hymn is also attributed. She is, furthermore, the subject of rather more interest in Luke 1–2 as a whole than is Elizabeth.

5.   The hymn as a whole reflects the situation of neither Elizabeth nor Mary.[25] Only v. 48 appears to tie the hymn to its narrative context and that verse reflects Mary's situation better than Elizabeth's. ταπείνωσις does not necessarily refer to the shame of barrenness. If Luke had wanted to refer to Elizabeth's shame he could have used a word such as ὄνειδος (v. 25). ταπείνωσις refers to the low or humble state of the speaker; it is that state which is characteristic of those who are ταπεινούς (v. 52). The word is used frequently in this sense

in the OT.[26] The speaker calls herself 'maidservant' as Mary does in v. 38 and so is one of the 'poor'.[27] She is henceforth to be 'called happy' as Mary has already been called by Elizabeth (v. 45; cf. v. 42). The claim of v. 48b that all generations would call the speaker happy would be strange and extravagant on Elizabeth's lips; it is natural on Mary's. There is certainly a reference to Hannah's prayer (1 Sam. 1.11) here but Luke's description of the birth of Jesus is at several points influenced by the story of Samuel's birth.[28] The dependence on Hannah's prayer (1 Sam. 1.11) at this point is not, therefore, a sign that the hymn was originally attributed to Elizabeth.

6.   The attribution of the hymn to Mary must, by any reckoning, have been very early indeed. Only a very widespread veneration could plausibly account for the near unanimity of the textual tradition. There is no convincing evidence of such veneration of Mary in the early period.[29]

There are further severe problems with the hypothesis that the hymn should be attributed to Elizabeth. If, as Harnack and almost all subsequent proponents of the theory have held, the original reading was simply, 'and she said', one would expect this reading to survive at some point in the textual tradition. It does not.

Furthermore, to attribute the hymn to Elizabeth is to ignore the structure of the narrative at this point. Dibelius[30] pointed out many years ago that it would be very strange for Elizabeth to break into a lengthy hymn praising God for her own pregnancy immediately after hailing Mary 'the mother of her Lord' in the most extravagant terms. One would expect a response from Mary. Moreover, the progression of thought in the passage indicates clearly that Mary must have spoken the Magnificat. As we have seen, there is a consistent promise–fulfilment–praise progression in Luke 1–2.[31] Just as Luke attributes a hymn to Zechariah when the word of the angelic annunciation is first fulfilled, so he would have attributed a hymn to Mary in similar circumstances.

The overwhelming textual support for the reading, the wording of Luke's insertion, v. 48, and the structure of Luke 1–2 as a whole make it highly probable that Luke meant to attribute the Magnificat to Mary. The reading 'Elizabeth said' may be the result of a simple error in the Latin textual tradition. Perhaps, a scribe inadvertently left out the name Mary, and a corrector misled, conceivably, by the very considerations which have appeared so powerful to Loisy, Harnack, and company, supplied the name Elizabeth. Such an error would adequately explain the few appearances of the reading 'Elizabeth said'.[32]

The Form of the Poem

The Magnificat is not only magnificent in itself; it has provoked magnificence in others. Many of the great theologians of the church have in their contemplation of the psalm been so stirred as to produce prose of unwonted beauty. Those fathers of the church whose interpretations are preserved in Aquinas's catena[33] on the text of Luke, and the great reformers, Luther and Calvin, all have written of the Magnificat in such a way that the modern reader can hardly fail in turn to be stirred. Some of these interpretations will be quoted in the course of the exegesis of the hymns.

On the other hand, there are those who see nothing unusually powerful in the Magnificat and the other hymns of Luke 1–2. 'To suggest that Luke wrote these [the hymns] is not to posit any very exalted skill on his part.'[34] The Magnificat, Drury contended, is, like the other hymns of Luke 1–2, a mere pastiche of OT fragments. It is true that there is hardly a word in the psalm which does not come from the OT but this does not mean that the Magnificat and the other psalms of Luke 1–2 are not creations of considerable literary merit.

> The use of the language of tradition is not necessarily a sign that creative ability is lacking. Traditional language is language already heavy with meaning. It carries the weight of its use in the past, and a skilled poet can awaken this past meaning and use it for his own purposes. In the case of the Magnificat there seems to be a deliberate attempt to speak so that one always hears the echoes of the biblical tradition in the background. This act of praise gains in power because in it reverberate Israel's many acts of praise in response to God's deeds. For the purpose of this psalm this must be so since it wishes to celebrate the deed which fulfills Israel's hope.[35]

The most obvious poetic device in the poem is parallelism which appears in 46b//47, 51a//51b, 52a//52b, 53a//53b, 55a//55b. This gives an OT air to the hymn even before one examines the individual words and phrases of the hymn. The parallelism can be synonomous (46b//47) or antithetical (52a//52b).[36]

As it stands the hymn displays the following simple structure.

46-47	Word of Praise
48	First Motive Clause + saying about the future
49a	Second Motive Clause
49b-53	Statements amplifying the second motive clause
54-55	Summary

It is possible that v. 48, which alone links the hymn to the context and which displays several Lucanisms, was added by Luke to adapt the hymn to its present narrative position.[37] Aside from this verse the unity and integrity of the psalm are clear.[38]

Without v. 48 the hymn displays, as was argued earlier, the characteristic structure of the declarative psalm of praise, word of praise + reason for it (God has acted). The amplifying statements, however, contain motifs which are characteristic of descriptive praise.[39] That God feeds the hungry is, for example, a statement which appears in a number of the OT descriptive psalms of praise. In the OT psalms, however, it is never said that God *has* done those things for which he is praised but that he *does* them. Descriptive praise in the OT praises God for what he does regularly. In the Magnificat, however, the verbs of which God is subject are aorist. He *has done* these mighty deeds.

This brings us to the most difficult point of interpretation in the psalm. What do the aorists of vv. 51-53 mean? The first possibility is that these verbs do speak of God's regular, recurring action; they are 'gnomic'. This was an especially popular solution of the problem among the older commentators,[40] and is not without value. Verses 49b and 50 quite obviously speak of God's abiding character and the aorist of v. 47 does not simply refer to a past event. Furthermore, these verses are deeply affected by the OT discussion of the constant problem of divine justice. There are, however, few examples of the gnomic aorist in NT Greek.[41] This problem is somewhat obviated if one accepts Schmid's suggestion that the aorists are literal translations of Hebrew perfects which can have a 'gnomic' sense.[42] This interpretation suffers, however, from the fact that it treats the verbs of vv. 51-53 in isolation. It ignores the fact that they explicate the verb of v. 49, ἐποίησεν, which is also aorist and which seems to point to a particular action or series of actions by God. Again the series of aorists in vv. 51-53 are summed up by vv. 54-55 which again seem to point to some definite fulfilment of God's promise to the fathers.[43] Furthermore, the aorists in the Benedictus once again refer to a specific act, the raising up of the Messiah of David's line.[44] That the aorists of vv. 51-53 are 'gnomic' is too simple a solution; it does not do justice to the complexity of the poem.

It might seem, then, that these verbs describe a particular event in the past.[45] To do so is after all the normal function of aorist verbs. Raymond Brown wrote, 'The aorists refer to a definite action in the past, namely, the salvation brought about through the death and resurrection of Jesus'.[46] This is very probably true in principle. But one must still ask, Where have the mighty been pulled down and where have the humble been lifted up? The Magnificat's answer to these questions is not a simple one. To treat the aorists as if they speak only of a particular event in the past is to lose sight of the eschatological tension present in the hymn. It 'flattens' the psalm's perspective on salvation. Although the aorists point back to a particular event, the 'Christ event', they also anticipate what is to come. They are, in some sense, 'eschatological'.

That there is an eschatological dimension to the hymn was clearly recognized, as we have seen, by Gunkel.[47] According to Gunkel the aorists correspond to the Hebrew prophetic perfect. Such verbs speak of future events as if they were past because the prophet speaks from the vantage point of the final fulfilment of God's purposes. Gunkel's analysis can be only partially correct, however. As was shown in an earlier chapter, the hymns of Luke 1–2 have the form of declarative psalms of praise. Their primary reference is *back* to some event in the past. To treat these verbs simply as prophetic perfects which are oriented only to the future once again destroys the eschatological tension of the hymn. It ignores the fact that these verbs are embedded in a psalm the orientation of which is to a specific event in the past. A more complex solution which respects the richness of the hymn's conception of salvation history is therefore necessary.

The hymn thanks God because he 'has done great things'. He has acted to save the speaker and the people. The particular saving act to which the hymn points is, as the climax of the hymn makes clear, a decisive help to Israel which fulfills the promise inherent in the nation's history. This decisive help is, it would appear, the coming of Jesus Christ.[48] The hymn speaks at its beginning and at its conclusion in a fairly straightforward way of an event which has occurred in the past. This provides the basic framework of the psalm. The event, however, is not significant only for the moment. Rather, it is absolutely characteristic of God and it has consequences which reach into the age to come. In fact, so decisive is the event that one can speak as if the age to come had already arrived, in the aorist. The coming of Jesus Christ was the guarantee that God's purposes were, in principle, already worked out. The Magnificat speaks of a past event with future, indeed eternal, consequences. This eschatological tension between the fulfilled and the yet to be fulfilled is not entirely uncharacteristic of the New Testament.

Such an interpretation of the aorists of the Magnificat is far from unusual. Many scholars, Plummer, Schürmann, Lohfink, Tannehill and Schotroff, to name but a few, have interpreted the aorists in this way.[49]

There have been several attempts to divide the Magnificat into strophes. Schürmann found in the hymn two strophes (46-50 and 51-55)[50] but Ramaroson found three (46-50, 51-53, 54-55)[51] and Plummer four (46-48, 49-50, 51-53, 54-55).[52] There are certainly changes in emphasis in the poem; there is, for example, a shift through the poem from the individual to the national. But 'strophes' may be too dignified a term for these changes. The movement of thought through the poem is a relatively smooth progression; the seams in the poem are not strongly marked and the content of the various sections are so closely intertwined that over-definite divisions are not to be desired.[53] No more elaborate structure than that which I have outlined above seems necessary.

Almost every commentator makes note of the similarity between the Magnificat and Hannah's song (1 Sam. 2.1-10). As we have seen, some even consider the former an imitation of the OT psalm. This similarity can be overemphasized, however. Creed's chart of OT parallels to the Magnificat demonstrates that in every verse except 48a there are closer verbal links to other parts of the OT than to Hannah's song.[54] There is also a considerable amount of material in the OT psalm to which one can find no parallel in Mary's song; only the reversal theme of the middle part of Hannah's song is markedly similar. The idea of reversal of fortunes is, however, a rather common motif in the ancient world.[55] Moreover the reversal is not described in the same manner in the two hymns. The slight similarity between the two hymns springs partly from the fact that the Magnificat is a part of that tradition of Jewish psalmody of which Hannah's song is a fine example. This similarity may, however, explain why Luke put the Magnificat, rather than the Benedictus, in Mary's mouth.[56]

The Immediate Context of the Hymn

The Magnificat forms the climax of the Visitation scene which serves to link the two parallel stories about John and Jesus.[57] That Elizabeth greets and blesses Mary as 'mother of my Lord' is a sign that the promise of the angel, that she would bear the Messiah (vv. 30ff.), had been fulfilled. To Elizabeth's blessing Mary responds with the Magnificat. The psalm, therefore, takes its place in one of the three promise–fulfillment–praise progressions of Luke 1–2.[58]

There have been attempts to place the hymn elsewhere in the birth stories. Bultmann, believing it to be a hymn of Elizabeth, placed it after v. 25.[59] Leaney[60] placed it after 2.20 and Sahlin placed it in the mouth of Zechariah after 1.64![61] As we have seen, there is no reason to assign the hymn to Elizabeth, so Bultmann's hypothesis is unnecessary. Leaney's suggestion offers no real advantage and Sahlin's seems entirely eccentric.[62] One wonders why those who recognized that the hymns of Luke 1–2 are but loosely tied to their contexts and consist of rather general praise should seek alternative settings for them within the birth stories. There is no reason to suppose that the hymns, once cut loose from their present moorings, would necessarily wash up on the shores to which Bultmann, Leaney and Sahlin assigned them.

COMMENTARY

The Word of Praise

46b. The psalm begins with a burst of exultation, 'My soul magnifies the Lord'. Commentators are agreed that 'my soul' and the paralleled 'my spirit' do not refer here to entities within the human personality but are simply periphrastic ways of saying 'I'.[63] Origen asked rhetorically, 'Now if the Lord could neither receive increase or decrease, what is it that Mary speaks of, 'My soul doth magnify the Lord'?'[64] But here the verb means to declare great, rather than to make great.[65]

47. The word of praise continues, adding in parallelism to v. 46, 'And my spirit has rejoiced in God my saviour'. The shift in tense from the present 'magnifies' to the aorist 'has rejoiced' is puzzling. It may be an ingressive aorist[66] or reflect the Hebrew imperfect + waw consecutive.[67] It would be dangerous to read too much into the aorist; it appears to function in precisely the same way as the present

of v. 46b.[68] Mary rejoices in 'God my saviour'. Since the NT occurrences of the word 'saviour' cluster in writings such as the Pastoral Epistles this phrase may look like a later Christian expression. In fact, the expression 'God my saviour' appears frequently in the LXX, most notably at Habakkuk 3.18, to which this verse is very similar. It usually represents the Hebrew 'God of my salvation'.[69] It may be that early Christians saw in this verse an allusion to the name of Jesus.[70] That this was the author's intention is doubtful, however. The allusion to Habakkuk 3.18 explains the occurrence of the expression here. That God is here called 'saviour' anticipates the enumeration of his saving acts later in the poem.[71] Salvation is connected with the coming of Jesus here, in the Benedictus (1.69), and in the Nunc Dimittis (2.30).[72]

Although Habakkuk 3.18 is the most exact parallel to the verse, the vocabulary of the Magnificat has been influenced by many other OT passages.[73] Jones is doubtless correct in asserting: 'It [the couplet] looks like a quotation, but it is not. It is freshly minted.'[74]

The First Motive Clause

48a. At this point, in accordance with the pattern of declarative psalms, the reason for praise is given. 'He has looked with favour on the low estate of his maidservant.' It has earlier been argued that this verse is an interpolation,[75] so the evidence for this supposition need not be rehearsed here. By alluding to the words of two OT mothers, Hannah (v. 48a) and Leah (v. 48b), the hymn makes clear that the speaker praises God for the gift of a son. She is the Lord's δούλη (cf. v. 38). Sahlin and many other scholars have argued that the maid-servant is the 'daughter of Zion' as in 4 Esdras 9.45 and is thus a personification of Israel;[76] but such an identification goes beyond the evidence, as Raymond Brown has shown.[77] The 'maidservant' of v. 48 is a particular individual in contrast to the 'servant' of v. 54 which is Israel.[78] Mary is not, however, simply speaking as an individual. Because God has looked on her low state, ταπείνωσις, those of low estate, ταπεινούς (v. 52), are exalted. What God does for her he does for a whole people. That Mary speaks for the people is also shown by the change from first-person singular self-references of the first part of the hymn (vv. 48, 49) to the first-person plural of the conclusion, 'our fathers' (v. 55). The 'I' who speaks in the hymn is both a particular individual, Mary, and the representative of God's people. Something very similar would have been true of the original hymn if it indeed lacked v. 48. The speaker would still praise God as representative of the community.[79]

God has 'looked upon', that is, 'looked with favour', upon the low state of his maidservant. The word here rendered 'low estate' has sometimes been interpreted as the shame of barrenness by those who attribute the hymn to Elizabeth.[80] Older Catholic scholarship and, more recently, H. Schürmann have seen in this word the 'humility' of the Virgin.[81] But 'true humility ... never knows that it is humble',[82] so this interpretation has been rejected by most modern commentators. The word ταπεινούς, it is widely agreed, refers to Mary's objective state. She is of 'low estate' and thus one of the ταπεινούς (v. 52).[83]

48b. This half verse represents a parenthetical glimpse into the future. Mary is to be called 'happy' by all future generations. Elizabeth had begun the chain of macarisms (v. 45)[84] which was to continue to all generations. The use of the future here indicates that the aorist of v. 48a is not a 'prophetic' use of the past tense. If the aorist were prophetic it would not be necessary to switch to a future to speak of events yet to come. The event alluded to in v. 48 has occurred but it will have future consequences.

The OT background of the verse is clearly the word of Leah (Gen. 30.13).[85] The verse contains, therefore, two clear references to significant OT mothers. Its inclusion seems to tie the hymn to its context and makes Mary the speaking 'I' of the hymn.[86]

The Second Motive Clause

49a. 'For he who is mighty has done great things for me.' Another, somewhat more general motive for praise is given.[87] The Lord can be magnified, declared *great*, because he has done *great* things.[88] This motive clause also anticipates the remainder of the hymn. The 'great things' are the 'mighty acts of God'.[89] The verse seems to allude to Deuteronomy 10.21 where the mighty acts of God are those connected with the Exodus.[90] In the Magnificat the mighty acts are specified in vv. 51ff.[91] This motive clause, unlike the first, has, therefore, links both with the introduction to the hymn and its later sections. Δυνατοί are usually human in the OT, but the word is occasionally used of God, as the divine warrior who rescues his people.[92]

Amplifying Statements

49b-50. Verse 49b belongs with v. 50 rather than with v. 49a. Two general statements are made about God's nature: he is holy and he is merciful. Descriptive psalms of praise characteristically praise both God's majesty and his goodness.[93] In this couplet the Magnificat conforms to that pattern.

The background of v. 49b is Psalm 111.9, a verse to which the Benedictus also alludes (Lk. 1.68).[94] God is to be held holy becuase he does great and fearful things for his people. There is a certain resemblance between this statement and the first petition of the Lord's prayer.[95] The verse is a nominal sentence rather than a relative clause, 'whose name is holy', which is a Hebraism.[96]

50. 'And his mercy is from generation to generation (to those who fear him).' God's 'mercy' is his covenant love for his people.[97] There is no exact parallel to the formula εἰς γενεὰς καὶ γενεάς in the LXX but very similar expressions occur.[98] The OT background of this verse is clearly Psalm 105.17: 'The steadfast love (ἔλεος) of the Lord is from everlasting to everlasting upon those who fear him'. The allusion to this psalm is the only justification for the traditional versification of the hymn. Without that OT background it might seem preferable to attach 'those who fear him' to the next verse, viz. *'to those who fear him* he has shown strength with his arm, but he has scattered those who are proud in the imagination of their hearts'. Verse 51 begins a series of three couplets in antithetical parallelism in each of which God shows his mercy to his people but punishes his people's enemies. In the traditional division of verses, v. 51a lacks a recipient of God's mercy to balance the 'proud' of v. 51b. Taking 'those who fear him' with 51a supplies that lack.[99] It would also improve the parallelism of 49b and 50 for there is nothing in the former verse which corresponds to 'those who fear him'. A glance at a Hebrew reconstruction of the text shows that the balance of word mass, so important to Hebrew poetry, would also be improved by taking these words with what follows.[100]

Even if this division of the verses is not accepted it is clear that those who fear him are the ones for whom God acts in v. 51.[101] 'Those who fear him' are those who acknowledge God's sovereignty.[102] That God acts graciously to those who fear him is no new idea. It appears, for example, frequently in the Psalter,[103] and at several points in the Psalms of Solomon.[104]

51. At this point the hymn changes its focus from what God is to

what he has done. The aorist verbs, as we have seen, look back to the coming of Jesus Christ, but also express vividly the sure consequences of that coming.

Behind the first half of this verse lie Psalms 89.11 and 118.15. Here God is pictured again as a warrior, whose strong arm rescues his people and shatters his enemies. The divine warrior language of v. 51a reminds one of the title 'mighty one' of v. 49. Furthermore, both verses use the same verb ἐποίησεν. In effect, this verse 'rephrases v. 49a'.[105] By doing so v. 51 links the more general statements of God's activity with the more personal ones of the first part of the hymn.

The expression 'shown', or literally 'made', strength is not a native Greek one.[106] The 'arm' of God is a symbol of his power[107] and is frequently connected with the Exodus events.[108]

The second half of the verse introduces a new theme, that God acts not only *for* those who depend on him but *against* those who refuse to do so.[109] The 'proud' are those who are self-sufficient; they look down on the humble (v. 52) but not up to God.[110] In effect, they are the opposite of those who fear him (v. 50). Pride is characteristic of the enemies of God's people.[111] The location of this particular form of pride is the heart, the centre of the reasoning power.[112]

52-53. The following two verses form one unit of thought. They make use of the common classical and OT motif of the reversal of fortunes.[113] Their unity is indicated by a clear chiastic structure.[114] If a work which God does against the wicked can be designated as A and a work for his people by B, the structure of the quatrain is: AB BA. The quatrain as a whole is paralleled by 1 Samuel 2.7-8 (Hannah's song) but its individual members more closely resemble various other texts.

The first line declares that God has pulled the rulers down from their thrones. The language of this half verse is reminiscent of Job 12.19 and Sirach 10.14. In contrast to this God has 'lifted up those of low estate'.

At this point we have touched upon a matter which has keenly interested Biblical scholars for many years. Who are 'those of low estate' or, more simply, the 'poor'? There is a voluminous literature on the poor, both in the Bible as a whole and, more specifically, in the Gospel of St Luke. To discuss the problem in depth would certainly demand an entire volume.[115]

The problem that must chiefly concern us is, quite specifically,

Who are the 'poor' in the Magnificat? In the first place it is obvious
that they are the opposite of the 'proud' (v. 51), the 'mighty' (v. 52a),
and the 'rich' (v. 53a). They are 'those who fear God' (v. 50), the
'hungry' (v. 53b), and ultimately, Israel (v. 54). Most importantly,
they are those for whom God has acted (vv. 51ff.).

Behind the Greek word ταπεινούς may well lie the Hebrew עֲנָוִים or
עֲנִיִּים, familiar to the reader of the Psalms. The complex of ideas
associated with the 'poor' in the Magnificat finds its antecedent in the
Psalter. There several words are used to describe the poor and
afflicted and these, in turn, are rendered by several Greek words in
the LXX. These words so cluster together, however, that one is
justified in treating them together. According to the Psalter God
delivers a 'poor' or 'humble' people but humbles the arrogant (Ps.
18.27). He saves the poor man (here πτωχός) and his angel encamps
around those who fear him (Ps. 34.6-7). (For that reason, according
to this psalm, one may 'magnify' the Lord [Ps. 34.3].) The nation
Israel can be called the 'poor' (Ps. 72.2; 149.4). Above all, the poor are
those whom God saves (Ps. 34.18; Ps. 35.10 [πτωχόν]; cf. Prov. 3.34).

There seem to be three closely related elements in the use of
language about the 'poor': attitude, situation and national identity.
The poor are not only the destitute; they are those who depend
utterly on Yahweh. They are, however, also very often those who live
in real affliction and so cry to Yahweh because of their need. They
are also the recipients of salvation; God sees their weakness and
delivers them from it. Finally, the word can be a self-designation for
Israel.

None of these aspects of the word are irrelevant to the Magnificat.
The word ταπείνωσις derives its strength and power there from the
many layers of meaning given it by its ancient Biblical use. Those of
low estate certainly share the ultimate dependence on Yahweh
characteristic of the OT poor. Their situation has been one of need
and perhaps is so still. But here we have a significant development.
That rescue of the poor which is characteristic of God has been
definitively achieved. Those who sing the hymn may be the poor and
afflicted but they are already the saved poor. They are also Israel,[116]
but they are the Israel whom God has helped. By reference to the
companion hymn, the Benedictus, we know the nature of that help:
God has visited and redeemed his people by sending the Messiah of
David's line, Jesus Christ.[117] By doing so God has achieved the final
definitive deliverance of his people.[118] But the word ταπεινούς

ought not to attract all attention. It is marvellously appropriate here not only because its use calls forth a particularly rich array of OT associations but because it has obvious opposites, the proud and the rich. This suits the intention of this section of the hymn which states clearly that God has reversed the orders of society.[119]

That God reverses the orders of society, pulling down those who are high and raising up the lowly, is a sign of his righteousness and sovereignty.[120] Calvin put it well:[121]

> [Mary] teaches us that the world does not move and revolve by a blind impulse of fortune but that all the revolutions are brought about by the Providence of God, and that those judgments which appear to us to disturb and overthrow the entire framework of society, are regulated by God with unerring justice.

E. Hamel[122] has argued that this reversal motif should be closely connected with the problem of the prosperity of the wicked (cf. Ps. 73). To affirm that God destroys the prosperous wicked and, by a very slight extension of the same idea, lifts up the oppressed, is to confess that his administration of the cosmos is righteous. The reversal of fortunes shows that God does not suffer the evil rich indefinitely to enjoy the benefits of their wickedness. They are sent empty away.[123]

That God had reversed the normal order of things by raising Jesus from the dead was an insight which seemed thoroughly to have impressed itself on first-century Christians.[124] 'The stone which the builders rejected has become the head of the corner' (Lk. 20.17 and other texts). Moreover, the establishment of a church of the 'foolish in the world' reversed natural expectations (1 Cor. 1.26). And those who preached the Gospel, it was claimed, had 'turned the world upside down' (Acts 17.6).[125] There seems to have been a strong sense among early Christians that God, by his acts among them, had definitively reversed the natural order of human life. Verses 52-53 of the Magnificat may be influenced by this widespread Christian perception.

Raymond Brown has argued vigorously that Luke obtained his canticles from a group of Jewish Christian Anawim. After noting several instances in which the Qumran community designated itself as the 'poor', Brown stated:

> It is not farfetched then to suggest that Luke got his canticles from a somewhat parallel community of Jewish Anawim who had been

converted to Christianity, a group that unlike the sectarians at Qumran would have continued to reverence the Temple and whose 'Messianism was Davidic'.[126]

To enter into the debate about whether a distinctive party of Anawim, in fact, existed would be fruitless.[127] It can be said, however, that one ought not to deduce the existence of such a group from the reference to 'those of low estate' in the Magnificat. The Magnificat and Benedictus make use of so many motifs drawn from the Psalter that it would be almost surprising if the theme that God saves the 'poor' did not find its place among them. The language of the Magnificat is highly stereotyped and any attempt to make sociological observations on the basis of it is perilous.

Nevertheless, one must observe that in the Magnificat the reversal of fortunes is a matter of rejoicing. Such a reversal can, in other circumstances, be seen as a disaster.[128] Only 'he who is down need fear no fall', and only he who objectively is of 'low estate' will rejoice that God has reversed human fortunes. It is possible, therefore, that this language was used not only because it was resonant with tradition but because, to some degree, it fitted the circumstances of the Jewish-Christian community in which the hymns originated.

There are two equal but opposite dangers which threaten the interpreter of these verses. One danger is to see in them only the political and economic revolution of the oppressed masses.[129] This sort of interpretation ignores the stereotyped OT nature of the language and the role of this segment of the psalm within the composition as a whole. On the other hand a complete spiritualization of the psalm is also a danger.[130] These verses are meaningful not only because they reverberate with the language of a revered tradition. They express the confident hope of those who first used the hymn that in the final days, the arrival of which had been guaranteed by the resurrection of Christ, their material lot would be bettered. There would then be genuine political and social revolution. Many modern commentators rightly understand these verses as referring to both a spiritual and a concrete reality.[131]

These verses, then, describe the great act for which God is praised, the coming of Christ, in stereotyped OT language. This present act is completely characteristic of God's dealing with humanity but, as the aorists make clear, it is the ultimate and definitive such act.

Summary

54. The hymn then summarizes the 'great things' for which God is praised: he has 'helped Israel'. The verb ἀντιλαμβάνειν means 'to take hold of to support'.[132] Israel is called servant as at Isaiah 41.8, 44.1, etc.[133] What has been done for Mary has consequences for Israel.

All three of the infancy hymns emphasize strongly that God has done something for 'Israel'. 'He has helped Israel' (1.54). The God of Israel has 'visited and redeemed his people' (1.68). The present salvation is a 'glory for thy people, Israel' (2.32). The Jewish Christians to whom the composition of these hymns probably ought to be attributed here identify themselves with Israel. This is not necessarily an exclusive identification; there may well be no intention of denying the name 'Israel' to their unbelieving fellow Jews. It is simply that all the history of God's dealing with Israel points forward to the salvation which the Church confesses in the Magnificat (v. 55). There is certainly no hint here of a rejection of Israel by God. Inasmuch as there is not even direct evidence of a concept of the church as the 'remnant of Israel'[134] the hymn may come from before the point at which the unbelief of the majority of Jews had become a theological problem. The act for which God is praised is the whole salvation event comprised by the life, death and resurrection of Christ.[135] It is here claimed, it would seem without any self-consciousness, that in this act God has helped 'Israel'.

Further definition of the 'help' to Israel is added by the use of an explanatory infinitive. One finds a similar use of the infinitive in the Benedictus.[136] In fact, the same infinitive μνησθῆναι appears in the Benedictus (v. 72).

55. At this point one comes across an assertion which is repeated with even greater emphasis in the Benedictus (vv. 72-73), and implied by the Nunc Dimittis (2.30-31): the present salvation is the fulfillment of ancient promise. It is the culmination of salvation history. Like v. 72 of the Benedictus the language appears to be coloured by the memory of Micah 7.20, but it may well be that 'only a Christian would weave together these Old Testament expressions into such a decisive affirmation'.[137]

The promise was 'to our fathers and to Abraham and to his seed forever'.[138] The figure of Abraham reappears in the Benedictus (v. 73). Indeed, Father Abraham reappears with some regularity in Luke–Acts as a whole. 'God's promise to the fathers, from Abraham onwards, is a theme which runs through the whole of Luke's two-volume work.'[139] He appears as the recipient par excellence of that promise which now finds its fulfillment.

The psalm ends with the phrase εἰς τὸν αἰῶνα, 'forever'. Such a formula very frequently ends a psalm[140] and it should not be attached too closely to any preceding part of speech. The formula has two functions: it states that the present salvation is not ephemeral but will last for all time and it marks the end of the psalm.

Summary

The Magnificat declares with exultant joy that God the Saviour has acted decisively for Israel. This decisive help is best explained as the coming of Jesus Christ and, more specifically, his death and resurrection. This is an event which, from the viewpoint of the poet, is one which has already occurred, but it is also one which has future, indeed eternal, consequences. The hymn uses motifs familiar from frequent use in the OT to describe the present salvation. It is also strongly emphasized that this present and future salvation is firmly rooted in Israel's past. The present salvation, with all its future consequences, is a fulfillment of God's past promises to his people.

THE BENEDICTUS

Translation

68   Blessed is the Lord God of Israel,
        for he has visited and redeemed his people.
69   He has raised up a horn of salvation for us
        in the house of David his servant,
70   just as he promised through the mouth of
        his holy prophets of old,
71   salvation from our enemies,
        and from the hand of all those who hate us,
72   showing mercy to our fathers and remembering his holy
        covenant,
73   the oath which he swore to Abraham our father,
74   to allow us, free from fear, delivered from the hands of the
        enemies,
75   to serve him in holiness and righteousness all our days.[1]
76   And you, child, shall be called
        prophet of the Most High,
        for you will go before the Lord to prepare his ways,
77   to give knowledge of salvation to his people
        through the forgiveness of their sins
78   in the heartfelt mercy of our God
        through which the rising light from on high has visited us[2]
79   to shine on those sitting in darkness and in the shadow of death;
        to guide our feet into the way of peace.

Textual Notes

1. The Koine tradition adds τῆς ζωῆς. This may be safely rejected as a later expansion. There is another textual problem here which is not reflected by the English translation. B and a few other manuscripts offer a dative of time while the vast majority of manuscripts give the more classical accusative. See BD, 108. The latter is probably a correction of the former.

2. This is the only textual variant of real importance in the Benedictus but it is, unfortunately, an almost insoluble one. The future ἐπισκέψεται is attested by א*, B, a few other manuscripts, and the Syriac tradition. The aorist, ἐπεσκέψατο, is found in אᶜ, A, C, D, the Koine tradition, many other manuscripts and the Latin tradition. The UBS and the Nestle editions of the NT read the future but Tischendorf read the aorist. Scholars are likewise divided by the issue. Grundmann, *Lukas*, 74; Klostermann, *Lukas*, 28; Robinson, 'Detection', 280 n. 3; Lagrange, *Luc*, 62, preferred the future. Brown, *Birth*, 373; Jones, 'Psalms', 38; Benoit, 'L'Enfance', 185, preferred the aorist. Sahlin offered a characteristically unusual explanation (*Messias*, 296): the aorist was changed to the future when the hymn was shifted from its original position after Lk. 2.28. In its present position the future was necessary because Jesus had not yet been born. Jones, 'Psalms', 38, implied that the difficulty goes back to a confusion over the translation of a Hebrew imperfect with waw consecutive. It is possible that the aorist resulted from the assimilation of the verb to the tense of the same verb in v. 68. On the other hand, the verb may have been assimilatd to the much nearer future of v. 76. Brown argued that the aorist is the *lectio difficilior* (*Birth*, 373), and should, therefore, be accepted. If the aorist was original an inclusio is formed with v. 68; so Lagrange, *Luc*, 62; Benoit, 'L'Enfance', 185. The problem is an immensely difficult one but the aorist, as the more difficult reading, seems preferable.

The Form of the Text
There is one overriding question concerning the Benedictus. Is the psalm, as we have it now, a unitary composition? The question is justified in that there is an obvious break in the psalm after v. 75. To that point the finite verbs are aorist and the hymn speaks in praise of God. In v. 76, however, the tense shifts to the future and Zechariah addresses the infant John directly. There have been three solutions of the problem: 1. that the hymn is a unitary composition; 2. that vv. 76-79 were added to the original psalm which ended at v. 75; 3. that Luke inserted v. 76 or vv. 76-77 into a pre-existing hymn.

1. The hymn is a unitary composition. We may leave aside those who can mantain the unity of the psalm either because they attribute its composition to Zechariah on the occasion described in the text, or to Luke himself. There remain, however, several variants on this basic theme. First, there are those who find in the Benedictus a complicated poetic structure, the presence of which guarantees the unity of the hymn. J. Wragg, A. Vanhoye and P. Auffret have seen a complicated chiastic structure spreading out from v. 72, involving the repetition of key terms.[1] One may admire these scholars for their

ingenuity but one can hardly avoid the conclusion that their arguments are rather far-fetched. That the hymn expanded from a central point such as the statement of v. 72 is contrary to the insight of C. Westermann, that the core of psalms such as the Benedictus lies in the one-sentence exclamation of praise, 'word of praise + reason for it: God has acted'.[2] Moreover, that the original proposal of Vanhoye ignored certain repetitions of vocabulary, Lord (vv. 68, 76), mercy (vv. 72, 78), way (vv. 76, 79), etc., has already been noted by Auffret himself.[3] Furthermore, the chiastic theory does not explain why certain key terms such as 'Blessed', 'redemption' and 'to serve' (which is the goal of the saving act of God) are not repeated. Nor does it give an adequate explanation of the utter change of direction at v. 76. Surely the poet could have repeated what are actually rather standard biblical expressions without this obvious break in the flow of thought of the poem. There is certainly repetition in this poem, and some of it is doubtless deliberate, but it is unlikely that this repetition was organized under a scheme such as Vanhoye and others have suggested. The most telling objection against this analysis is a simple one, however; it 'does nothing to explain the progression of thought in the hymn'.[4]

M. Gertner has suggested that the Benedictus is a covert midrash on the Aaronic Blessing of Numbers 6.24-26.[5] That which links the two seemingly disparate parts of the poem is a dependence on the seven key concepts of that OT blessing. Gertner's argument is not always entirely clear: he argues both that the hymn was an older Jewish midrash,[6] and that it was shaped by Luke to make it apply explicitly to John and Jesus,[7] and yet is a compositional unity. The seven concepts of Numbers 6.24-26, blessing, being gracious, giving light or shining, etc., are so common that it is not entirely surprising that these words, or others related to them by the elastic rules of midrashic interpretation, appear together. Furthermore, all seven concepts would appear in the hymn even without vv. 76-77.[8] Gertner's interpretation may, it seems, be safely laid aside.

There are also scholars who maintain the unity of the Benedictus without recourse to analysis of the structure. Jones, Gaston and Marshall have affirmed that the Benedictus is best considered a unitary composition.[9] The 'onus probandi', Jones affirmed, is on those who would deny the unity of the hymn.[10] However, both Jones and Gaston also claimed that the hymn had existed independently of its present narrative context. Like the other hymns of Luke 1–2, it probably arose in Jewish-Christian circles.[11] Neither scholar has suggested, however, a Sitz im Leben which would account adequately for the address to the child. While most of the hymn is, indeed, generalized praise of God which could have arisen in the worship of the early church, it is hard to imagine vv. 76f. in any context very different from that presupposed by the narrative. In the infancy narrative itself, those verses make sense; as a part of early Christian worship they do not.

Leaney and Sahlin have suggested an alternative setting for the hymn. They claimed that the hymn has been transposed to its present location from its original setting on the lips of the prophetess Anna at Luke 2.38.[12] In this case the child is obviously not John but Jesus (that the 'child' was originally Jesus is also argued by Gaston and Robinson[13]). This theory falls down on two counts, however. First, no adequate explanation has been given to account for the transposition of the hymn to its new location. Sahlin[14] argued that Luke felt compelled to place the hymn on Zechariah's lips as a replacement for the Magnificat which he had already transplanted to its present position and made a speech of Mary. But this is to multiply improbabilities. One wonders why the Magnificat, if it was originally a speech of Zechariah, contains feminine self-references! Secondly, the description of the prophet of v. 76 is so heavily influenced by the synoptic description of John that the most reasonable interpretation must surely be that John himself is the 'child' to whom v. 76 is addressed.[15]

It seems, therefore, that those who would preserve the unity of the Benedictus have not adequately explained the abrupt shift in v. 76.

2. A simple and widely held solution to the problem is that vv. 76-79 are an addition to 1.68-75 designed to adapt the hymn to its present situation. This position has been argued by, among many others, H. Gunkel, P. Winter, J. Gnilka, P. Vielhauer and G. Lohfink.[16] The first section of the hymn might be Jewish (Gunkel, Winter, Vielhauer and Gnilka) or Christian (Lohfink). The most common explanation of the second half of the hymn, vv. 76-79, is that these verses formed a genethliakon or birthday ode.[17] A variation on this particular analysis was offered by H. Schürmann who saw in 1.67, 76-79 the original conclusion of the baptist legend into which a Christian messianic song had been interpolated.[18] Such a structural analysis is, with respect to the psalm itself, identical to that offered by Gunkel and others.

This theory explains the abrupt break in the hymn at v. 76. The strongest point in its favour is that 'eternity' formulae such as 'all our days' (v. 75) appear to conclude many OT psalms.[19] Of the various forms of the theory perhaps the most persuasive is Schürmann's, for it explains most clearly the origin of vv. 76-79. While this theory is a plausible one it does not, in my judgment, explain the structure of the hymn as adequately as the third option, which now must be discussed.

3. It has been suggested that Luke inserted v. 76 or, more likely, vv. 76-77 into the hymn in order to adapt an originally independent psalm to its present context. The former solution was proposed by Bultmann,[20] the latter by Dibelius, Benoit, George and Brown.[21] Bultmann's proposal was rather tentative; it serves only to indicate the minimum which must be removed in order to resolve the structural difficulty. The latter proposal, which has been most strenuously argued by Benoit, must be seriously considered, however.

Before laying out the evidence for this theory one objection must be dealt with, that 'all the days of our lives' is a formula which marks the conclusion to a psalm. Benoit was able to point to two instances, Psalms 90.14 and 128.5, in which this formula did not mark the conclusion of a psalm.[22] A closer look at the evidence shows that Benoit could well have stated his case more strongly. In fact, this 'beliebte Schlussformel'[23] does not appear as a concluding formula in any of the Psalms which are referred to by Schürmann, Vielhauer and Gnilka.[24] The usual concluding formula is some variation of εἰς τὸν αἰῶνα. Only in Psalm 23.6 does there appear a formula, 'all the days of my life', which is similar to the Benedictus and here, it should be noted, the formula does not actually conclude the psalm. Another sentence appears before the end of the poem. Only in Isaiah 38.20 does a formula similar to that in the Benedictus function as a 'Schlussformel'. In contrast to this, the expression, 'all our (my) days', appears at Psalms 27.4, 90.9, and, as Benoit noted, at 90.14 and 128.5 in positions other than the end of their respective psalms. There is, however, a common factor to all these occurrences, excluding 90.14 but including 23.6 and Isaiah 38.20. The expression is connected with some particular blessing on the part of God. In two cases, Psalm 27.4 and Isaiah 38.20 it is explicitly connected, as in the Benedictus, with continual worship of God. Considering this evidence, it appears that the expression 'all our days' is not necessarily a formula which marks the conclusion of an originally independent psalm.[25]

Since the evidence in favour of the theory that vv. 76-77 is an insertion has been adduced earlier in the work I shall summarize it only briefly at this point.[26] In vv. 78-79 the non-specific,general, praise of God characteristic of vv. 68-75 resumes. The people of God are again spoken of in the first person singular: 'through the heartfelt mercies of *our* God . . . has visited *us* . . . to guide *our* feet'. This contrasts markedly with v. 77, 'the forgiveness of *their* sins'. In the final two verses of the Benedictus the vocabulary of the hymn is again explicitly drawn from the OT and shows no signs of Luke's hand.[27] A striking illustration of this can be seen in the 26th edition of Nestle's Greek New Testament. In the margin of the text of the Benedictus are listed those texts which form the OT background to the psalm. In vv. 68-75, 78-79 there is barely room to list all the references. In vv. 76-77, on the other hand, only references to Luke appear except for Malachi 3.1 and Isaiah 40.3 which are, of course, quoted in Luke's gospel.

This theory is strengthened if the aorist rather than the future is taken to be the original reading in v. 78, but it does not depend on it. An independent hymn consisting of Luke 1.68-75, 78-79 would probably have used the aorist in v. 78 as in the rest of the hymn. Verses 78-79 would then recapitulate the thought of vv. 68-69. But it would have been quite natural for Luke himself to have altered the aorist of the original hymn to the future when he adapted the hymn to its present use. This theory of Benoit and others appears most adequately to explain the abrupt break in the flow of thought of the Benedictus.

There have been several attempts to divide the hymn into strophes. Benoit himself advanced a theory which accorded with his belief that vv. 76-77 had been added by Luke. He suggested that the hymn contains three strophes, each containing the same internal structure.[28] The last strophe is a brief recapitulation of the psalm as a whole.[29]

	Strophe 1	*Strophe 2*
The Saving Act of God	68 (visited, etc.)	72 (shown mercy, etc.)
Biblical Preparation	69-70 (promise to David)	73-74 (Promise to Abraham and patriarchs)
Resulting Salvation	71 (deliverance from enemies)	75 (serving without fear)

Benoit noted that the salvation which resulted from the act of God corresponds to the Biblical preparation. Deliverance from enemies corresponds to the mention of David the warrior, the service of God to the possession of the land promised to the patriarchs.[30]

Then, if one leaps over vv. 76-77, one finds in the final strophe a brief recapitulation which employs the same structure as that of the first two strophes.

Saving Act	78 (visited)
Biblical Preparation	79a (reference to illumination promised by prophets, esp. Isaiah)
Result	79b (the ways of peace)

Essentially the same structure has been suggested by Brown.[31]

Benoit's analysis of the structure of the psalm is illuminating but may be over-refined. It is true that certain themes are reiterated but the hymn gives the impression of a rather ramshackle construction. There is no great distinction, in reality, between the saving act itself and the result of the act. Rather, one amplifying description of the act is piled on another. There are certainly changes in emphasis in the hymn but, as was the case with the Magnificat, 'strophe' may be too dignified a term for the phenomenon. Benoit's analysis does, however, illuminate the progression of these changes in emphasis. It also clarifies the role of vv. 78-79. These verbs serve to recapitulate the psalm as a whole, reminding the hearer that the saving act consists of God's mercy visited (vv. 68, 78a) on us in the person of the Davidic Messiah (κέρας, v. 69, ἀνατολή, v. 78b).[32]

Perhaps the structure of the Benedictus may be best outlined as follows:

Word of Praise	68a
Motive clause	68b
Statements amplifying the Motive Clause	69-75
Prophecy concerning John	76-77
Recapitulation	78-79

The Benedictus does not display synonomous parallelism as clearly and exactly as the Magnificat. Ths feature is present, however, in a rough fashion in vv. 68-69, 71-73 and 79.

An attempt to place the hymn in a particular liturgy, such as the Paschal celebration of the early Palestinian Church,[33] would be fruitless. The most that can be said is that the hymn looks back to Jesus 'aus der Sicht der nachösterlichen Gemeinde'.[34]

The Immediate Context of the Hymn

In v. 64 we read that Zechariah spoke 'blessing God'. In v. 67, the actual introduction to the psalm, it is said that Zechariah 'prophesied'. The Benedictus, in its present form, supplies the words for both occasions.[35] The prophecy concerning John answers the question of the neighbourhood, 'What will this child be?' This may explain why Luke inserted the hymn after a new introduction in 1.67 rather than after v. 64.

The hymn, in its present context, speaks of Jesus Christ. His coming is the truly significant event. It is only because John's birth is so closely connected with the coming of Jesus, the Davidic Messiah, and is, indeed, a sign of that coming, that Zechariah can praise God so triumphantly. The gift of John to the aged couple is a sign of the certainty of the coming of the Messiah, Jesus. It is not at all surprising, therefore, that the figure in view in most of the Benedictus is not John but Jesus the Messiah.

COMMENTARY

The Word of Praise, v. 68a

As we have seen, the Berakah with which the psalm begins is a familiar OT formula.[36] On several occasions similar formulae are linked with David or David's son (1 Sam. 25.32; 1 Kings 1.48; 8.15; cf. 2 Chr. 2.12). It is, of course, necessary to supply a verb when one translates these formulae. A certain anomaly becomes apparent when one considers their usual English translations. When the blessing addresses God directly the indicative is usually supplied, 'Blessed *art* thou', but when it speaks of God in the third person, one usually finds the subjunctive 'Blessed be the Lord'. Supplying a subjunctive makes the formula hortatory.[37] Several scholars have insisted that the subjunctive must be supplied here,[38] but it is difficult to see why this should be so. R. Deichgräber surveyed those cases in which the LXX supplied a verb in short nominal words of praise and found the indicative to be predominant.[39] The preference for the indicative is especially marked in those instances in which the word of praise begins with 'blessed' and in the NT and early Christian writings.[40] It appears that the indicative ought to be preferred, 'Blessed is the Lord'. The one praised is the 'Lord God of Israel' (cf. Acts 13.17), a title which sets the Jewish tone of the whole psalm.

The Motive Clause, v. 68b

God is praised because he has visited and redeemed his people. The verb 'visited', ἐπεσκέψατο, corresponds to the Hebrew, פקד, a verb which often points to acts of gracious favour on the part of God.[41] In Psalm 106.4, for example, the verb is simply translated 'help' by the RSV.[42] The verb is aorist and ought to be interpreted in its normal sense as referring to something which has happened in the past. The content of this gracious help is then spelled out more clearly. He has redeemed his people, literally 'performed redemption'. Lohfink claimed that the appearance of this expression, rather than the aorist of λυτρόω, indicates that the saving action of God is not yet over, thus maintaining eschatological tension. This is probably an attempt to read too much into the text. There is little difference between this expression and Luke 24.21, 'We had hoped that he was the one to redeem (λυτροῦσθαι) Israel'. The Benedictus simply affirms what the two disciples had only hoped.[43] As Sahlin noted, the exact expression does not appear in the OT but the thought is closely paralleled by Psalm 11.9.[44] The recipient of God's favour is 'his people', i.e. Israel. The Jewish-Christian community of origin, at the point of composition of the hymn, did not differentiate itself from Israel nor, apparently, did it see the church as a replacement of Israel after the flesh. This same attitude is also shown by the many allusions to the history of Israel which appear in the psalm. One wonders if this indicates that the hymn originated before the problem of Jewish unbelief became a pressing one.

Amplifying Statements

At this point the poem amplifies in a series of statements the meaning of the act for which God is praised.

69. As has been shown earlier, this verse affirms that God has raised up the Messiah from the House of David.[45] Harnack thought that ἤγειρεν referred to the resurrection of Christ.[46] While this thought may well have occurred to Christian users of the hymn, the primary meaning of the verb on this occasion is to 'bring into existence'.[47] The phrase 'David his servant' appears to be a liturgical formula adopted from Judaism and taken into Christian worship.[48] It reappears at Acts 4.25 and Didache 9.2. The latter occasion is particularly significant, for there David is called 'servant' in connection with his role as ancestor of Jesus, as appears to be also the case in the Benedictus. This qualification of David as 'servant' shows that

Lohfink may have erred when he claimed that the 'house of David' meant 'Israel als heilsgeschichtliche Grösse'.[49] The verse praises God for the raising up of a Messiah of David's line.

70. This verse breaks the flow of the hymn; without it v. 71 would follow v. 69 quite naturally. The phrase also reappears almost verbatim at Acts 3.21. Moreover, as we have seen, this verse displays several Greek rather than Hebrew syntactical features.[50] It has been suggested, therefore, that Luke may have added this verse to the hymn.[51] Other scholars, however, have pointed to the links between this verse and early liturgical language[52] and have suggested that both this verse and Acts 3.21 are ultimately dependent on such language. R. Brown even claimed that the identity of this verse with Acts 3.21 may indicate their common origin within the early Jerusalem community.[53] He also pointed out, rightly, that this verse parallels the thought of 1.55 and 1.73 and so concluded that it was probably original to the hymn.

That the verse was original or that Luke added it are not the only options, however. This verse may have been an accretion accumulated during its use in the liturgy of the early church. One might suppose, given the Greek syntax of the verse, that any such addition may have been made by the Greek speaking church. If so, this might indicate that Luke himself was not responsible for the translation of the hymns. As it is, the hymn looks back to a history of prophetic promise. Nathan's prophecy, 2 Samuel 7.12-16, may be particularly in mind. It is worth noting that the aorist in this verse cannot be 'prophetic', that is, speaking of the future as if it were past.[54] The expression 'holy prophets' appears only in later Jewish writings (Wis. 11.1; 2 Bar. 85.1). That those prophets existed ἀπ' αἰῶνος is a slight exaggeration; the words mean merely 'from of old'.[55] The verse as a whole insists that the raising up of the Messiah from David's house is not something new; it is rooted in Israel's history. The present salvation is the fulfillment of ancient promise.

71. The connection between this verse and v. 69 is difficult. σωτηρίαν could stand in apposition to κέρας σωτηρίας[56] or function as an additional description of the whole event alluded to in 1.68-69.[57] The latter seems more likely. The salvation here envisaged consists of national redemption. At this point the OT background of the text is of the highest significance. In this verse lies an allusion to Psalm 106.10 which recalls God's deliverance of his people at the Red Sea. The present salvation is described in relation to *the* great

saving event of the past, the deliverance from Egypt. It could almost be described as a new Exodus.[58] This typological description of the 'salvation' of this verse means that the deliverance spoken of is not simply from Roman domination. Rather, it symbolizes God's response to the 'Heilsnot' of his people,[59] their need of rescue from all that prevents them from serving him in 'holiness and righteousness'. The enemies, who are doubtless both national and individual, are not specified.

72. The OT allusions of the hymn had focused first on David (vs. 69, 70), then on Moses and the Exodus (v. 71). At this point the patriarchs come into view although, as Brown has pointed out, the oath/covenant language is also applicable to David.[60] The use of non-articular infinitives is reminiscent of Luke 1.54 and may be a Semitic construction.[61] It is difficult to know whether they describe the purpose or the result of God's action.[62] Perhaps, with God as subject, there is little difference between the two. The use of the infinitive to pile clause on clause is characteristic of the hymn as a whole. Such a series of inifinitives is not unknown in Hebrew poetry.[63] The expression 'showing mercy to our fathers', μετὰ τῶν πατέρων, is a difficult one.[64] Does this mean that the patriarchs only now receive God's mercy? Or are they even co-workers with God in procuring salvation for Israel?[65] While it is true that it was believed that the patriarchs were still in existence (Lk. 13.28; 16.23), they appear in the hymns primarily as recipients of promise rather than of salvation. In the Benedictus, as in the Magnificat, the fathers are primarily connected with the oath or covenant made in the past (cf. Lk. 1.55). Salvation, which involves the remembering of that oath, is primarily for 'present-day' Israel. But this salvation of Israel is also a continuation of God's mercy to the fathers.[66] The rough parallelism of the verse makes it likely that 'showing mercy', or more literally, 'doing mercy', and 'remembering the covenant' are roughly equivalent.[67] The term 'holy covenant' appears only in late Judaism.[68]

73. The content of the covenant is then specified. It consists not of a two-sided agreement but of an 'oath to Abraham'. Oath, ὅρκον, which is accusative, stands in apposition to διαθήκης, which is genitive. It appears that the case of ὅρκον has been assimilated to that of the relative pronoun ὅν.[69] The etymological allusions to 'Zechariah' and 'Elizabeth' found in this verse by Laurentin are 'mere accident'.[70]

The oath in question is to Abraham, as in, for example, Genesis

22.16ff.[71] The psalm has thus completed a rapid review of OT history. The saving act is not new; its roots reach back through David (v. 69), Moses and the Exodus (v. 71), to Abraham, the father of the people. 'The law of Moses, the prophets and the psalms' are here made to speak of Christ.

74. At this point the hymn gives the content of the oath. The infinitives of vv. 74 and 75 relate back, however, not only to the oath of v. 73, but continues to describe the purpose and the result of the saving act described in vv. 68ff.[72] The infinitive with article may correspond to the Hebrew ל + infinitive,[73] but is also a common feature of Lucan style.[74] It is difficult to differentiate between the functions of articular and non-articular infinitives in the Benedictus. They seem to be used interchangeably. The adverb ἀφόβως modifies the participle, 'being delivered' and the infinitive 'to serve' which appears in v. 75.[75] The participial phrase, 'being delivered from the hand of the enemies' refers back to v. 71. Once again, the enemies are not specified.

75. The ultimate goal and result of God's saving action is finally reached, 'to serve him in holiness and righteousness'. The ultimate purpose of national liberation is therefore cultic; the political interest of the poem is subordinated to the religious.[76] To serve 'in holiness and righteousness' is an allusion to Joshua's solemn exhortation to Israel (Jos. 24.14). There, the people are commanded to serve God in holiness and righteousness in the land which has been given them.[77] Here also the purpose of God's saving action is that the people should serve him aright. While the formula 'all our days' is not necessarily a concluding formula,[78] it does sometimes function as a solemn signal that the climax of a poem has been reached (Ps. 23.6; 128.5). In the original hymn, if our reconstruction is correct, only the recapitulation remained.

76. At this point in the poem as we have it, however, Zechariah turns to the child, who, in this context at least, is certainly John.[79] His prophecy answers the question voiced in v. 66, 'What then will this child be?'[80] The change in direction in the poem is, as has been noted, a dramatic one. Perhaps the most striking change is the appearance of the future rather than the aorist. The future verb 'you will be called' is equivalent to 'you will be acknowledged as'.[81] προφήτης ὑψίστου is, as has been noted many times,[82] a Messianic title in Testament Levi 8.15 but here stands in conscious subordination to Luke 1.32. John is to be called 'prophet of the Most High',

but Jesus 'Son of the Most High'. That the title 'prophet of the Most High' is, in itself, an 'Elias-Attribut', as Vielhauer claimed, is unlikely.[83] The vocabulary of the second half of this verse is drawn from the citation of Isaiah 40.3 which appears in Luke 3.4 with, perhaps, some influence of Malachi 3.1 as cited in Luke 7.27. There is only a slight verbal connection between this verse and Luke 1.17 which explicitly mentions Elijah.[84] The description of John's role in Luke 1.76-77 is essentially the same as that found in the body of the Gospel. John is here cast in the role of Elijah to no greater and no lesser degree than in Luke 3 or Luke 7.[85]

The identity of the κύριος of v. 76 has been disputed. All those who uphold the baptist provenance of the hymn would consider the κύριος to be God.[86] So also would those who consider the child of v. 76 to be Jesus, rather than John,[87] and others such as Klostermann, Lagrange, and Schürmann.[88] All these scholars argue that in Luke 1–2 κύριος, with the exception of 1.43 and possibly 2.11, refers to God, not Jesus. This must therefore also be the case in 1.76. The κύριος here is intended to be Jesus. Certainly for Christian readers, the Lord before whom John will go is Jesus.[89] Vielhauer, who argued so vigorously for the baptist provenance of the hymn, admitted that in the context of Luke 1–2 the Lord before whom John will go is the Lord whose mother Elizabeth greeted.[90] If, as seems likely, vv. 76-77 were composed for the sole purpose of relating the hymn to its context, the κύριος of v. 76 may well be Jesus rather than God. The hymn would then present John in typical Christian fashion as forerunner of Jesus. The 'Lord', then, would be the same as the ἀνατολή, i.e. the Davidic Messiah of v. 78.

77. The delineation of John's role then continues. The infinitive τοῦ δοῦναι is epexegetical and appears to be parallel to ἑτοιμάσαι. 'Knowledge of salvation' is not an expression found in the OT, NT or the Testaments of the 12 Patriarchs, nor can a Hebrew equivalent be found in the Qumran writings.[91] The meaning of 'knowledge of salvation' is, however, more closely defined by the addition of the phrase ἐν ἀφέσει ἁμαρτιῶν.[92] The expression 'forgiveness of sins' is a favourite of Luke's; 8 of 11 NT occurrences are found in Luke–Acts.[93] The most important such occurrence for understanding its use here is Luke 3.3: John preached 'a baptism of repentance for the forgiveness of sins'. That role is anticipated in 1.77.[94]

'Knowledge of salvation through the forgiveness of sins' then is to be the result of John's preparatory activity. Luke here attributes to

John a role of extreme importance in salvation-history. That 'knowledge of salvation' comes from his activity is testimony to his power. John's role is not an independent one, however; he is certainly subordinate to the κύριος of v. 76, who is the ἀνατολή of v. 78. His significance lies in the fact that his appearance as forerunner guarantees the appearance of the Messiah, 'the one who is to come'.

This subordination of John to Jesus, a feature of all the gospels, explains the presence of the prophecy at this point in the hymn. The hymn has already described the present saving act of God by reference to the history of Israel from David to Abraham. It has expressed the purpose of God's activity (v. 75). At this point it is ready to recapitulate its contents by presenting again the Davidic Messiah under the image of the ἀνατολή. John, as forerunner, appeared before the Messiah. His role is therefore described here, immediately before the culminating description of the Messiah himself.

Recapitulation

At this point the hymn again describes the Davidic Messiah. In v. 69 he appeared under the image of the horn; here he reappears under the image of the ἀνατολή, the rising light from on high. If, as seems probable, ἀνατολή translates the Hebrew צמח, the same combination of titles appears in the 15th Benediction of the Shemoneh Esreh. 'Cause the shoot of David to shoot forth quickly and raise up his horn by thy salvation . . . Blessed art thou, Lord, who causest the horn of salvation to shoot forth.' The exact meaning of ἀνατολή has been much disputed.[95] In the LXX it translates צֶמַח, the 'sprout' of David,[96] which became a Messianic title in Judaism,[97] and early Christianity.[98] The word ἀνατολή contains within it both the reference to a rising 'sprout' from Jesse and to a rising light.[99] There seems, therefore, no reason to seek an alternative explanation involving the use of the verb ἀνατέλλω.[100] The metaphor may well be somewhat mixed, combining as it does the image of the 'sprout' and 'rising light'. The alternative explanations are equally difficult, however. 'Suns' or 'stars' which rise (ἀνατέλλω) do not do so from 'on high'. The difficult image can only be understood when one remembers that the 'rising light', in as much as he is the subject of the verb 'visit',[101] and comes ἐξ ὕψους, that is, from God, is clearly a person.[102] This person is the Messiah of David's line who attracts to himself various images. He is at once 'horn' (v. 69), and 'sprout' and 'rising light' (v. 78). The combination of these metaphors is found again in Revelation 22.16, 'I am the root and offspring of David, the bright morning star'.[103] The one who 'visits' in Luke 1.78 is the one who speaks in Revelation 22.16, Jesus the Messiah of David's line.

He is to come 'through the heartfelt mercy of our God'. To be more accurate, mercy is here associated not with the heart, but with the 'bowels', σπλάγχνα, the seat of emotions.[104] The phrase is only loosely linked with the description of John's role in vv. 76-77.[105]

79. The role of the ἀνατολή is then defined by means of two infinitives, ἐπιφᾶναι and τοῦ κατευθῦναι.[106] In v. 79a, 'to shine on those who sit in darkness and in the shadow of death' shows that the image of the ἀνατολή is here understood primarily in terms of light.

The words are particularly rich in OT allusions. Behind this text lies the wording of Psalm 107.10 and the description of the work of both the Davidic Prince (Is. 9.2), and the Servant of the Lord (Is. 42.7).[107] Those who sit in darkness are doubtless the people of Israel as in Isaiah 9.1. This impression is confirmed by the ἡμῶν of the parallel line, 'to guide *our* feet'. This corresponds to the other first person plural references of vv. 68-75. These, it will be remembered, are 'his people' who are saved by the God of Israel (v. 68). The use of language drawn from Isaiah and of the imagery of light anticipates the Nunc Dimittis, 'a light for revelation to the Gentiles'. The darkness in which the people sit is a symbol of their utter need and oppression. As the OT background shows it is the darkness of the prison cell (cf. Is. 42.7; Ps. 107.10). To these captives the Messiah will proclaim liberty (Lk. 4.18). He will guide their feet into the way of peace, a fitting climax to the hymn. 'The way of peace', a phrase which appears in Isaiah 59.8, leads to that wholeness which is God's eschatological gift. One is reminded here of the words of the Nunc Dimittis (Lk. 2.29), 'Now you are letting your servant depart in peace' and of the Gloria, 'Peace to those on whom his favour rests'. Peace 'indicates the eschatological salvation which is already present as the power of God'.[108] It is for this that God 'has visited and redeemed his people'. It may be that the way of peace is the same as the 'way of salvation' of Acts 16.17 which is opened by the proclamation of the Gospel.[109]

Summary

This hymn repeats two themes already found in the Magnificat. These are: that God has acted to save Israel and that the present salvation is rooted in Israel's past. More specifically, this great salvation is the direct fulfilment of God's promises to his people.

In the coming of salvation the infant John, whom Zechariah addresses in the second half of the psalm, has an important role. He is to be forerunner of the Messiah and will prepare his ways. John's birth is therefore the certain guarantee that the 'rising light from on high' will shortly shine on his people. It is he, the Davidic Messiah, who is the truly important figure in the hymn.

THE NUNC DIMITTIS

Translation

29. Now you are letting your servant go in peace, Master, according to your word.
30. for my eyes have seen your salvation,
31. which you have prepared before the face of all the peoples,
32. a light for revelation to the Gentiles[1] and glory for your people Israel.

Textual Note
There is only one textual problem in the Nunc Dimittis; D omits the word ἐθνῶν from v. 32. All the remaining witnesses include the word. The preponderance of external witnesses is not the only reason for considering the word original, however. The Gentiles feature prominently in the several texts from Deutero-Isaiah to which the poem alludes, Is. 42.6; 49.6; 51.4; 52.9-10. Furthermore, the presence of ἐθνῶν seems required by the use of the word Ἰσραήλ in v. 32b. The parallelism of the two stichs, 32a and 32b, is flawed without it. (Admittedly, one could argue that this was the reason the word was secondarily inserted into the text.) Leaney, *Luke*, 100, suggested that D omits the word 'Gentiles' because of a grammatical difficulty: one would naturally expect a dative here as in the texts which form the LXX background to the verse. Simple error would appear to be a more likely explanation of the omission which does not occur in other Western texts. The word also easily finds its place in attempts to reconstruct the putative original Hebrew text. See, for example, H. Sahlin, *Messias*, 266; R. Aytoun, 'Hymns', 275. It seems best, therefore, to follow the reading of the majority of texts at this point.

The Immediate Context of the Hymn
This hymn fits rather more neatly into its narrative context than the Magnificat and Benedictus fit into theirs. Its statement that the

speaker is being let go in peace suits the situation of the aged Simeon. This has led to the suggestion that, if the hymn ever existed separately, the story of Simeon must have been composed around it.[1] Although this suggestion seems unpersuasive, it may well be that Luke has worked over this part of his tradition more carefully than the material in ch. 1.[2] Nevertheless, the hymn could be omitted without disruption to the narrative. If the Nunc Dimittis were omitted 2.33 would follow 2.28 in precisely the same manner as 1.65 follows 1.64; in both cases wonder would follow an unspecified blessing of God.[3] The narrative may originally have mentioned Simeon's praise without explicitly giving its content, just as it mentions Anna's praise without quoting it (2.38).[4] The chief problem here, however, is not that the narrative makes no sense without the hymn; it is that the hymn may make no sense without its narrative context.

Whether or not the poem circulated independently, the present context of the hymn is important for its proper exegesis. The Nunc Dimittis, like the other two infancy hymns, forms the climax of a promise–fulfilment–praise progression. In Simeon's case the promise had been that he would see the Lord's anointed before his death. The fulfilment of this promise he receives into his arms (v. 28). Thereupon he 'blesses' God in the words of the Nunc Dimittis.

The context of the hymn is an overpoweringly Jewish one. The physical setting is the Temple of Jerusalem. Jesus' parents were there in obedience to Israel's law. Simeon, 'righteous and devout', is, in a sense, the personification of expectant Israel.[5] This pious man, Luke informs us, was looking for the 'consolation of Israel'.[6] Moreover, the word of prophecy added at the conclusion of the hymn, vv. 34-35, primarily concerns the effect of Jesus upon Israel. All this must be kept in mind when interpreting a hymn which speaks of 'revelation to the Gentiles'.

The Form of the Hymn

The poetic structure of the hymn is relatively obvious: it consists of three bicola or couplets, the last of which contains synonymous parallelism.[7] But to note the structure is not to describe the form of the poem adequately. Several commentators have suggested that it is a prayer.[8] More commonly it is treated as a hymn.[9] While the two categories are not to be completely separated it seems that the latter is the more accurate description of the poem. Although the hymn, unlike the Magnificat and Benedictus, addresses God directly it does not make a request to him. The verb in v. 29, ἀπολύεις, is a simple present indicative, 'Now you are letting your servant depart in peace'.[10] Verse 29 as a whole is best considered a somewhat extravagant word of praise. Certainly Luke's introduction treats it as if it were a hymn, 'And he *blessed* God and said'. Verse 29 appears to reflect Jacob's words upon seeing Joseph alive and well (Gen. 46.30). That these words were considered to be an expression of praise is shown by the expansion of the Biblical account in Jubilees 45.3-4, 'And Israel said unto Joseph: "Now let me die since I have seen thee, and now may the Lord God of Israel be blessed . . . It is enough for me that I have seen thy face . . . ".'[11] Here the statement concerning readiness for death stands in parallel to what is clearly a hymnic expression.

If this interpretation of the psalm's first line is correct it can be seen that the hymn displays the same basic structure as the Magnificat and Benedictus:

29	Word of Praise
30	Motive Clause
31-32	Statements Expanding the Motive Clause

This is the typical structure of the kernel of the declarative psalm of praise.

If it is concluded that the hymn once had an existence apart from its narrative context the question of Sitz im Leben immediately arises. To what use was the hymn put? D. Jones offered three different suggestions: 1. that it was a liturgical response to the conclusion of worship, 2. that it was spoken upon discharge after a successful battle, 3. that it was a liturgical piece used before the death of a believer.[12] Jones appeared to consider the last the most likely of the three:[13]

> It may not be far from the mark to hazard the guess that the Nunc Dimittis reflects an early Christian response to the death of a believer, at a time when the coming of the Lord was regarded as imminent. With these words a believer was ready to fall asleep in Christ.

As Jones himself pointed out, the first two solutions do not do justice to the use of ἀπολύεις as a euphemism for death.[14] The third possibility is certainly not subject to that objection, but it remains implausible. It seems unlikely that the church had developed rituals

for the death of believers at the early stage of which Jones speaks.
Certainly, Jones offered no evidence of the existence of such rituals.

It seems more likely that the Nunc Dimittis, like the Magnificat
and Benedictus, was part of the general hymnody of the early church.
All three thank God for the advent of the Messiah. The reminiscence
in v. 29 of the words of Jacob, i.e. Israel, is instructive here. There is
evidence that it was thought that Jacob longed to see the day of the
Messiah.[15] Perhaps the Jewish Christian community here personified
itself as 'Israel' and declared, echoing the words of Genesis 46.30,
that the long-expected Messiah had come. Its joy is the joy of 'Israel'
upon seeing the beloved son.

The Nunc Dimittis shares another characteristic with the Magnificat and Benedictus: it is a mosaic of OT allusions. However, the
allusions in Simeon's song are drawn from Deutero-Isaiah rather
than primarily from the Psalter as is the case in the first two infancy
hymns.[16] These allusions are artfully woven together into a hymn of
'suppressed rapture and vivid intensity'.[17]

COMMENTARY

The Word of Praise.

29. The hymn begins with an emphatic 'now'. Throughout the
infancy narratives there is a sense that the present moment is the
time of salvation: 'For behold, from *now* on . . . ' (v. 48); 'Unto you is
born *this day* . . . ' (2.11).

> The entire third Gospel is presented as the fulfilment of messianic
> time. The frequency with which Luke employs the adverbs now
> (*nun*) and today (*semeron*) underscores the fact that the time of
> salvation has begun with Christ.[18]

ἀπολύεις is sometimes considered to be modal in force,[19] but most
commentators apparently consider it a normal present indicative.
'More probably, in enabling Simeon to see the Messiah, the Lord is
already carrying out part of the process of letting him die in peace.'[20]
This process now begins for Simeon.[21]

Although the expression 'let depart in peace' can refer to a simple
earthly parting,[22] in this case the verb ἀπολύεις is clearly a
euphemism for death.[23] The expression therefore becomes comparable
to the words of Jacob on seeing Joseph (Gen. 46.30). But Simeon
'saw' one greater than Joseph,[24] and for this blessing he praises God.

The tone of this statement contrasts strongly with that of the prophetic Essene mentioned by Josephus who was also willing to go down into death, but in despair.[25]

Another image is suggested by the juxtaposition of the words δοῦλος and δέσποτα, namely the manumission of a slave. By using this pair of words Simeon acknowledges his utter subjection to God.[26] Δέσποτα occurs occasionally in the LXX as the translation of אדני. In the NT it is applied to God primarily in liturgical language such as Acts 4.24 or Revelation 6.10. It recurs in later Christian prayers as well.[27]

In the present context, 'according to your word' refers back to the promise to Simeon that he would not die before seeing the Lord's Messiah. In a wider sense, however, the phrase corresponds to the thought expressed in 1.55, 73: the present salvation is a fulfilment of God's past promise. ἐν εἰρήνῃ appears at the end of the couplet in an emphatic position. It doubtless corresponds to the Hebrew שלום.

> On the basis of OT and Rabbinic usage εἰρήνη thus acquires a most profound and comprehensive significance. It indicates the eschatological salvation of the whole man which is already present as the power of God.[28]

Peace is an essential characteristic of the Messianic kingdom (Ps. 72.7; Zech. 8.12; Is. 9.6). It is 'into the ways of peace' that the dayspring will guide his people (Lk. 1.79), and peace is promised by the angels to those on whom God's favour rests (2.14). Simeon is among that number; he is 'der erste Erlöste'.[29]

The Motive Clause

30. The motive for praise is now given: 'for my eyes have seen your salvation'. This is clearly a periphrastic way of saying, 'I have seen'. According to v. 26 Simeon had been promised that before death he would see 'the Lord's Christ'. Now, he declares, he can die in peace because he has seen 'your salvation'. It is clear, therefore, that Luke intends us to understand 'salvation' as 'the Lord's Christ' and to see the infant Jesus as both. 'Salvation' is here not the usual feminine noun but σωτήριον, the neuter adjective used substantively. It is not only salvation itself, but also the one who brings salvation.[30] It is posssible that there is in this word a deliberate etymological allusion to the Hebrew root of the name Jesus. Σωτήριον appears only four times in the NT and three times in Luke–Acts, here and at Luke 3.6

and Acts 28.28. Its presence here is probably due to a reminiscence of Isaiah 40.5, 'all flesh shall see the salvation, σωτήριον, of God'. That quotation from Isaiah 40 also appears in Luke 3.4-6 as a description of the work of John the Baptist as forerunner of the Messiah. In seeing God's salvation Simeon is but the first of 'all flesh'. This pious Jew, the personification of Israel, in accepting Jesus as 'salvation', will even be joined by the Gentiles: 'Let it be known to you then that this σωτήριον of God has been sent to the Gentiles. They will listen' (Acts 28.28).[31]

Amplifying Statements
31. The nature of the 'salvation' of v. 30 is now more carefully defined. This salvation of which Simeon speaks has been *prepared* by God.[32] This is an unusual combination of ideas.

> The idea of the preparation of *salvation* is unique and in the light of what follows, this must mean the providential preparation of salvation through Israel's history, according to prophecy and promise until the time of fulfilment which is now recognized.[33]

Once again we meet that theme which is prominent in the Benedictus and Nunc Dimittis: the present salvation finds its roots in those divine promises which so mark Israel's history.[34]

'Before all the peoples, λαῶν'. The question immediately arises, 'Who are the "peoples"?' G.D. Kilpatrick has pointed out that in the only other occurrences of the plural of λαός (Acts 4.25, 27), the word must refer to the tribes of Israel.[35] Nowhere, he asserted, does Luke use the word λαός of Gentiles. He suggested, therefore, that the 'peoples' of v. 31 are likewise the tribes of Israel. This interpretation of the verse is unpersuasive; it has met with little acceptance among commentators. The use of λαοί in Acts 4.25, 27 is influenced by the language of Psalm 2, and cannot, therefore, be used as a criterion for determining Luke's usage of the word.[36] Furthermore, the Nunc Dimittis, if it was not composed by Luke, would not necessarily display Luke's characteristic usage of words. Certainly it is the Gentiles, not the tribes of Israel, who are mentioned in the OT texts, especially Isaiah 52.10, which seem to lie behind this part of the Nunc Dimittis. Finally, both Gentiles, ἐθνῶν, and Israel are mentioned in the following verse which explains the nature of the salvation prepared before all the peoples. It seems best, therefore, to translate λαῶν as 'peoples', that is, Israel and the Gentiles.

At this point, however, we come face to face with the question of the Gentiles' share in salvation. Sahlin, in the interests of his theory that Proto-Luke contained no universalism, argued that the Nunc Dimittis affirms only that the Gentiles will witness God's salvation, not that they will participate in it. The Nunc Dimittis, he argued, does not go beyond the hope expressed in Deutero-Isaiah that the Gentiles will witness Israel's vindication. Whether there is universalism in Deutero-Isaiah is a thorny problem which cannot be discussed here.[37] The question that must concern us is whether there is universalism in the Nunc Dimittis. That question cannot be considered apart from a discussion of v. 32.

32. 'A light for revelation to the Gentiles and glory for your people Israel.' The verse as a whole is connected to vv. 30-31 by means of the word 'light' which stands in loose apposition to 'salvation' and explains its nature. Light is particularly associated with the Gentiles in the texts which form the OT background to this verse: Isaiah 49.6 and 51.5 (LXX). Similarly 'glory' stands in apposition to either 'light' or 'revelation', probably the former. Glory is a word associated with Israel in Deutero-Isaiah, interestingly, in close connection with salvation.

> I will bring near my deliverance; it is not far off and my salvation
>   will not tarry;
> I will put my salvation in Zion, for Israel my Glory. (Is. 46.13).[39]

Salvation, then, consists of light for the nations and glory for Israel. The positions of the Gentiles and of Israel are exactly parallel in the construction of the verse. It is hard to believe that their positions are not also parallel with respect to the reception of salvation. It appears, therefore, that v. 32 envisages the Gentiles sharing with Israel in the salvation of God. This is the conclusion of almost all the commentators.

'Salvation' is not only the event but the one who brings salvation, that is, the Messiah. Because of the structure of the poem, he is also, therefore, 'light', as in the Benedictus (1.78), and the 'glory' of Israel.[40]

The expression φῶς εἰς ἀποκάλυψιν is a difficult one. In what sense does revelation pertain to the Gentiles?[41] In the NT when a genitive follows ἀποκάλυψις, it normally identifies that which is revealed or the one from whom revelation comes, not the ones to whom it is granted. Here, however, it is clear that the Gentiles are neither the ones revealed nor the ones who do the revealing.

Sahlin used this difficulty to justify an unusual theory. He suggested that the translator here misunderstood his Hebrew original.[42] There is no Hebrew noun which means revelation. The translator must, therfore, have supposed, wrongly in Sahlin's view, that he was reading an infinitive, probably piel, of the verb גלה. The unpointed text would read אור לגלות גוים. Such a text could also mean, however, 'a light for the dispersion among the Gentiles'.[43] This reconstruction is certainly possible; it is precisely that given by Aytoun who was not in any way searching for mistranslations.[44] The objection to Sahlin's theory is not, therefore, a linguistic one. It is that the OT allusions in the verse are to passages which speak of something that is done to or among the Gentiles, not to the diaspora (Is. 49.6; 42.6; 52.10). In Isaiah 49.6, for example, the Servant is 'a light *to the Gentiles*'. One can be 'enlightened' by considering the two occurrences of the phrase 'light to the Gentiles' in Deutero-Isaiah (Is. 42.6; 49.6). That phrase is, in the LXX, φῶς ἐθνῶν. A genitive appears where one might normally expect a dative. The phenomenon in Luke 2.32 is exactly similar, perhaps under the influence of those OT antecedents. Perhaps the best word on the subject comes from Lagrange, 'l'expression est difficile à analyser, mais l'idée est claire'. The light is for the purpose of revelation to the Gentiles. It will affect them.

By comparison, the second half of the couplet is easy to understand. The saviour will also bring glory to Israel. It was thought that in the last days God would give glory to Israel (Is. 46.13; 60.1, 19). This expectation had now been fulfilled. It is not entirely clear whether glory is parallel to light or to revelation. Either is grammatically possible but the OT background which associated light with the Gentiles and glory with Israel suggests that the former is more likely.

Summary
The Nunc Dimittis picks up anew two themes familiar from the Magnificat and Benedictus, that God has acted decisively to save Israel and that this salvation is rooted in Israel's past. It fulfils God's word. The hymn also introduces the Gentiles, however. They, too, are to have a share in this great salvation. The salvation which Simeon holds in his arms is both a light for the Gentiles and the glory of God's people Israel.

PART THREE

THE SIGNIFICANCE OF THE HYMNS

The three Jewish Christian hymns of Luke 1–2 occupy a special place in Luke–Acts: they stand at the head of the two volumes. It appears that Luke himself may well have inserted them into their present prominent positions[1] and one might well ask why he did so.

There may be several answers to this question. Perhaps Luke, like most Christians through the ages, simply considered them too beautiful and moving to ignore; one can only applaud his taste. Certainly they are useful for expressing the exultant joy of those Jewish proto-Christians in whose mouths they are placed. These psalms thus greatly enrich the infancy narratives themselves. But neither of these considerations adequately explains the position of the hymns. Their praise is so general that they could, theoretically, have been placed in the mouth of any believing Jew in the entire two-volume work and they would doubtless have enriched any narrative into which they might have been inserted. They stand, however, at its very head.

It seems reasonable to suppose that the evangelist placed them at the head of his work because they contain themes which would reappear later in his writings. They are the overture which sets out certain motifs which will recur in the body of the composition.[2] Two such themes or motifs are prominent in the hymns and in Luke–Acts as a whole. These are: 1. promise and fulfilment and 2. the restoration of Israel. In the remaining pages of this work I shall attempt briefly to discuss these two themes.

This is not an attempt to describe Lucan theology as a whole. Nor is it an attempt to subsume all Lucan theology under the two themes of prophecy and fulfilment and the restoration of Israel. Luke–Acts seems to defy all attempts to impose a rigorously consistent theological framework upon it; there are doubtless other themes of importance in the work.

There are also individual words or expressions found in the infancy hymns which recur in Luke–Acts; these have been noted in the course of the exegesis and cannot be considered again at this point.[3] It was mentioned in the course of the exegesis of the Magnificat that a considerable body of literature has arisen on the theme of the 'poor' in Luke–Acts. This word appears in the Magnificat in connection with the idea of the 'reversal' of the orders of society, which, it was suggested, was a not infrequent one in early Christian literature.[4] For two reasons I shall not, however, discuss these themes again at this point. First, these themes appear only in the Magnificat and not in the other two hymns. Secondly, they appear to be a part of the general description of a saving act of God which the Magnificat summarizes as a help for Israel. It is this theme, the decisive help for and restoration of Israel which, as we shall see, recurs in the other hymns of Luke 1–2. The present discussion is only an attempt to show that the two themes mentioned above, promise and fulfilment and the restoration of Israel, are present in the hymns and also are themes which play significant roles in the work as a whole.

1. *Promise and Fulfilment*
The hymns of Luke 1–2 assert that promise and fulfilment are characteristic of salvation history. This is shown by their position in the narrative: each culminates a promise–fulfilment–praise progression.[5] It is also a recurring motif within the hymns, finding explicit expression in each of the three psalms. The present salvation has come about:

> just as he spoke to our fathers
> to Abraham and to his seed, forever. (1.55)

and,

> just as he spoke through the mouth of his holy prophets from of
>   old. (1.70)

In redeeming his people God has

> shown mercy to our fathers
> remembering his holy covenant
> the oath which he swore to Abraham our father. (1.72-73)

The present salvation is 'according to your word' (2.29).

The same theme is also implied by less direct allusions to prophetic words. The Benedictus, for example, declares that the work of the ἀνατολή is to shine on those sitting in darkness and in the shadow of death, an allusion to Isaiah 9.2 and its description of the ideal Davidic prince. The Nunc Dimittis too, is full of allusions to the Servant songs of Deutero-Isaiah. These OT texts are examples of what has been spoken 'through the mouths of the holy prophets from of old'. Not unconnected with this motif is the psalms' characteristic use of the OT to explain the present salvation in terms of God's past dealing with his people. By loose allusions to the relevant portions of the OT it becomes clear that the present fulfilment is like the Exodus (1.50, 51, 71) or the raising up of David (1.69), or the conquest of Canaan (1.75).[6] There is promise inherent in the whole of God's dealing with his people; this promise is now definitively fulfilled. The present salvation has its roots in Israel's history. It has been anticipated either by explicit promise or by saving actions which once anticipated that saving strength now fully shown forth in Jesus Christ. There is, therefore, already an idea of 'salvation-history' in the psalms of Luke 1–2. This is not 'salvation-history' in the sense of Conzelmann's analysis with three distinct epochs. At best there are two epochs, the past which has been characterized by promise, and the present which is the time of fulfilment.[7]

This is hardly a unique NT viewpoint. As is well known, Matthew very frequently gives 'proofs from prophecy', especially in his infancy narratives, and this feature also occurs once in Mark.[8] It is certainly present in the infancy narratives even without the hymns.[9] But it is also a viewpoint which is characteristic of the rest of Luke–Acts.

Scholars have long recognized that there is in Luke–Acts the the theme of promise and fulfilment.[10] In recent years, however, it has been more strongly emphasized, partly as a corrective to Conzelmann's work.[11]

Both Luke and Acts assert at many points that the present salvation is a fulfilment of God's promises. The appearance of John fulfils what is 'written in the book of Isaiah the prophet' (Lk. 3.2ff.). Jesus reads from the scroll of Isaiah and announces, 'Today this scripture has been fulfilled in your hearing' (Lk. 4.21). The risen Christ 'beginning with Moses and all the prophets . . . interpreted to them in all the scriptures the things concerning himself' (Lk. 24.27). The gift of the Spirit is 'what was spoken by the prophet Joel' (Acts 2.16). Perhaps the clearest expression of the motif comes from Paul,

'And we bring you the good news that what God has promised to the fathers this he has fulfilled to us their children by raising Jesus' (Acts 13.32). Moreover, even the obduracy of some Roman Jews confirms what the Holy Spirit said to the fathers 'through Isaiah the prophet'. Examples could easily be multiplied.[12]

The examples just given suffice to show, however, that the theme of promise and fulfilment is invoked at key junctures in Luke–Acts. The motif also appears elsewhere in Luke–Acts but its presence at these turning points is significant; the theme binds together different parts of Luke's work.

It is also significant that this theme appears, for the most part, in material peculiar to Luke. It would be theoretically possible to assign this interest in promise and fulfilment to a source but the spread of the theme throughout the two-volume work suggests that its presence ought to be ascribed to the redactional interest of Luke himself.[13]

The position of the hymns of Luke 1–2 at the head of the two volumes is but another striking example of the author's use of the motif of promise and fulfilment. By placing the hymns of Luke 1–2 in their present position Luke announces to the reader that this theme of promise and fulfilment will be a vital one in the work as a whole.

2. *The Restoration of Israel*
The fulfilment takes place in the coming of Jesus Christ 'of whom the prophets have spoken'. It is of extreme importance to note that the fulfilment is for Israel:

> He has helped Israel his servant (Lk. 1.54).

Moreover, it is the 'God of Israel' who is blessed in the Benedictus (1.68), and the present salvation is the glory of God's people Israel (2.32). Furthermore, it is several times stressed that those for whom God has acted are descendants of Abraham and the patriarchs (1.55, 72-73).[14] These hymns apparently declare that God has acted decisively for Israel. According to Luke 24.21 Cleopas says to the stranger on the Emmaus road, 'We had hoped that he [Jesus] was the one to redeem Israel'. The Benedictus declares that through the same Jesus Christ God has actually done so (1.68).

The hymns of Luke 1–2, then, declare that God has done something decisive for Israel: he has 'visited and redeemed' it. Is it possible that this theme too is developed in the rest of Luke–Acts? The scholarly world has not neglected the question of the role of

Israel in Luke–Acts,[15] but the estimate of that role has varied widely. It is fair to say, however, that attention has been focussed more on Israel in Acts than in Luke's Gospel.[16]

A widely held opinion is that Luke emphasized in Acts the 'rejection' of Israel, in two senses of the word: the people of Israel as a whole has rejected God's Messiah and God has therefore rejected the people.

> It [Acts] traces back to the apostolic age the rejection of the gospel by the Jews. It shows how the People, despite all the efforts of the early Christian preachers and the persuasiveness of their arguments from Scripture, rejected the gospel; it argues that the rejection was long ago foretold in the Book, to which Christians alone—pious men like Stephen, now hold the key.[17]

The hearts of the Jews have been hardened (Acts 28.26-27). Because of this rejection Paul and with him the church are free to turn to the Gentiles; 'they will listen' (Acts 28.28; cf. 13.46; 18.6). The presupposition of the Gentile mission is, therefore, the rejection of the Jews.

> Yet the Christian mission need not have become the purely Gentile mission which in fact it was in Luke's day: it was to the Jews that salvation was first offered again and again. It was not until they refused it by their vilification of Jesus that the emissaries of Christianity turned to the Gentiles.[18]

There is considerable evidence to support this understanding of Acts, particularly in the three apparently programmatic statments, Acts 13.46, 18.6 and 28.28. Nevertheless, the Norwegian scholar, J. Jervell, has vigorously disagreed with this viewpoint.[19] Jervell has offered three theses which spell out an alternative understanding of Israel's relation to the gospel. These are:[20]

> (1) Luke does not describe a Jewish people who, as a whole, reject the early Christian message, and in which the believing Jews are exceptions. The numerous references to mass conversions of Jews, on the one hand, and the narratives about the rejection of the message, as well as the persecutions incited by Jews, on the other hand, show us that the missionary proclamation has divided Israel into two groups: the repentant and the unrepentant.
>
> (2) In Acts, 'Israel' continues to refer to the Jewish people, characterized as a people of repentant (i.e., Christian) and obdurate Jews ... The portion of Jews who believe in the Messiah and are

willing to repent appears as the purified, restored, and true
Israel... For Luke this relationship is the presupposition for the
Gentiles' sharing in the promises...
(3) From the beginning of the mission it is certain that according to
Scripture and in agreement with the missionary command, the
Gentiles have a share in salvation. Sharing in salvation, however
means having a share in the promises of Israel. Thus, the mission
to Gentiles is fulfilment of Scripture in the sense that the promises
must first be fulfilled to Israel before Gentiles can share in
salvation.

As is declared in thesis 1, Jervell's starting point was the observation
of the fact that Luke frequently reports mass conversions of Jews.[21]
There are fewer reports of mass conversions of Gentiles and these, it
is to be noted, are not 'pure' Gentiles, i.e. Gentiles not already
connected with the synagogue.[22]

The reports of Jewish conversions in Jerusalem progress arith-
metically in preparation for James's statement in Acts 21.20 that
there are tens of thousands of believing Jews, but the reports of
conversions outside Jerusalem are not ordered in any particular
way.[23] This emphasizes the success of the Gospel in Jerusalem itself.
Furthermore, it is not only the Jews of Jerusalem, the very heart of
Israel, who most willingly accept the gospel, it is 'those Jews who are
faithful to the law, the real Jews, the most Jewish Jews, that become
believers'.[24]

There is, of course, also opposition to the gospel; reports of
conversions alternate through Acts with accounts of rejection leading
eventually to persecution.[25] Some discussions of Jervell's work
underestimate the importance of this point.[26] Jervell did, in fact,
recognize that there was, according to Acts, considerable opposition
to the gospel. Because this had been so strongly emphasized in other
analyses of Luke–Acts, he did not, however, discuss the rejection
motif as extensively as the acceptance one. Jervell's thesis is not, after
all, that Israel as a whole had accepted the gospel and thus been
restored but that it had, according to Luke, been divided by the
gospel. Such a thesis *demands* recognition of the rejection motif. It
might be, however, that Jervell, in his attempt to persuade the
scholarly world that Luke also represents many Jews as accepting the
gospel, did not give enough weight to the opposite reaction, the
rejection of the gospel.

There is not enough space here thoroughly to discuss Jervell's exegesis of the many relevant texts but a brief mention must be made of his understanding of James's quotation from Amos 9.11 (Acts 15.16-18).[27]

16. After this I will return, and I will rebuild the dwelling of David, which has fallen; I will rebuild its ruins, and I will set it up,
17. that the rest of men may seek the Lord, and all the Gentiles who are called by my name,
18. says the Lord, who has made these things known from of old.

According to Jervell this quotation must mean that in some sense the dwelling of David has been rebuilt; the accession to Christianity of Gentiles such as Cornelius is proof of this. This fulfils the Jewish hope 'that at the end of time the Gentiles will be included in the restored Israel'.[28] The coming in of the Gentiles is a decisive sign of the fulfilment of God's ancient promise to Israel.

Jervell's understanding of the reason for the Gentile mission is therefore the opposite of the usual one.

> One usually understands the situation to imply that only when the Jews have rejected the gospel is the way opened to the Gentiles. It is more correct to say that only when Israel has accepted the gospel can the way to Gentiles be opened. The acceptance of the message took place primarily through the Jewish Christian community in Jerusalem. The unrepentant portion of the people cannot hinder the fulfilment of the promises to Israel. In fact, the opposition is the fulfilment of prophecy.[29]

God has 'visited' his people Israel through Jesus Christ (Lk. 1.68, 78). Through the preaching of those who have accepted Jesus as Messiah God then 'visits' the Gentiles to take from them 'a people for his name' (Acts 15.14). The order is 'the Jew first, then the Greek' (Rom. 1.16; 12.19; cf. Acts 13.46).[30]

Jervell also discussed the situation of the unrepentant portion of Israel. Those Jews who do not accept the gospel are 'purged' from the people in accordance with a pattern already established by Moses;[31] they thus lose their right to the name Israel. According to Jervell the decisive moment for the Jews is past. When the gospel reached Rome the gospel had been representatively proclaimed to the Diaspora and the time of mission to Israel was over.[32]

On the other hand, those Gentiles who accept the gospel are welcomed, not as a new Israel, but as Gentiles. They are accepted

without becoming Jews, that is, without the law. The preaching of
the apostles has 'given to Gentiles a share in the salvation that comes
from the repentant people of God'.[33] The Gentile church is, in
effect, founded on the Jewish-Christian believers.

At this point we may turn back to the hymns of Luke 1–2. If, as I
have argued in the course of this study, they are early Jewish-
Christian psalms, they fit marvellously well with this analysis of
Luke's theology. It seems possible that Luke has inserted them into
their present position at the head of his work in order to anticipate
the motif of the restoration of Israel accomplished by the apostolic
preaching of the gospel.

That the infancy narratives as a whole accord well with Jervell's
analysis of Luke's theology has already been suggested in 1976 by L.
Gaston.[34] Gaston's otherwise excellent study is, however, marred by
an apparent desire to cling to Sahlin's Proto-Luke hypothesis.[35] It
seems far more likely that the restoration motif represents a redactional interest of Luke rather than a characteristic of a Jewish-
Christian source. Sahlin never took his projected study of the
theology of Proto-Luke beyond the third chapter of Luke so it is
difficult to know what detailed arguments he would have adduced to
prove the existence of a unified Semitic source extending as far as
Acts 15. However, his argumentation with respect to the infancy
narratives often seems rather eccentric. One is hardly tempted,
therefore, to depend on Sahlin's conclusions regarding the rest of the
Gospel and Acts 1–15. It seems likely that any Semitic sources
behind Acts 1–15 are short accounts interspersed among original
Greek pericopes.[36] But even so one still has to account for a
redactional interest on Luke's part. He was the one who collected
and arranged these stories within the framework of Acts as a whole.
Moreover, Jervell's analysis depends on the analysis of materials
drawn from Acts as a whole, even from parts of Acts beyond the
utmost possible bounds of Proto-Luke. It is to the composer of the
two-volume work in its entirety that we ought to attribute an interest
in the restoration of Israel.

It is to this writer, to Luke himself, that we ought also to attribute
the inclusion of the hymns of Luke 1–2. Luke has placed these
psalms in the mouths of 'those Jews who are faithful to the law, the
real Jews, the most Jewish Jews', the very sort of Jews who, according
to Jervell, became believers.[37] They announce in the most vigorous
tones that God has done something definitive for Israel: 'He has

visited and redeemed his people' (Luke 1.68). I suggest that it is more reasonable to suppose that these psalms stand at the head of a book which sees an Israel repentant and restored, at least partially, rather than an Israel rejecting the gospel and therefore rejected by its God.

There is even a hint in the Nunc Dimittis of the mission to the Gentiles. While the Magnificat and Benedictus describe only a deliverance for Israel the Nunc Dimittis also speaks of 'a light to the Gentiles'.[38] As appears to be the case in Acts, God's mercy culminates in light reaching the Gentiles. But the Gentiles do not replace Israel in the Nunc Dimittis; they receive mercy alongside Israel. There seems, on the other hand, to be no hint in the infancy hymns of the rejection of the gospel by some Jews. While Luke 2.34-35 seems clearly to speak of a division within Israel, the hymns themselves look only on the more joyful side of salvation history.[39] They anticipate only 'the tens of thousands faithful to the law' of Jerusalem (Acts 21.20).

One thing remains to be said. In light of the belief expressed not only by most modern critics but also by Paul, Romans 9–11, that the mission to the Jews had been largely a failure, Luke's emphasis on the redemption of part of Israel may seem puzzling. This puzzlement may, however, be reduced if one considers the origin of the infancy hymns. These hymns, I have argued, originated in an early Palestinian Jewish-Christian community. These Jewish-Christians apparently believed that through Jesus Christ God had 'helped Israel' and had 'visited and redeemed his people'. They were the ones who in their hymns spoke as if they were, in effect, all Israel. Is it surprising then that Luke considered the Jewish-Christians of Palestine to be the human foundation of the Church? No, all Israel had not rejected the gospel and God had certainly not rejected Israel. These Jewish-Christians among whom the hymns had originated were living evidence to the contrary. The Jewish-Christian church was, in a sense, the foundation of the wider church according to Luke's theological structure. But the Jewish-Christians, among whom should be numbered those who had composed and used these hymns, were in another sense also the foundation of Luke's theological structure. Because they existed Luke could declare that God had not rejected all Israel but rather had redeemed a part of it.

We have come then to the end of our journey through the pre-Biblical history of the hymns of Luke 1–2. By taking these hymns which had originated in a Jewish-Christian community and placing them at the head of his gospel, Luke preserved them and offered them to the world. He thus gave them a place of honour not only in Luke–Acts but in the life of the Church. The Church into whose worship they quickly passed over is now almost entirely a Gentile one. But in using these hymns the Church takes up and declares anew its Jewish heritage. Just as Luke suggested, we in the Gentile Church are built on the foundation of pious Israelites who received the gospel with joy. We are built upon not only 'the foundation of the apostles and prophets' whose activities are recounted in Acts but also the humble sons and daughters of Abraham, whose worship still echoes in the hymns of Luke 1–2. In a sense these hymns, like the one whose coming they honour, are, therefore,

> a light for revelation to the Gentiles,
> and glory for your people Israel.

NOTES

Introduction

1. Hereafter, Brown, *Birth*.
2. Gunkel, *Introduction*, 10.
3. A rather similar definition of the hymn comes from an acknowledged expert on hymns, St Ambrose: 'A hymn is a song containing praise of God. If you praise God but without song you do not have a hymn. If you praise anything that does not pertain to the Glory of God, even if you sing it, you do not have a hymn. Hence a hymn contains the three elements: *song* and *praise* of God' (*De cantu et musica sacra*, I, 14. This is the translation that appears in E. Werner, *Sacred Bridge*, 207). Ambrose adds here the very useful distinction that a hymn's praise is directed towards God.
4. Gunkel, 'Lieder', 46ff., and *Einleitung*, 80.
5. Westermann, *Praise of God*, 115.
6. Westermann, *Praise of God*, 23, 31.
7. Westermann, *Praise of God*, 122ff.
8. Westermann, *Praise of God*, 23.
9. See, for example, Aytoun, 'Hymns', 274-88.
10. See Deichgräber, *Gotteshymnus*, 39.

The Origin of the Hymns

1. See, for example, Geldenhuys, *Luke*, 84-5 and Machen, *Virgin Birth*, 75-101, esp. 95, 97.
2. Marshall, *Luke*, 46. Marshall also stated, however, 'The lack of Christian colouring suggests that the present hymn fits no situation better than that of Mary herself, although this does not necessarily mean that Mary herself composed the hymn at the precise occasion in the text' (*Luke*, 79). The exact implications of this statement are unclear. Does Marshall mean that Mary herself composed the hymn on some other occasion? On the other hand, did someone else compose it for the purpose of enriching this particular narrative?

3. J. Wragg argued that the hymns were ancient Jewish psalms (*Infancy Narratives*, 270ff.). They could thus be quoted by Mary and Zechariah on the occasions described in the narrative. The Magnificat had been a psalm connected with an oral cycle of poetry about Ruth (*Infancy Narrative*, 284-87), which was remembered as Mary's favourite (p. 279). The Benedictus culminated in a prophecy like Is. 9 and Mal. 4. The similarity between this prophecy and his own situation caused it to come to Zechariah's mind after the birth of his son (*Infancy Narratives*, 298). A person whose doctrine of scripture demands that the hymns of Luke 1–2 represent the very words of the characters to whom they were attributed would do better to ignore this theory in favour of the traditional explanation of their origin, that they were composed by the people in question. This position was most ably defended by the rugged American conservative, J.G. Machen, in *Virgin Birth*, 75-101. Somewhat more likely is Schürmann's contention that the basis of the Magnificat, 1.46-50 which goes back to Mary, has been fleshed out by the addition of the more general praise found in the remainder of the hymn (*Lukas*, 78ff.). This only falls foul of the evident links between the first and second parts of the hymn. See the exegesis of the Magnificat in Part Two below.

4. Harnack, 'Magnificat', 538-66.

5. Erdmann, *Vorgeschichte*, 31ff., agreed with Harnack with respect to the Benedictus but not the Magnificat. Morgenthaler, *Zeugnis II*, 76-77, supposed that Luke composed the hymns after a careful study of Jewish eschatological hymns, a curiously academic hypothesis. Schmithals, in the most recent commentary on Luke, has argued that Luke composed both the Magnificat and Benedictus (*Lukas*, 31, 34).

6. Gunkel, 'Lieder', 43-65.

7. Creed, *Luke*, 306-307; Sparks, 'Semitisms', 133, 135f.; Goulder and Sanderson, 'Genesis', 12-30; Tinsley, *Luke*, 34; Drury, *Tradition*, 49-51; Turner, 'Relation', 100-109. Turner is sometimes listed among those who believe that the hymns were composed by Luke as, for example, by Brown in *Birth*, 348. Turner does not specifically give an opinion as to the origin of the hymns and does not completely deny the possibility of Semitic sources in these chapters (pp. 100, 108). On the other hand he does mention that the hymns are particularly Septuagintal and that 'Here are traces of a mind which revelled in the cadences of the Greek Old Testament' (p. 101), by implication, Luke.

8. Creed, *Luke*, 306 (cf. p. 22), for a specific reference to Harnack's article.

9. Cadbury, *Luke–Acts*, 192-93. Tannehill, 'Magnificat', 263-75. See also Hendrickx, *Infancy*, 78.

10. Cadbury, *Luke–Acts*, 6.

11. This position is apparently held by Brown, *Birth*, 349-50.

12. See below, pp. 50-66.

13. Gunkel, 'Lieder', 52. One might well hesitate over Gunkel's assumption that Luke was a Gentile and therefore completely unfamiliar with Jewish forms.

14. See below, pp. 67-85.

15. Brown, *Birth*, 350, n. 34.

16. Drury, *Tradition*, 50.

17. Drury, *Tradition*, 50. See also the very similar statement by Turner quoted in n. 7 above.

18. In fact, this argument by itself may not even prove capacity. Most English clergymen of the 17th century were familiar with the source of John Bunyan's vocabulary and allusions. Yet how many among them, even among those of a literary bent, had the capacity to write *The Pilgrim's Progress?* The hymns of Luke 1-2 may not be the literary masterwork that Bunyan's tale is but the analogy surely indicates that vocabulary drawn from a source which is common property can be, in itself, no evidence of authorship by any particular individual. Composition of hymns like those of Luke 1-2 requires a particular literary skill which is not demonstrated elsewhere in Luke–Acts.

19. It is worth noting here that Luke certainly did not compose the first half of Lk. 19.37; these words are drawn from the common tradition (cf. Mt. 21.19; Mk 11.10). The second half of Lk. 19.37, the Gloria in excelsis, and several passages in Revelation were identified as 'Siegesrufe' by Deichgräber, *Gotteshymnus*, 39. There is no reason to suppose that Luke composed either Siegesruf.

20. See, for example, Brown, *Birth*, 347f., and below, pp. 20-21 and 26 of the present work.

21. Bultmann, *Synoptic Tradition*, 363. Cf. Minear, 'Luke's Use', 116.

22. Drury, *Tradition*, 50.

23. Cadbury, *Luke–Acts*, 192.

24. Winter, 'Magnificat', 328-47.

25. Brown, *Birth*, 348.

26. The history of the scholarly controversy over the proper attribution of the Magnificat has been outlined by S. Benko in 'Magnificat', 263-75. See the brief discussion of this textual problem on pp. 108-13 of this book.

27. Harnack, 'Magnificat', 538-66.

28. Harnack, 'Magnificat', p. 540. The assumption behind this method, that Luke's LXX was substantially the same as ours, is a dubious one. See Kahle, *The Cairo Geniza*, 209-64, or Jellicoe, *Septuagint*, 78ff. Nevertheless, Harnack's method does remove from consideration those words and expressions which are obviously biblical and therefore cannot be used as evidence for or against Lucan authorship. But see also Jeremias's careful study, *Sprache*. In this book Jeremias examines all the hymns for traces of

Luke's hand. See especially pp. 60-63, 73-76, 95-96. Jeremias considered these hymns to be traditional with the exception of a few minor Lucan insertions.

29. Hawkins, *Horae Synopticae*, 198.

30. Spitta, 'Magnificat', 61-94.

31. Machen, 'Hymns', 1-38.

32. This flaw may stem from the presupposition that Hannah's song of 1 Sam. 2 is the model for the Magnificat. It is significant that Harnack's argument occurs in an article, the main purpose of which was to prove that the hymn ought to be attributed not to Mary but to Elizabeth whose situation is superficially more similar to Hannah's. He was, therefore, ready and willing to see the parallels between this hymn and Hannah's, but in so doing overlooked other OT passages which may also have been sources for the Magnificat. It would be foolish to deny the fact that there are resemblances between the two hymns. The similarities are there, similarities in thought, vocabulary and setting. The similarity in setting may, perhaps, have led Harnack to overestimate the similarity in vocabulary.

Harnack traced the vocabulary of vv. 46, 47 and 53 back to Hannah's hymn. These verses can be more easily derived from other passages in the LXX. See the charts of parallels in Creed, *Luke*, 303ff.

33. Machen, 'Hymns', 5.

34. Hawkins, *Horae Synopticae*, 15.

35. Machen, 'Hymns', 15.

36. Brown, ·*Birth*, 336.

37. This should really be counted as only one occurrence since the second incidence of the expression is merely a repetition of the action of the previous verse.

38. Machen, 'First Two Chapters', 219.

39. Very useful charts which lay out in parallel columns the hymns and their Old Testament sources can be found in Creed, *St. Luke*, 303ff., and in Brown, *Birth*, 358-60 (Magnificat), 386-89 (Benedictus), and 458 (Nunc Dimittis). Creed's charts present the Greek texts, Brown's the English.

40. The reminiscences of the account of Samuel's birth are not confined to the Magnificat; they also partially shape the story of Jesus' presentation in the Temple. See Brown, *Birth*, 451, and Burrows, *Infancy*, 1-41. Burrows contended that the entire infancy story is shot through with reminiscences of the account of Samuel's birth. Many of Burrow's arguments may be dismissed but enough remain to convince the reader of the strong influence of the OT birth story on its NT counterpart.

41. That v. 48 is an insertion into the original hymn is held by, among others, Gunkel, 'Die Lieder', 57-58; Brown, *Birth*, 8 n. 28; Grundmann, *Lukas*, 63.

42. Harnack, *Physician*, 217.

43. Sahlin, *Messias*, 158ff. Observations such as these led Sahlin to place the Benedictus in the mouth of the prophetess Anna at Lk. 2.38 and the Magnificat after Lk. 1.64, the first introduction. While Sahlin's reconstruction is unconvincing (the feminine self-references in the Magnificat sound very odd in Zechariah's mouth) his game of hymnic musical chairs bears testimony to the looseness with which the hymns occupy their present positions.

44. This position was held by Gunkel, 'Die Lieder', 46, 58ff. A survey of scholars who hold this and other positions on the question can be found in Marshall, *Luke*, 87.

45. Benoit, 'L'Enfance', 169ff., and Brown, *Birth*, 381.

46. Machen, 'Hymns', 16.

47. Brown, *Birth*, 386-89.

48. See the discussion of the tense of ἐπεσκέψατο in the exegesis of the Benedictus (Part Two, below).

49. Harnack, *Physician*, 206-209.

50. See below, p. 50 for a longer discussion of this point.

51. Harnack, *Physician*, 217.

52. Machen, 'Hymns', 20.

53. See Yadin, *War Scroll*, 324-29.

54. The hymns would still be similar in structure if v. 48a remained. One would then simply have two motive clauses rather than one. Verse 48b, the word about future blessings, does, however, break the pattern outlined here. That this half verse alone should be excised was the opinion of Mowinckel, *Psalms II*, 123 n. 51. But for the reasons advanced above it seems best to consider the whole verse a Lucan insertion (cf. Brown, *Birth*, 357).

55. George, *Luc*, 61-62.

56. See the chart in Brown, *Birth*, 468.

57. George, *Luc*, 62.

58. Jeremias, *Sprache*, 95.

59. George, *Luc*, 62.

60. See below, pp. 84, 145.

The Original Language of the Hymns

1. Knox, *Sources*, II, 40.

2. That not all the hymns were composed in the same language is suggested by Machen, *Virgin Birth*, 98, and by George, *Luc*, 62.

3. The most common version of this opinion is that the narratives and hymns of ch. 1 come from baptist circles while ch. 2 is a Christian composition. See below, pp. 88-94.

4. The best presentation of the evidence is in Paul Minear's important essay, 'Luke's Use', 111-31.

5. Laurentin, 'Traces I', 449-54. Laurentin presented an excellent summary of scholarly opinion with respect to the four options. A more recent survey, although only of those who hold Aramaic or Hebrew source theories, can be found in McHugh, *Mother*, Note I, 'An Aramaic or Hebrew Source for the Lucan Infancy Gospel', 435-37.

6. Laurentin, 'Traces I', 451.

7. Laurentin, 'Traces I', 451-52.

8. Laurentin, 'Traces I', 452.

9. See the discussion of the languages of Palestine in the first century AD in Fitzmyer, 'The Languages of Palestine', in *Aramaean*, esp. pp. 32-38.

10. Plummer, *Luke*, xxvi (cf. also pp. 7, 46).

11. See Dalman, *Words*, 39; Lagrange, *Luc*, lxxxvii. Sparks put it most baldly, 'There are no traces of Aramaic whatsoever: the idiom is Biblical Hebrew' ('Semitisms', 135).

12. Dalman, *Words*.

13. Dalman, *Words*, 39-40.

14. Dalman, *Words*, 42.

15. Dalman, *Words*, 42.

16. Fitzmyer, *Aramaean*, 46.

17. Dalman, *Words*, 38.

18. Dalman, *Words*, 14-15.

19. Dalman, *Words*, 224. Much the same argument appears in Sparks, 'Semitisms', 133.

20. Gunkel, 'Lieder', 46, 58ff., and Winter, 'Magnificat', 347.

21. Winter, 'Two Notes', 158ff.

22. Box, 'Gospel Narratives', 96-97, and *Virgin Birth*, 46-48. Winter's argument is somewhat contradictory at this point. The ἀνατολή is either God or the Messiah, but not both.

23. Box, *Virgin Birth*, 47, claims that both the Syriac verb and noun cognates are 'constantly used of light and splendour'. Cf. Gnilka, 'Hymnus', 229.

24. Box, *Virgin Birth*, 47.

25. Box, *Virgin Birth*, 47. Box only specifically mentioned Cant. R. to 3.6.

26. Dalman, *Words*, 4.

27. On the background to the use of ἀνατολή here see Gnilka, 'Hymnus', 227-32. It may be noted that T. Jud. 24.4, possibly a gloss, calls the Messianic figure 'Branch of the Most High', βλαστὸς τοῦ ὑψίστου. This occurs only a few lines after the reference to Num. 24.17.

28. See above, pp. 21-25, for a discussion of Harnack's method.

29. Harnack, *Physician*, esp. Appendix II, pp. 199-218.

30. Only Gaechter among modern commentators would seek to minimize Luke's contribution to the final form of these chapters (*Maria*, 14-17).

31. Moulton, *Grammar*, I, 13-19; II, 481-83.

32. Moulton, *Grammar*, I, 18.

33. Moulton, *Grammar*, II, 482.

34. Moulton, *Grammar*, II, 483.

35. Creed, *Luke*; Sparks, 'Semitisms'; Turner, 'Relation'; Goulder and Sanderson, 'Genesis'. Of these discussions Turner's is the most specific and detailed. As it was written as a response to an article by Paul Winter it will be discussed below (pp. 40-42) in connection with that article. Sparks's article was mainly concerned to cast doubt on the Proto-Luke hypothesis, so only a small part of his discussion is directly relevant to the infancy narratives. The only significant argument offered is essentially the same as that of Dalman concerning the word ἀνατολή ('Semitisms', 133). Creed's discussion (*Luke*, 306-307) is brief and seems to depend on Harnack. Goulder and Sanderson delineated the parallels between Luke 1-2 and the OT, especially Genesis. That there are no sources behind Luke's narrative is more assumed than proved in their article.

36. Cadbury, *Luke–Acts*, 192-93.

37. *The Evangelist's Calendar* is obviously a more advanced descendant of the article of which Goulder had been co-author 20 years earlier, 'Genesis'.

38. Goulder, *Calendar*, esp. p. 102.

39. I should judge that a thorough examination of the OT parallels to Luke 1-2 would show that they had been drawn from many parts of the OT in an eclectic manner and that the lectionary texts of Goulder's theory are not of any special importance among them.

40. Oliver, 'Purpose', and Tatum, 'Epoch', attempted to fit the infancy stories into Conzelmann's three-fold division of redemptive history by describing these chapters as the Epoch of Israel. This attempt must be judged to be a failure for it ignores the many signs in Luke 1-2 that the time of fulfillment has already dawned. The hymns in particular emphasize this theme strongly.

41. See McHugh, *Mother*, Note 1, 437, for a list of scholars who have held this position.

42. Burney, *Aramaic Origin*, 101.

43. Wellhausen, *Einleitung*, 27-28; Torrey, *Four Gospels* and *Translated Gospels*; Manson, *Teaching*, 27; Burney, *Aramaic Origin*, 101ff.

44. Torrey is not, of course, the only scholar who has attempted to find such mistranslation. He is, however, the most thorough, with one exception, in finding possible mistranslations. The exception is Sahlin in *Messias*. However, Sahlin's attempts to reconstruct the underlying Hebrew text of the birth stories seem to be intended not to prove the existence of that text but rather to show the theological tendencies Sahlin supposed it to have possessed.

45. Torrey, *Translated Gospels*, 84, 87.

46. Torrey, *Translated Gospels*, 26, 28f.

47. Franklin, *Christ the Lord*.
48. Torrey, *Translated Gospels*, 28.
49. Torrey, *Translated Gospels*, 73.
50. Torrey, *Translated Gospels*, 84ff.
51. Torrey, 'Medina'.
52. Black, *Aramaic Approach*, 12, added a variation to Torrey's theme by suggesting that in first century usage מדינה specifically referred to *the province*, that is, Palestine. However, as Marshall rightly remarked (*Luke*, 80), Mary was already in Palestine and had, therefore, no need to hasten there.
53. The argument was accepted not only by such scholars as Laurentin, Winter, and Sahlin, but temporarily by F.C. Burkitt (see the quotation of a personal letter to Torrey in *Translated Gospels*, 86) and more recently by Jeremias, *Sprache*, 56.
54. Torrey, *Translated Gospels*, 85.
55. Brown, *Birth*, 332; Marshall, *Luke*, 80.
56. This passage is listed in this way in Moulton and Geden's *Concordance*. Perhaps our supposed careless scribe so understood the word.
57. In both these cases the underlying Hebrew word for city is עיר and Ἰούδα is left undeclined.
58. The argument concerning Lk. 1.39 is the only one I should consider incorrect. The rest are inconclusive rather than incorrect.
59. Burrows, *Infancy*, 1-41, suggested that the story of Jesus' birth depends on the MT version of Samuel's birth. Brown, *Birth*, took special note in his charts of OT parallels of those expressions which, in his judgment, depended on the LXX rather than on the MT. Resch, *Kindheitsevangelium*, listed all likely and many unlikely parallels to the text both in the LXX and in the MT but apparently did not compare them for the purpose of determining the original language of the text.
60. Winter, 'Observations'; Turner, 'Relation'; and Winter, 'On Luke'.
61. Winter, 'Observations', 113f.
62. Winter, 'Observations', 114.
63. Turner, 'Relation', 101.
64. Winter, 'On Luke', 222.
65. Winter, 'On Luke', 222.
66. Turner, 'The Relation', 102.
67. Winter, 'On Luke', 223.
68. Winter, 'On Luke', 223.
69. Winter, 'Observations', 116.
70. Turner, 'Relation', 102. The LXX passages are: Wis. Sol. 11.21; Dt. 8.17; Jdt. 13.13; Ps. 89(90).11; Ps. Sol. 17.2.
71. Both Winter and Turner brought forward other evidence to support their positions. Winter suggested that the use of κύριος for God rather than

Jesus in these chapters proves dependence on a source and dealt with Lk. 1.17, and 2.13, 34 as he did with the texts mentioned in the body of this chapter. Turner challenged Winter with respect to Lk. 1.17 and concluded his article by listing the occurrences in the rest of Luke–Acts of certain 'Hebraistic' idioms of Luke 1–2. This latter procedure reinforces the argument that Luke had a definite influence on the final shape of his infancy narratives but does not rule out the possibility that he made use of a Hebrew source or sources in their composition.

72. Turner, 'Relation', 101.

73. Winter, 'On Luke', 222.

74. That the Greek Bible of the first century need not have been precisely the same as ours is clear. On the development of the text of the Greek Bible see the discussion in Kahle, *Cairo Geniza*, 209-64, and Jellicoe, *Septuagint*, 67-156. Similarly, the exact shape of the text of the Hebrew OT cannot be established with certainty. See Cross, *Ancient Library*, 120-45. An example of the false conclusions ignoring this difficulty can lead to may be found in Brown, *Birth*. In his chart of the OT background of the Nunc Dimittis Brown implied that the Greek version of Is. 40.5 must have provided the vocabulary for Lk. 2.30 because, unlike the MT, one presumes, it contains the word 'salvation'. That word is also present in the Isaiah text from Qumran, however. See also note 76 below.

75. Winter, 'On Luke', 224. In fact, Lk. 1.37 is more nearly a quotation than most of the passages discussed here.

76. Brown did not specifically state his opinion on the question of the original language of the hymns but implied that it was probably Greek. In his charts of OT parallels to the hymns he used an asterisk to denote those parallels which, in his opinion, most closely resemble Luke in the LXX rather than the MT (*Birth*, 358-60, 386-89, 458; see also note 74 above). Brown did not, however, mark those cases in which the parallel is more exact in Hebrew or only exists in that language, e.g. the Hymn of the Return in 1 QM XIV 4-5 or the 15th Benediction of the Babylonian version of the Shemoneh Esreh. The connection between Luke's text and some of these parallels is rather tenuous and in most cases several OT passages can be claimed as parallels to each line in the hymns. The slight differences between the Greek and Hebrew versions of the OT in those parallels is insignificant because, once again, Luke's words are not quotations.

77. Laurentin, 'Traces I' and 'Traces II'. In the latter article, pp. 12-13, n. 1, Laurentin listed the names of those scholars who had previously found etymological allusions and the verses in which they had found them. The first name on Laurentin's list is that of J.J. Wettstein, from 1751. It should be noted, however, that not all of these investigators concluded that the presence of these allusions proved the existence of a Hebrew original. For example, Burkitt, 'Magnificat', 220-27, shared Harnack's views on the origin

of Lk. 1–2 but used the etymological allusions in the Magnificat to argue that the hymn ought to be attributed to Elizabeth.

78. Laurentin, 'Traces II', 13.

79. Laurentin was quite willing to cite LXX usage as evidence when it appeared to bolster his case. See, for example, 'Traces I', 441f., n. 2. The concordance from which the figures given in this chapter were drawn is Hatch and Redpath's *Concordance*.

80. In Ps. 35.27, 40.16, and 70.4, μεγαλύνω is used in parallel with ἀγαλλιάω as in the Magnificat and translates גדל in all three cases.

81. Laurentin, 'Traces II', 9.

82. Laurentin, 'Traces I', 443.

83. There is some uncertainty about the etymological derivation of the name but Laurentin found the allusions in the supposed use of the verb רום. See 'Traces II', 17-18.

84. There may well be a connection between Ps. 89, a Messianic Psalm, and the hymns of Lk. 1–2, which appear to celebrate the coming of the Davidic Messiah. However, the example of Ps. 89 does show that the coincidence of these Hebrew roots is not necessarily due to the desire to create etymological allusions.

There are a number of other locations in the Bible at which several of the concepts discussed above coincide. To mention but a few, the Mary/Jesus combination, ישע/רום, occurs in Pss. 12, 18, and 57 in addition to Ps. 89.

85. The mention of the prayer may, however, be due to the influence of the account of the angelic appearance of Dan. 10.12, or possibly the wording of Sir 51.11.

86. Torrey is, of course, an exception. The argument of *Translated Gospels* is that all four gospels were translated from Semitic originals. Box, 'Gospel Narratives', 82, suggested that this verse alone derives from a Semitic source.

87. The significance of the name Peter was certainly well known (Mt. 16.18 and parallels).

88. Some have found Laurentin's reasoning persuasive. See, for example, Wink, *John the Baptist*, 64ff., and, in substance, Flood, 'Magnificat', 209. Flood, however, also agreed with Winter's suggestion that the hymns of Lk. 1 were originally songs of victory from the Maccabaean wars. One would have thought the combination difficult if not impossible.

89. Tannehill, 'Magnificat', 264, 273.

90. Black's position with respect to the original language of the hymns is not entirely clear. In his treatment of them he seems to proceed on the assumption that they were composed in Aramaic (*Aramaic Approach*, 151-55). Then, in an 'Additional Note on the Original Language of the Lucan hymns' (p. 156), he wrote, 'A decision as between Hebrew and Aramaic is difficult to make, though the tendency now appears to be to assume the former'.

91. Zorell, 'Magnificat'; Aytoun, 'Ten Hymns'; Box, *Virgin Birth*, 68. See also Gunkel, 'Lieder', 48ff.; Sahlin, *Messias*, 175, 266, 299; Mowinckel, *Psalms*, II, 124, n. 1.

92. Aytoun, 'Ten Hymns', 277.

93. Zorell's confidence ('Magnificat', 754), that he could reproduce the exact text of Luke's source by the use of OT parallels was misplaced. The parallels are only allusions and are therefore too imprecise to enable one to do what Zorell proposed.

94. Aytoun suggested the removal from the Magnificat of either Lk. 1.51 or 52, or 55b ('Ten Hymns', 282-83), and from the Benedictus, 1.69b, 70 and 73 (p. 283). He must also add from time to time a few Hebrew words not represented by our text, in Lk. 1.46, 76, for example.

95. Zorell managed to fit everything in the Magnificat into his scheme ('Magnificat', 754f.). Mowinckel excised Lk. 1.48a (*Psalms*, II, 123 n. 1).

96. Aytoun, 'Ten Hymns', 283.

97. Aytoun, 'Ten Hymns', 285.

98. One could also compare Sahlin's treatment of the Magnificat as a series of 10 qinah (3 plus 2) verses and the criticism of that arragement in Mowinckel, *Psalms*, II, 124, n. 54. Mowinckel excised v. 48a and found 8 '4 plus 3' bicola in the Magnificat.

99. The uncertainty of the appeal to metre is illustrated by the nature of the Qumran Hodayoth which are, of course, Hebrew psalms. 'There is no regular metre in 1QH' (Mansoor, *Thanksgiving Hymns*, 24). See also Kraft ('Poetic Structure', 17): 'One cannot escape the judgment that such regularity of metre as seems fairly sure in the canonical psalms does not exist here. The variety of metrical structure in these poems seems to amount almost to metrical chaos.'

100. The common factor in the methods of all the scholars listed above is the counting of stressed syllables in key words. This method is not necessarily the only one, however. In America a method which counts all syllables, not just the stressed ones, has become popular. See, for example, Stuart, *Early Hebrew Metre*, esp. pp. 1-50, and the foreword by Freedman, in the reissue of Gray, *Hebrew Poetry*, vii-xlvi.

101. Gottwald, 'Poetry, Hebrew', *IDB*, III, 834f.

102. It is partly because the speeches of Luke 1–2 do not possess 'parallelism of thought and word-mass' to nearly the same degree as the hymns that they should not be considered 'hymns' as well.

103. Gunkel, 'Lieder', 52.

104. Mowinckel, *Psalms*, II, 122-25.

105. Brown, *Birth*, 246.

Raymond Martin's Method

1. R.A. Martin, 'Syntactical Criteria' and 'Aramaic Sources'. In the latter article Martin applied the first nine criteria of his system, that is, the ones he had developed at that point, to Luke 1–2. He concluded that Luke 1–2 are translation Greek.

2. R.A. Martin, *Syntactical Evidence of Semitic Sources in Greek Documents*, hereafter *Syntactical Evidence*. I am grateful to the SBL and to Dr Martin for permission to quote from the book. I must also thank Dr Martin for correcting several errors in a rough draft of this chapter (any remaining errors are mine, not his) and for informing me of three articles in which he has published the results of the application of his method to other texts. These are: R.A. Martin, 'Syntactical Evidence of a Semitic Vorlage of the Testament of Joseph', 'Syntax Criticism of the Testament of Abraham', and 'Syntax Criticism of the LXX Additions to the Book of Esther'.

3. R.A. Martin, *Syntactical Evidence*, v.

4. See pages 5-38 of *Syntactical Evidence*.

5. Martin is aware of this problem. See *Syntactical Evidence*, 6.

6. Martin studied the following texts composed in Greek: 2–3–4 Maccabees, papyri (not specified), Polybius, Herodotus, Thucydides, Xenophon, Diodorus, Dionysius and Josephus.

7. It appears that the idea of using this phenomenon as a criterion came from N. Turner's article 'Relation'. See *Syntactical Evidence*, 16.

8. Martin has erred here in expressing percentage as a decimal figure. For example, with respect to Genesis the number should be either 3% or .03 separated articles for every unseparated one. It is not .03%!

9. Martin excludes the following adjectives from his count: numerals, πᾶς, πολύς, ἕτερος, ποιός, αὐτός.

10. Martin excluded from his data the use of the dative with forms of λέγω, εἶπον, and δίδωμι.

11. See Table 3 in the appendix to this chapter for a more detailed presentation of the results. The table reproduces the results outlined on p. 39 of Martin, *Syntactical Evidence*.

12. Martin, *Syntactical Evidence*, 45.

13. See Table 4 for the figures in question. A more detailed presentation of these results may be found in the tables in *Syntactical Evidence*, 49, 51, 53.

14. Martin, *Syntactical Evidence*, 45.

15. Martin, *Syntactical Evidence*, 52.

16. Martin, *Syntactical Evidence*, 50.

17. Martin, *Syntactical Evidence*, 52.

18. Martin, *Syntactical Evidence*, 87.

19. Martin, *Syntactical Evidence*, 97.

20. It is generally conceded (and here the adverb is, I think, appropriate) that the same author composed both Luke and Acts.

21. This phrase was used by L. Gaston in 'Tradition', 212.

22. See Table 5 in the appendix to this chapter for a more detailed presentation of the results.

23. C. Chatfield, *Statistics for Technology*, 138. I wish to thank Mr G. Walsham of Fitzwilliam College, Cambridge, for assisting me with this question. It need hardly be said, however, that any statistical errors are mine rather than his.

24. The result for chapter 1 (excluding 1.1-4) was -12, for chapter 2, -5. I tentatively suggest that Luke slightly expanded his source in the account of Jesus' birth and presentation, thus introducing more original Greek characteristics.

25. The review may be found in *CBQ* 37, 1975, 592-3.

26. I shall assume the correctness of the two-source theory in this chapter.

27. See, for example, C.C. Torrey, *Translated Gospels*, and other works, and more recently, J.C. O'Neill, 'The Synoptic Problem', 273-85.

28. The sample was extended beyond the end of the first chapter in order to obtain a text of more than 50 lines in length.

29. R.H. Charles, *Revelation*, cxliii. This conclusion seems to have found wide agreement among commentators although Torrey in *Apocalypse* argues for translation from Aramaic. But see John Sweet, *Revelation*, 16, where Charles's position is essentially reaffirmed.

30. See Table 3 in the Appendix to this chapter.

31. The New Testament is obviously full of this sort of Greek and one might well expect it to be the middle term between translation and original Greek. It is not entirely surprising, therefore, that the results for the passages studied here fall into the gap between the two types of Greek. Moreover, those texts which were certainly composed in Greek, albeit by a 'Hebrew of the Hebrews', do show predominance of original Greek frequencies. The texts from the Gospels, which may rest on an Aramaic substratum, show fewer such frequencies. In Revelation, the Greek written by an author thinking in Hebrew, the translation Greek frequencies predominate, although not so strongly as in most of the translated Greek studied by Martin.

The Form of the Hymns

1. The many parallels in vocabulary to the OT can be explained, as we have seen, by the theory of conscious imitation of the LXX. Furthermore, any such parallels found in extra-canonical literature could be explained as the result of common dependence on the OT. Similarly, the form of Luke's hymns may also be the result of imitation of OT patterns. I intend to suggest that a study of the hymns contained in the apocrypha and pseudepigrapha can show us the form of Jewish psalms of the period; some or many of these may have been composed for their present literary contexts. Luke may, it

could be argued, have done the same. These formal parallels cannot, therefore, be considered completely to preclude Lucan authorship.

2. Gunkel, 'Lieder', 53. Gunkel concerned himself in this article only with the Magnificat and Benedictus.

3. Brown, *Birth*, 350.

4. Westermann, *Praise of God*, 115.

5. Mowinckel, *Psalms*, II, 122-23. The epiphany psalms were, according to Mowinckel, a sub-group of the hymns of praise particularly associated with the feast of Tabernacles (*Psalms*, I, 94).

6. Westermann, *Praise of God*, 23.

7. Westermann, *Praise of God*, 22.

8. See below, pp. 114-16.

9. Gunkel, *Einleitung*, 344.

10. The psalms which Gunkel considered to be eschatological could be interpreted in light of various hypothetical festivals, most notably Mowinckel's enthronement festival. That scholar denied that there were any true eschatological hymns in the Psalter (*Psalms*, I, 111; see also Additional Note VIII, vol. II, pp. 225-26).

11. The following is a list of possible eschatological hymns mentioned in the lists of either Gunkel or Westermann with a question mark beside those poems the identification of which as eschatological hymns I should consider either mistaken or doubtful: Is. 12.1-2(?); 4-6(?); 25.1-5(?); 26.1-6(?); 40.9-11; 42.10(?); 44.23; 45.8(?); 48.20; 52.9-10; 54.1; 61.10ff.; Dt. 32.43; Jer. 20.13; 31.7-9; 51.10?; Joel 2.21ff., Zech. 2.14; 9.9; Nahum 2.1; Zeph. 3.14-15; Tobit 13(?); Ps. 9.6-13; 16-17(?); 68(?); 75.2; 5-12(?); Ps. 98; Ps. 149. To this list might be added several hymns in the intertestamental literature. These poems will be discussed later in this chapter.

12. Gunkel found more than 200 examples of the imperative plural in the psalms. (*Einleitung*, 34).

13. This was considered by Gunkel to be one of the more obvious characteristics of the hymn (*Einleitung*, 42-43).

14. Gunkel, *Einleitung*, 276.

15. Westermann, *Praise of God*, 35.

16. Westermann, *Praise of God*, 31.

17. See Westermann, *Praise of God*, 25-30.

18. Other examples given by Westermann include: Ps. 13.6; 3.7; 10.17; 6.8; 54.7; 56.13; 31.17; 28.6; 31.21; 22.34.

19. Westermann could only point to two psalms of this type in the Psalter, Ps. 124 and 129. However, he groups with these psalms songs of victory such as Ex. 15.21, epiphany psalms, Judg. 5.4-5, Ps. 18.7-15 and the sentences of praise contained in the historical books.

20. Westermann, *Praise of God*, 87.

21. See Ps. 116.1; 56.12; 30; 1,3.

22. Westermann would prefer to read 'Let us sing' with the LXX.

23. Westermann, *Praise of God*, 107.

24. Westermann, *Praise of God*, 117.

25. Among the familiar motifs of descriptive praise are: God's condescension, i.e. he looks down upon his people to save them (Ps. 33.13, 18-19; 135.10; 105.12ff.), his reversal of society (Ps. 113.7-9), and the provision of food. Because of this Westermann sometimes appears to treat the Magnificat as if it were descriptive praise. This is probably the reason brackets appear around verses (1.46-55) in his identification of Luke's hymns as declarative psalms of praise (*Praise of God*, 115). However, these themes are used to expand and explicate the significance of the one great saving deed which the Magnificat declares or confesses. The composer has used common OT motifs to bring out the significance of the event of which he sings.

26. Westermann, *Praise of God*, 142-45.

27. Westermann, *Praise of God*, 144.

28. Kaiser, *Isaiah 13-39*, 197.

29. Gray, *Isaiah 1-39*, 425.

30. Westermann calls this an eschatological hymn (*Praise of God*, 144, n. 8).

31. Westermann, *Praise of God*, 144.

32. This is the translation found in E. Schürer, *The Jewish People*, II, 456-58.

33. See also 1 Macc. 4.30-33; Tobit 3.11ff.; 8.5ff.; 8.15ff.; 1QM XIII.7ff.; XVIII.7ff.; 1QapGen. 20.12-15; Jub. 25.15ff.; 1 En. 84.12ff.

34. The translation is that found in *APOT* (3 Bar. 17.3).

35. The translation is that of Fitzmyer, *The Genesis Apocryphon*, XXI.2-3, 59.

36. Other examples include: 1 Macc. 4.24; Tobit 11.16; Susanna 60; 2 Macc. 3.30; 8.27; 10.7, 38; 11.9; 12. 41; 15.29; 1 Esd. 4.62; 9.46; Jub. 8.20; 13.7; 16.26-27; 17.3; 22.6; 29.4; 31.25, 31; 32.1, 7; Adam and Eve 50.3; 1 Enoch 25.7; 27.5; 36.4; 41.7; 48.5; 61.9; 69.26; 71.11; 81.3, 10; 83.11, 90.40. Two exceptions to the general pattern are 2 Macc. 12.37, in which a hymn is sung in the midst of battle, and 2 En. 106.11, in which Noah is reported as praising God in the midwife's arms.

37. Gunkel, *Einleitung*, 40.

38. The translation is that found in *APOT*.

39. Tobit 12.6(?); Jdt. 13.14 (praise God); 13.17; Bel and the Dragon 38 (no word of praise); 1 Esd. 4.40; 8.25-7; Jub. 22.28 (no motive clause), 25.12; Apoc. Mos. 27.5 (no word of praise); 37.2; cf. Adam and Eve 47.1; 1 Enoch 22.14; 39.9-13; 48.10; 61.11; 4 Ezra 12.40 (poetic exhortation + motive clause). Where there is no remark beside the reference the introductory word of praise is 'Blessed'.

40. One ought also to mention the hymn-like confession of the mighty

ones who have been put down from their thrones in 1 En. 63 and the series of rhetorical questions somewhat reminiscent of Ps. 8 in tone, in 2 Bar. 75.

41. The structure of the psalm may be compared with the analysis of the declarative psalm of praise of the individual displayed in the chart on pp. 103-105, Westermann's *Praise of God*.

42. See *APOT*, I, 629; Eissfeldt, *Introduction*, 590; and Dancy, *Apocrypha*, 223. This procedure would be almost identical to that by which Luke may have adapted the Magnificat and Benedictus to their contexts.

43. The translation is that of Mansoor, *Thanksgiving Hymns*. This introduction, with only slight variations, appears 14 times in the Hodayoth. Mowinckel, 'Hodayot 39.5-20', 270, suggests that the expression should be translated as a voluntative, 'I will praise thee'.

44. In 1QH V. 20 this formula is a correction inserted by a second hand replacing the more usual formula, 'I praise thee' (Mansoor, *Thanksgivng Hymns*, 134 n. 10). The benediction occurs 5 times in 1QH.

45. Cross, *Ancient Library*, 122-23.

46. These psalms were published by Sanders, *Psalms*, and by Starcky, 'Psaumes Apocryphes', 353-71. One psalm, the apostrophe to Zion, appears in both collections.

47. Sanders, *Psalms*, 76, from which the translation of the psalm is also taken (p. 78).

48. Noth, 'Psalmen', 1-23.

49. Delcor, 'Cinq nouveaux psaumes esséniens?', 85-102; Philonenko, 'L'Origine', 35-48.

50. The translation is that found in Mingana, 'Christian Documents', 496.

51. Yadin, *War Scroll*, 324-29; von der Osten-Sacken, *Gott und Belial*, 100-105; Davies, *War Scroll*, 85-88.

52. Y. Yadin, *War Scroll*, 324-26. A text of this passage containing slight variants was published by Hunzinger, 'Fragmente', 131-51.

53. See the charts of parallels in Ryle and James, *Psalms of Solomon*, xci-xcii.

54. Ps. Sol. 2.37ff.; 3; 5; 10; 17.1-2; 18.1-4.

55. Ps. Sol. 13; 15.1-5; 16.1-5. There are also benedictions at the conclusion of Ps. Sol. 5 and 6.

56. Robinson, 'Hodajot-Formel', 194-235.

57. Robinson, 'Hodajot-Formel', 210.

58. Robinson, 'Hodajot-Formel', 203. He adds that only two benedictions occur in the apostolic fathers.

59. Lehmann, 'Talmudic Material', 403.

60. Sanders, *Psalms*, 65. This translation depends on the reconstruction of Noth, 'Psalmen', 18. This reading of the Syriac is also presupposed in Delcor, 'Cinq nouveaux psaumes esséniens?', 99, and Magne, 'Le Psaume 154 et le Psaume 155', 96.

61. Mingana, 'Christian Documents', 494; Strugnell, 'Apocryphal Psalms', 275; Lührmann, 'Weisheitspsalm', 90; Skehan, 'Syriac Apocryphal Psalms', 157.

62. Lührmann, 'Weisheitspsalm', 95.

63. Magne, 'Le Psaume 154 et le Psaume 155', 102.

64. These psalms were published by Starcky, 'Psaumes Apocryphes', 353-71. The translations of the psalms are taken from Starcky's article.

65. Starcky, 'Psaumes Apocryphes', 366, 369.

66. I have argued earlier that Lk. 1.48 and 1.76-77 are Lukan additions to the original hymns designed to fit them to their present literary contexts. I am here concerned with the hymns in their original shapes.

67. This interpretation will be defended at greater length in the exegesis of the Nunc Dimittis.

68. These introductions also do not employ the usual language of Christian praise which tends to express itself in words of 'thanks'. The Benedictus is one of only four benedictions in the NT. See Robinson, 'Hodajot-Formel', 203-10.

69. There would be a perspective shift in the Benedictus if one were to consider 1.76-77 an original part of the hymn. This perspective shift is quite different from the comparable shifts in the true eschatological hymns, however.

The Community of Origin

1. See the examples of Jewish poetry adduced earlier. Aside from this poetry there are several references in Philo to the composition or singing of hymns. He records of the Therapeutae: 'Then the President rises and sings a hymn composed as an address to God, either a new one of his own composition or an old one by poets of an earlier day ... After him all the others take their turn (Philo, *Contemplative Life*, 80 [Loeb edn, IX, 162; cf. 164-65], and *De Agricultura* [Loeb edn, III, 148-49]). These last two references appear to describe antiphonal choirs of men and women which reenact the singing of the choir by the Red Sea, Ex. 15.

2. Brown, *Birth*, 350.

3. Winter, 'Magnificat'.

4. See above, pp. 80-81.

5. Winter, 'Magnificat', 342.

6. Winter, 'Magnificat', 331.

7. Cf. Brown, *Birth*, 350.

8. Winter, 'Magnificat', 333-34.

9. 'Commentators are agreed that the Chronicler used the Psalms and that they are therefore older than his work' (Myers, *1 Chronicles*, 121).

10. It is surprising that Winter treated the Benedictus in this manner since he made reference in this connection to the so-called 'Hymn of the Return' (1QM XIV. 4ff.) which is, of course, a hymn after battle. See 'Magnificat', 332-33.

11. See the discussion of this point below, pp. 95-96, and in the exegesis of the Benedictus.

12. Brown, *Birth*, 350.

13. *APOT*, II, 648. 'Danach würde in v. 5f. mit scharfer Polemik auf die Errichtung des hasmonäischen Königtums Bezug genommen und diese als Usurpation des Davidkönigtums charakterisiert' (Schüpphaus, *Die Psalmen Salomos*, 66).

14. Ryle and James, *Psalms of Solomon*, xci-xcii.

15. Gryglewicz, 'Die Herkunft', 267.

16. His attribution of the Gloria in excelsis to Pauline circles ('Die Herkunft', 270), is especially surprising.

17. See the charts of OT parallels in Creed, *Luke*, 303ff.

18. Brown, *Birth*, 458.

19. Gryglewicz found six Gründworter which the brief Nunc Dimittis shares with the Benedictus. Despite this congruence he supposed that the former hymn did not come from the same Jewish-Christian community as the Benedictus but rather from one in touch with Johannine traditions ('Die Herkunft', 267-68, 270).

20. Mann, 'Historicity', and Flood, 'The Magnificat', esp. 206-207. However, the latter scholar also appears substantially to accept Laurentin's theory that the hymns contain etymological allusions to the names of characters in Luke 1-2 (p. 209). One would have thought it rather difficult to hold these opinions simultaneously.

21. See above, p. 70.

22. Wink presents a lengthy list of scholars who have found a Baptist source in Luke 1 (*John the Baptist in the Gospel Tradition*, 60, n. 1). Most of these names will recur in the notes below.

23. Dibelius, *Täufer*, 73-74; *Tradition*, 125; *Jungfrauensohn*, 3, 14.

24. Erdmann, *Vorgeschichte*, 31.

25. Bultmann, *Synoptic Tradition*, 297. It should be noted that although Bultmann considered the Magnificat part of the Baptist legend he agreed with Gunkel with respect to the ultimate origin of the hymns. Cf. also Völter, *Erzählungen*, 22ff.; Erdmann, *Vorgeschichte*, 31; Kraeling, *John the Baptist*, 169. Kraeling made a considerable error at this point in supposing that 'It has been suggested by no less a person than Adolf Harnack that to the repertory of Baptist hymnody used by the writer of the Christian Nativity Story there should be added as a second element the Magnificat'— referring in this connection to Harnack's article 'Magnificat'. As we have seen, Harnack actually argues that the hymns were composed by Luke himself.

26. See the discussion of the text-critical problem connected with the proper attribution of the Magnificat and also the exegesis of this verse below, pp. 108-13, 118-19.

27. See above, pp. 21, 25.

28. Bultmann, *Synoptic Tradition*, 296; Goguel, *Jean-Baptiste*, 73; Vielhauer, 'Benedictus', 30.

29. But see Robinson, 'Detection', 280-81, who argues that the whole hymn including v. 76 was originally applied to Jesus.

30. See below, pp. 95-96.

31. Bowen, 'John', 99.

32. Bowen, 'John', 101.

33. Bowen, 'John', 102. The section of the Protevangelium which describes the threat to the infant John may be a later addition (22.3ff.). Origen knew the Protevangelium but described the death of Zechariah in a manner entirely different from the account in ch. 22. Moreover, the oldest manuscript of the Protevangelium shows signs that 22.3ff. may have been added to it. See *NTA*, I, 373.

34. Völter, 'Apokalypse des Zacharias', 247-49; *Erzählungen*, 27; Schonfield, *The Lost Book of the Nativity of John*, 43. Schonfield gives no reason for the deletion of the reference to David. Cf. also Scobie, *John the Baptist*, 55, who argued that the phrase 'from the house of his servant David' was a gloss because it spoiled the metre of the reconstructed Hebrew poem. It appears that he is here dependent on Aytoun, 'Hymns', 284, whom Scobie cites p. 51, n. 2). But, as I have shown above (pp. 46-49), Aytoun's reconstruction is hardly to be trusted and excising a phrase on the basis of it is unwarranted. Furthermore, the excision is not extensive enough. An allusion to David remains even in the phrase 'horn of salvation'. See further below, pp. 95,96.

35. Völter, 'Apokalypse des Zacharias', 248.

36. Völter, 'Apokalypse des Zacharias', 249.

37. Völter, 'Apokalypse des Zacharias', 249.

38. See above, pp. 27-28.

39. See below, p. 95.

40. Bultmann, *Synoptic Tradition*, 296; Vielhauer, 'Benedictus', 30; Kraeling, *John the Baptist*, 168; Thyen, 'Βάπτισμα', 115. All four refer explicitly to Gunkel in their notes. Kraeling errs once again in assuming that Gunkel argued that the hymns are baptist. In addition, Goguel argued that the first part of the Benedictus is a 'psaume messianique' which refers to a Davidide, but he does not mention Gunkel in his discussion of the question (*Jean-Baptiste*, 74).

42. Bultmann, *History of the Synoptic Tradition* 296; Vielhauer, 'Benedictus', 30; Goguel, *Jean-Baptiste*, 73-74.

43. Thyen, 'Βάπτισμα', 115.

44. Vielhauer, 'Benedictus', 30.

45. Vielhauer, 'Benedictus', 30-31.

46. Cf. Lk. 1.43.

47. Vielhauer, 'Benedictus', 42.

48. Vielhauer, 'Benedictus', 43.

49. See above, pp. 67-85.

50. Many scholars deny the existence of a baptist source. See, for example, Wink, *John the Baptist*, 58ff.; Brown, *Birth*, 246-47; Benoit, 'L'enfance', 169ff.; Robinson, 'Detection', 279 n. 2. But even if there was a baptist source behind the account of John's birth it had probably been Christianized by the time it got to Luke by means of the addition of the parallel account of Jesus' birth. This is affirmed even by some supporters of the baptist source theory. Cf. Bultmann, *Synoptic Tradition*, 296; Winter, 'Literary Problem', 261. My own use of Martin's method of determining the presence of Semitic sources which is described earlier in this work would at least support this position. The John and Jesus section of ch. 1 are syntactically indistinguishable; both are equally Semitic.

51. See above, p. 93.

52. Ps. 41.14; 72.18; 89.53; 106.48. The first is a 'Psalm of David' and the middle two are full of Davidic references. The reader may remember that in rebuttal of Laurentin's argument that Luke 1–2 are full of etymological allusions to Mary, John, etc. I showed that the Hebrew roots of those names all occurred in Ps. 89 (see above, pp. 44-45). That comparison shows that certain important concepts appear together both in that 'Davidic' psalm and the ones in Luke.

53. See Deichgräber, *Gotteshymnus*, 40-43.

54. See above, pp. 34-35.

55. See the charts of parallels in Ryle and James, *Psalms of Solomon*, ci-cii.

56. Some of these parallels consist of little more than the common use of a single word.

57. Wilcox, *Semitisms*, 73, Table 5. See also with respect to Lk. 1.70, 74-76.

58. Wilcox, *Semitisms*, 73.

59. All the language in the parallels listed by Wilcox ultimately derives from the OT.

60. See the exegesis of this passage, below, pp. 149-50.

61. Klijn, 'The Study of Jewish Christianity'; Kraft, 'In Search of Jewish Christianity'; Munck, 'Jewish Christianity in Post-Apostolic Times'; Murray, 'Defining Judaeo-Christianity'; Quispel, 'The Discussion of Judaic Christianity'; Riegel, 'Jewish Christianity: Definitions and Terminology'.

62. This definition recalls the simple statement of Munck: 'A Jewish Christian is the same as a Jew who has become a Christian' ('Jewish Christianity' in *Aspects du Judéo-Christianisme*, 87). The reader may wish to know how the hymns fare when a more specific definition of Jewish Christianity is applied.

To this 'ethnic' definition of Jewish Christianity some scholars add doctrinal ones. Thus Hort wrote, 'The only Christianity that can properly be called Judaistic is that which falls back to the Jewish point of view ... It ascribes perpetuity to the Jewish law' (*Jewish Christianity*, 5). Schoeps used the term to designate the Ebionites who held, among other opinions, an adoptionist Christology (*Jewish Christianity*, 9, 61-62). Schoeps's treatment of the subject does not differ greatly from that of Baur who appears to consider the Jewish Christians as identical with Paul's opponents and calls the Ebionite Pseudo-Clementines 'Jewish Christian' (*The First Three Centuries*, I, 55). A different sort of definition is offered by Daniélou: 'Jewish Christianity should be understood to refer to the expression of Christianity in the thought forms of late Judaism' (*Jewish Christianity*, 11 n. 21). Longenecker presented a two-part definition, the first part of which is essentially the same as Daniélou's. The second criterion is geographical; Jewish Christianity is that Christianity which is dependent upon the church of Jerusalem. A chronological element may also be mentioned. Munck believed that true Jewish Christianity perished in AD 70 ('Jewish Christianity in Post-Apostolic Times', 103-104; cf. Brandon, *Fall of Jerusalem*). Scholars like Schoeps and Strecker, on the other hand, concentrated on the later Jewish Christianity exemplified by later (sometimes heterodox) writings (Schoeps, *Jewish Christianity*; Strecker, appendix to Bauer's *Orthodoxy and Heresy*, 241ff. See also Klijn and Reinink, *Patristic Evidence for Jewish Christian Sects*).

Several of these definitions cannot be applied directly to the hymns of Luke 1-2. The hymns do not mention the Law and have only a very rudimentary Christology. Nevertheless, it can be said that they ascribe perpetuity, if not to the law, at least to the covenant with Israel. It is clear, however, that the hymns easily fit Daniélou's definition. Nothing is more obvious than that they 'express themselves in the thought forms of late Judaism'. With respect to geography and chronology it appears that the hymns originated in Palestine before AD 70.

63. Westermann, *Praise of God*, 115; Gnilka, 'Hymnus', 238; Brown, *Birth*, 350-55; Jones, 'Psalms', 44; Benoit, *L'Enfance* (for the Benedictus), 186.

64. Brown, *Birth*, 354; cf. Ellis, *Luke*, 65.

65. Schneider, *Lukas*, 62; Delling, *Worship*, 90-91; Ernst, *Lukas*, 85 (94); Luce, *Luke*, 91; Manson, *Luke*, 276n; Reicke, *Luke*, 31.

66. The hymns embedded in the epistles do not display the characteristic structure of the declarative psalm of praise described earlier in this chapter.

The Meaning of the Hymns

1. George, *Études*, 44-45; Brown, *Birth*, 248-49.
2. The significance of Brown's own solution to this problem will be discussed in the excursus which appears on pp. 102-107.
3. Brown, *Birth*, 250.
4. Dibelius, *Täufer*, 67. This analysis is preferred by George, *Etudes*, 44 n. 2, and by Wink, *John*, 59. I concur in their estimate of its quality.
5. See the exegesis of Luke 1.54-55, 72-73, and 2.29.
6. Brown, *Birth*, 251.
7. Dibelius, *Täufer*, 67.
8. Brown, *Birth*, 246.
9. Brown defined source as 'an oral or written consecutive narrative or collection of material' and said that the question about sources asks 'whether someone shaped such a narrative before Luke' (*Birth*, 241 n. 19).
10. This is claimed by Goulder and Sanderson in 'Genesis', by Goulder again in *Calendar* and by Drury, *Tradition*.
11. This process would be invalid if Luke were dependent on Matthew.
12. Brown, *Birth*, 257.
13. Brown, *Birth*, 251.
14. Brown, *Birth*, 252 n. 49.
15. See above, pp. 17-28.
16. Brown, *Birth*, 243.
17. This is argued by Flender, *St. Luke*.
18. Talbert, *Patterns*, 45.
19. Brown, *Birth*, 252 n. 49.
20. See above, p. 103.
21. See the table of annunciations in Brown, *Birth*, 156.

The Magnificat

1. Laurentin, 'Traces II'; 'Note-Annexe 2', 19-23.
2. Benko, 'Magnificat'.
3. The text of the decree of 26 June 1912 may be found in Laurentin, 'Traces II', 22.
4. In 1893 Loisy, under his own name, suggested the possibility that the original text read 'Elizabeth said'. See Loisy, *Évangiles*, 302 n. 1. In 1896 D. Völter independently advanced the Elizabeth hypothesis in connection with his argument concerning a baptist source in Luke 1 (Völter, 'Apokalypsis Zecharias', 255; see further, pp. 90-92 above.)
5. *De Psalmodiae Bono* 9.15-16; 11.11. For the text of this homily see Turner, 'Niceta', esp. 238-89.

6. See Benko, 'Magnificat', 265-66; Jacobé (A. Loisy), 'L'origine'. The article by Harnack is 'Magnificat', which was earlier discussed at length (see pp. 21-25 above). Benko seems to insinuate that Harnack was guilty of plagiarizing Loisy's work, ('Magnificat', 265). There is, as far as I see, not the slightest justification for this imputation.

7. See, for example, Durand, 'L'origine'; Hilgenfeld, 'Kindheitsgeschichte'; Spitta, 'Magnificat'.

8. Burkitt, 'Magnificat'.

9. Bernard, 'Magnificat'; Emmet, 'Magnificat'; Machen, *Virgin Birth*, 88-98.

10. Laurentin, 'Traces II', 22-23.

11. Davies, 'Ascription'; Danker, *New Age*, 15; Drury, *Luke*, 30.

12. Goulder and Sanderson, 'Genesis', 20 n. 2; Schürmann, *Lukas*, 72-73; Brown, *Birth*, 334-36; Marshall, *Luke*, 78.

13. Benko, 'Magnificat', 271.

14. The context makes it almost certain that Irenaeus wrote 'Mary' at this point. Cf. Harnack, 'Magnificat', 540.

15. See Zahn, *Lukas*, 750. See also Harvey, *Adversus Haereses*, II, 34 and 163 for the relevant texts.

16. This translation appears in Benko, 'Magnificat', 264 n. 2.

17. Zahn, *Lukas*, 749.

18. Barns, 'Magnificat', attempted to find support for the 'Elizabeth' reading in the catechetical instruction of Cyril of Jerusalem. His argument was effectively dismissed in a short note which the editor of *JTS*, F.E. Brightman, felt it necessary to add to the conclusion of the article. See Barns, 'Magnificat', 453.

19. This was noted by Spitta, 'Magnificat', 90-91, and by Zahn, *Lukas*, 746. More recent treatments of the subject have generally ignored this point. I am using the date ascribed to the writing by Cullmann, *NTA*, 372, who suggests the roots of the story go back to about AD 150.

20. The order is that of Harnack in 'Magnificat', 540ff.

21. Harnack, 'Magnificat', 542. Cf. Burkitt, 'Magnificat', 222. One other argument has been adduced in favour of the 'Elizabeth' reading. Burkitt argued that there is an etymological allusion to the name 'John' in ἔλεος (v. 50), which proves that the hymn properly belongs to John's mother ('Magnificat', 226). On the other hand, Laurentin argued that his etymological discoveries proved that the hymn ought to be attributed to Mary ('Traces II', 15-18. Neither argument is convincing. See the treatment of the question of etymological allusions above, pp. 42-46.

23. Schürmann, *Lukas*, 73 n. 211.

24. See above, p. 21.

25. See above, pp. 20-21.

26. Leivestad, 'Ταπεινός', 40ff.

27. Davies, 'Magnificat', suggested that such considerations led to an incorrect attribution of the hymn to Mary. His arguments could, however, suggest equally that the attribution to Mary is correct.

28. See Brown, *Birth*, 319; Burrows, *Infancy*, 1-40.

29. Marshall, *Luke*, 78. The Protevangelium of James which, as we have seen, is the first witness to the 'Mary' reading, does show considerable interest in the person and antecedents of Mary. One could even speak of 'devotion' to Mary (Cullmann, *NTA*, I, 374). The same book, however, also devotes considerable space to the person of Elizabeth and Zechariah. See especially chapter 23.

30. Dibelius, *Botschaft*, 14.

31. See above, pp. 101-102.

32. See also Lagrange, *Luc*, 45, who suggests that a scribe wrote 'et ait Maria Elizabeth' intending to clarify the narratve. The first name then dropped out of the text leaving the reading 'Elizabeth said'.

33. Aquinas, *Catena*.

34. Drury, *Tradition*, 49. Cf. Loisy, *Les Évangiles*, 299.

35. Tannehill, 'Magnificat', 265.

36. Tannehill suggested that there is synthetic parallelism in 51a//51b ('Magnificat', 266). This verse may be considered another example of antithetical parallelism if 'those who fear him' is read with v. 51 rather than with v. 50. See the treatment of this point on p. 120 above.

37. See above, pp. 21-25.

38. The suggestion of Marty that Luke added vv. 51-53 because of his Ebionitism ('Prières', 372), is highly unlikely. There is no structural or linguistic evidence to support his position. Schürmann's suggestion (*Lukas*, 73), that a more general hymn, vv. 51-55, was added to the original individual song of thanksgiving, 1.46-50, ignored the many links between the two halves of the psalm. See the exegesis of the relevant verses.

39. Westermann, *Praise*, 124-25, 130.

40. See, for example, Farrar, *Luke*, 56; Luce, *Luke*, 91; Robertson, *Translation*, 145. Such an explanation of the verbs seems also to be assumed by Calvin, *Harmony*, I, 60. Cf. Luther: these words 'are intended to set forth in general the works of God that He always has done, always does, and always will do' (*Magnificat*, 339). Cf. Bede in Aquinas, *Catena*, 47: 'For truly, through all generations of the world, by a merciful and just administration of Divine power, the proud do not cease to fall, and the humble to be exalted'.

41. See BD 171. Cf. Marshall, *Luke*, 84; Schürmann, *Lukas*, 75 n. 234.

42. Schmid, *Lukas*, 55. Cf. Loisy, *Les Évangiles*, 300. That the Hebrew can have this meaning is affirmed by Gesenius, *Grammar*, 312, who gives as examples Ps. 9.11, 13; 10.3; 119.40. See also Ramaroson, 'Structuram', 31, who suggested that Hebrew participles lay behind the Greek aorists.

43. ἐλάλησεν undoubtedly describes a past event.

44. See the exegesis of the Benedictus.

45. Several of the fathers saw in these verses a description of Christ's defeat of the Devil and of the dispersion of the Jews. See Aquinas, *Catena*, 46-47. See also the interpretation held by Winter, that the verbs refer to a Maccabean victory, 'Magnificat'.

46. Brown, *Birth*, 363.

47. See above, pp. 68, 70.

48. See above, pp. 94-98.

49. Plummer, *Luke*, 33; Schürmann, *Lukas*, 75; Lohfink, *Sammlung*, 26; Tannehill, 'Magnificat', 274 n. 26; Schotroff, 'Magnificat', 302.

50. Schürmann, *Lukas*, 70-71.

51. Ramaroson, 'Structuram', 34. Cf. W. Vogels, 'Magnificat', 280-81.

52. Plummer, *Luke*, 32. Brown saw in the hymn an introduction (46b-47) and three strophes (48a-50, 51-53, 54-55) (*Birth*, 357ff.).

53. On the interweaving of the thought of the poem see Tannehill, 'Magnificat', especially 272-75.

54. Creed, *Luke*, 303-304.

55. See Hamel, 'Renversement'.

56. That the hymns could, in principle, be placed in the mouth of other characters in Luke 1–2 is shown by Sahlin's rearrangement. He puts the Magnificat in Zechariah's mouth and the Benedictus in Anna's. See below, pp. 117, 130.

57. See above, pp. 100-102.

58. See above, p. 101.

59. Bultmann, *History*, 296.

60. Leaney, *Luke*, 26.

61. Sahlin, *Messias*, 159ff.

62. Sahlin's name will recur in the exegesis of the hymns in connection with rather unusual proposals. He often seems to have borrowed from the science of text-criticism the principle of preferring the most difficult reading with the aim of applying it to the task of interpretation.

63. Cf. 'your servant' and 'my eyes' in the Nunc Dimittis.

64. Aquinas, *Catena*, 42. Origen offered a fascinating homiletical answer to his own question. Having observed that Christ is the image of God and that we are to form our souls after that image, he wrote: 'When I have made my soul great in thought, word, and deed, the image of God is made great, and the Lord Himself, whose image it is, is magnified in my soul'.

65. Lagrange, *Luc*, 45. Cf. Lk. 1.58 where the same verb does mean 'to make great'.

66. Brown, *Birth*, 336.

67. Marshall, *Luke*, 82. It seems hardly likely that it refers back to the annunciation as was suggested by Plummer (*Luke*, 31) or that the word 'and'

replaces a Hebrew 'for' (Lagrange, *Luc*, 46). There are two motive clauses later in the hymn.

68. The verb ἠγαλλίασεν is active rather than the more usual deponent. Cf. Bauer, *Lexicon*. Other instances of the active are 1 Pet. 1.8; Rev. 19.7.

69. Cf. Ps. 24.5; 25.5; Mic. 7.7. See also Sir. 51.1. There was a tendency in the Psalms, according to Jones, to 'consider "salvation" personally so as to make it practically equivalent to "saviour"' (Jones, 'Psalms', 20). The word 'salvation' occurs regularly in the hymns, 1.69, 71, 77; 2.30. It may be a key concept in Luke–Acts (cf. Marshall, *Historian*, 92ff.).

70. Grundmann, *Lukas*, 64; Ernst, *Lukas*, 85.

71. Klostermann, *Lukas*, 19; Schürmann, *Lukas*, 73.

72. Cf. Lk. 2.11; and Brown, *Birth*, 360.

73. 'Magnify' and 'rejoice' appear together at Ps. 19.5 (LXX); 40.16; 70.4. The parallel between soul and spirit is found at Is. 26.9; Job 12.10; Dan. 3.39, 86. The last parallel, coming as it does in the Song of the Three Children, is especially noteworthy. To the couplet as a whole Ps. 35.9 and, to a lesser degree, 1 Sam. 2.1, are parallel.

74. Jones, 'Psalms', 21.

75. The first to suggest this seems to have been Weiss in his *Life of Christ*, I, 245. The evidence for this position has already been adduced on pp. 21-26. above.

76. Sahlin, *Messias*, 164. Sahlin used this argument to justify the very unlikely theory that the Magnificat belongs in the mouth of the male Zechariah. This does not, of course, render the argument itself false. See also Laurentin, *Structures*, 148ff.; Vogels, 'Magnificat', 282; Leaney, *Luke*, 22; McHugh, *Mother*, 37ff., 76; Gaston, *Stone*, 270.

77. Brown, *Birth*, 320ff.

78. Jones, 'Psalms', 21.

79. This shows the flaw in Jones's argument that v. 48 must be original because all three hymns involve a secondary personality, the maidservant of the Magnificat, the child of the Benedictus, and the servant of the Nunc Dimittis (Jones, 'Psalms', 21; God is the primary personality). Actually, *all* psalms of praise involve a secondary personality. God does not act in a vacuum; he always acts for a person or a people. There would, therefore, still be a secondary personality in the Magnificat even without v. 48. (Using these terms, the 'child' of 1.76ff. is actually the 'tertiary' personality.)

80. See, for example, Klostermann, *Lukas*, 19. Cf. 1 Sam. 1.11 where the word does carry this connotation.

81. Schürmann, *Lukas*, 73.

82. Luther, 'Magnificat', 215.

83. See Brown, *Birth*, 336, 361; Lagrange, *Luc*, 46; Ernst, *Lukas*, 85-86. This interpretation is quite acceptable to Catholic commentators who see in Mary 'an idealized representative of the Anawim who constituted the

remnant of Israel' (Brown, *Birth*, 353 n. 45). 'When she speaks of what God has done for her, she speaks of what God has done for Israel' (McHugh, *Mary*, 76).

84. Cf. Plummer, *Luke*, 32; Schürmann considered the angelic salutation to be the first such blessing (*Lukas*, 73).

85. Loisy, *Luc*, 96, claimed that the change from the OT 'women' to the Magnificat's 'generations', the only significant difference between the two texts, is designed to show that the speaker's son is greater than Leah's. The change may not, however, have been a deliberate one.

86. Cf. above, pp. 21, 25.

87. Marshall, *Luke*, 83.

88. Ernst, *Lukas*, 81. This verbal connection does not, however, justify any alteration in the order of verses as Black suggested (*Aramaic Approach*, 151).

89. The weakly attested variant μεγαλεῖα may be a reminiscence of Acts 2.11 (Plummer, *Luke*, 32; Brown, *Birth*, 337).

90. Cf. Dt. 11.7; Judg. 2.7.

91. Jones, 'Psalms', 23.

92. Ps. 45.2 (LXX 44.4; cf. 44.6); Zeph. 3.17.

93. Westermann, *Praise*, 131.

94. Jones, 'Psalms', 23. Cf. Ps. 99.1-3.

95. Lagrange, *Luc*, 48.

96. So, among others, Sahlin, *Messias*, 172; Marshall, *Luke*, 83; Klostermann, *Lukas*, 20.

97. See especially Ex. 20.6; 34.6ff. and in connection with David, 2 Sam. 7.15 (Brown, *Birth*, 337; Marshall, *Luke*, 83).

98. See Ps. 49.11; 89.1. The exact formula occurs in Test. Levi 18.8 (Brown, *Birth*, 337; Marshall, *Luke*, 83).

99. It is worth noting that in v. 53 the objects of God's mercy, the hungry, and of his wrath, the rich, appear before the relevant verbs—as would also be the case in v. 51 if this proposal were accepted.

100. See, for example, Sahlin, *Messias*, 175; Winter, 'Magnificat', 346.

101. So Brown, *Birth*, 337.

102. De Cantanzero, 'Fear', 166ff.

103. See, for example, Ps. 25.11; 34.9; 85.9; 103.11, 13, 17.

104. Ps. Sol. 2.33 (37); 13.12 (11); 15.13 (15).

105. Tannehill, 'Magnificat', 272. Cf. also Schürmann, *Lukas*, 75.

106. So, for example, Brown, *Birth*, 337, who, as we have seen, doubts that these hymns depend upon a Semitic *Vorlage*.

107. Ernst, *Lukas*, 86.

108. Marshall, *Luke*, 83; Brown, *Birth*, 337; Jones, 'Psalms', 25. Cf. Ex. 6.6; Dt. 4.34.

109. Tannehill, 'Magnificat', 276; Leuenberger, *Magnificat*, influenced by Luther, interpreted this as the work of God's 'left hand'.

110. Schoonheim, 'Vokabel', 242ff.

111. Jones, 'Psalms', 25, noted that the messianic Ps. Sol. 17 four times attributes this fault to the enemy: 6(8), 13(15), 23(26), 41(46).

112. Brown, *Birth*, 337; and cf. Obad. 3.

113. See especially Hamel, 'Renversement', 58ff.

114. This has been perceived by many commentators. See, for example, Tannehill, 'Magnificat', 267.

115. An excellent survey of the extensive literature on the subject may be found in a dissertation recently presented to Cambridge University: D. Secombe, *Possessions*, esp. 2-12, 19-48. On the discussion concerning the poor in the Psalms see van den Bergh, 'Ani', and on the discussion in Luke, see Mealand, *Poverty*, Appendix C, 'Studies of the Lucan attitude to wealth' (pp. 103-104).

116. Seccombe, *Possessions*, 91ff., argues vigorously that the ταπεινοί of v. 52 are Israel. This is of course true, but does not exhaust the implications of the word.

117. See above, pp. 95-97.

118. On the background and use of language about the poor, see Grundmann, 'ταπεινός', *TDNT*, VII, 1ff.; Bammel, 'πτωχός', *TDNT*, VI, 885ff.; Leivestad, 'ΤΑΠΕΙΝΟΣ'. On the use of this language in Luke–Acts see Johnson, *Literary Function*.

119. It is to be noted that God is the subject of these words. G. Gutierrez altered the meaning of the text when he stated after quoting these lines, 'True liberation will be the work of the oppressed themselves; in them, the Lord saves history. The spirituality of liberation will have as its basis the spirituality of the anawim' (Gutierrez, *Liberation*, 207). The 'spirituality of the anawim' recognizes that God alone can save. To believe that one saves oneself is, in fact, the spirituality of the proud. If this is forgotten the poor become, after the reversal, the new proud. Nevertheless, one can clearly see in these verses God's 'preferential option for the poor'.

120. Hamel, 'Renversement', 60ff.

121. Calvin, *Harmony*, 60. One detects here a difference in tone. To the burghers of Geneva revolution may well have appeared 'to disturb' society. Its essential rightness needed demonstration. To those who first used the Magnificat, as we have seen, it was a matter for great rejoicing.

122. Hamel, 'Renversement', 63-64.

123. The reversal motif appears at several points in the OT. See 1 Sam. 2.7; Job 12.19; 22.29; Ez. 21.26; Sir. 10.14; 11.4-6. There appear to be verbal reminiscences of Ez. 21.26, Job 12.19 and Sir. 10.14 in our passage. In Ez. 21 the reversal of fortunes is a sign of God's judgment upon Israel. As is the case in the Magnificat, reversal is cause for rejoicing in Hannah's song (1 Sam. 2.1-10). In the citations from Wisdom literature the references to the motif are part of general observations on the rules which govern the universe. In En. 46.5 and 1QM XIV. 11 the destruction of the powerful occurs at the end.

The theme here becomes specifically eschatological rather than simple observation of the way life normally works. Verse 53a seems to depend on Ps. 107.9. Ps. 107.10 appears to be behind the last line of the Benedictus (v. 79). Cf. also Ps. 24.11.

124. See Hamel, 'Renversement', 35-36.

125. See also the repeated use of the saying, 'Every one who exalts himself will be humbled and he who humbles himself will be exalted' (Lk. 14.11; 18.4; Mt. 23.12; cf. Mt. 18.4; 1 Pt. 5.6). The passive form does not conceal the fact that it is God who will do the humbling and exalting. See also the parable of the Rich Man and Lazarus (Lk. 16.19-31). The motif is also reminiscent of the blessing and woes of the Sermon on the plain (Lk. 6.2ff.). Cf. Schotroff, 'Magnificat', 306ff.

126. Brown, *Birth*, 352.

127. Seccombe, *Possessions*, 91ff., denies vigorously the existence of such a group.

128. Cf. Ez. 29.21 where the humbling of the mighty is a sign of God's judgment.

129. See Gutierrez, *Liberation*, 207-208. Cf. C. Maurras, a French socialist of the last century whose work is described in Hamel, 'Renversement', 56-57.

130. For an example of a completely spiritualizing interpretation see Lagrange, *Luc*, 50. Jones, 'Psalms', 26, also almost seems to spiritualize the hymn completely.

131. Brown, *Birth*, 363; Marshall, *Luke*, 84; Plummer, *Luke*, 37; Schürmann, *Lukas*, 76.

132. Brown, *Birth*, 334; Plummer, *Luke*, 33; Lagrange, *Luc*, 50. Cf. Acts 20.35; Sir. 2.6.

133. This use of language drawn from Deutero-Isaiah reminds one of the Nunc Dimittis.

134. This is suggested by Brown, *Birth*, 364.

135. Lohfink, *Sammlung*, 26.

136. Jones, 'Psalms', 27; Marshall, *Luke*, 85.

137. Jones, 'Psalms', 28.

138. Some scholars would assert that Ἀβραάμ is the indirect object of the infinitive 'to remember' (v. 54); 'remembering his mercy to Abraham . . .' Verse 55a in this interpretation is a parenthesis. See Marshall, *Luke*, 85; Lagrange, *Luc*, 51; and, with some slight variation, Plummer, *Luke*, 34. This seems an unnecessarily awkward interpretation. It seems better to see 'Abraham . . .' as standing in loose apposition 'to our fathers'. Such is the opinion of Schürmann, *Lukas*, 77 n. 252; Sahlin, *Messias*, 173, and Brown, *Birth*, 338. The variation between πρός (v. 55a), and the simple dative in v. 55b is not unknown. Tannehill, 'Magnificat', 271 n. 19, gives many examples of such a variation in Luke. One certainly need not agree with Ramaroson, 'Magnificat', 542, that this syntactic variation demands the

rearrangement of the order of verses.
    139. Dahl, 'Abraham', 151.
    140. See below, pp. 131, 191n.19.

The Benedictus

    1. Wragg, *Infancy*, 267; Vanhoye, 'Structure', 382-89; Auffret, 'Structure',
248-58. It appears that Wragg and Vanhoye independently hit on a very
similar structure. Auffret's article is a refinement of Vanhoye's proposal.
    2. See above, pp. 71-72.
    3. Auffret, 'Structure', 248. Auffret's own solution to this problem is to
superimpose upon Vanhoye's structure yet another chiasmus centred on
v. 76 ('Structure', 255). Even so Auffret's structure ignores several of the
word pairs he himself discovers ('Lord' and 'way').
    4. Marshall, *Luke*, 86. Marshall does, however, concede that there may
be 'certain elements of truth in the scheme'.
    5. Gertner, 'Midrashim', esp. 273-82.
    6. Gertner, 'Midrashim', 274.
    7. See, for example, Gertner, 'Midrashim', 281.
    8. Gertner saw the word 'face' behind ἐνώπιον in v. 76 and the verb 'to
be gracious' behind ἔλεος in v. 77. These words occur also in vv. 75 and 74
respectively.
    9. Jones, 'Psalms', 34; Gaston, *Stone*, 259; Marshall, *Luke*, 87; cf. Daube,
Judaism, 201. These scholars affirm that the change of direction at v. 76 is
not unknown in Jewish compositions but give no examples of such a change.
Sahlin, *Messias*, 290, offered Ass. Mos. 10.8 as an example of this phenomenon but that instance is only a slight change of topic within a consistently
future-oriented prophecy.
    10. Jones, 'Psalms', 34.
    11. Jones, 'Psalms', 47-48; Gaston, *Stone*, 261-62.
    12. Sahlin, *Messias*, 287; Leaney, *Luke*, 24-25.
    13. Gaston, *Stone*, 261; Robinson, 'Detection', 280. Robinson did allow
the possibility that the first part of the hymn was 'modelled' on traditional
material ('Detection', 281 n. 1).
    14. Sahlin, *Messias*, 287-88.
    15. See above, p. 94.
    16. Gunkel, 'Lieder', 58-60; Winter, 'Magnificat', 334; Gnilka, 'Hymnus',
219; Vielhauer, 'Benedictus', 35; Lohfink, *Sammlung*, 27.
    17. See Erdmann, *Vorgeschichte*, 31ff.
    18. Schürmann, *Lukas*, 85. It should be noted that, according to
Schürmann, the baptist legend was a Jewish-Christian, not baptist, account.
A somewhat similar theory has been offered by F. Hahn, *Titles*, 365-66.
Verses 68-75, 78, 79a are Christian additions to a baptist core. Verse 79b is

baptist. This theory has some of the characteristics of Schürmann's analysis and some of Benoit's, with, it appears, some influence on the part of Vielhauer.

19. Gunkel, 'Lieder', 59: Ps. 16.11; 18.51; 28.9; 29.10; 30.13. Cf. Schürmann, *Lukas*, 88 n. 52.

20. Bultmann, *History*, 296.

21. Dibelius, *Täufer*, 74; Benoit, 'L'Enfance', 182-86; George, *Luc*, 61; Brown, *Birth*, 379, 381. See above, pp. 26-28.

22. Benoit, 'L'Enfance', 185. Admittedly Ps. 128.5 is very close to the end of the poem.

23. Gnilka, 'Hymnus', 220.

24. Schürmann, *Lukas*, 88 n. 52; Vielhauer, 'Benedictus', 39 n. 59; Gnilka, 'Hymnus', 220. The three lists are almost identical. The references in question are listed in n. 19 above.

25. Cf. also 1QH XVII.14 where the expression does not end a psalm.

26. See above, pp. 26-28.

27. See the charts in Brown, *Birth*, 386-89.

28. Benoit, 'L'Enfance', 185-86. See also the structures advanced by Plummer, *Luke*, 39-40, and Loisy, *Les Evangiles*, 310, who divided the hymn into 5 strophes (68-69, 70-72, 73-75, 76-77, 78-79) and Lagrange, *Luc*, 58, and A. Loisy, *Luc*, 104, who found seven distichs or strophes in the material. Curiously, Benoit said that Loisy divided the hymn into *six* strophes! ('L'Enfance', 184 n. 1).

29. Benoit, 'L'Enfance', 184-86.

30. Benoit, 'L'Enfance', 185.

31. Brown, *Birth*, 381-82.

32. Benoit's analysis is also somewhat over-elaborate with respect to the recapitulation. The history of preparation is not explicitly mentioned as in vv. 70 and 73. At best it is suggested by the allusion to Is. 9 in v. 79.

33. See the tentative suggestion of George, *Luc*, 63.

34. Lohfink, *Sammlung*, 27.

35. Grundmann, *Lukas*, 69.

36. See above, pp. 71-72.

37. Wragg, *Infancy*, 287-89, called this formula 'jussive' apparently because of the usual English translation. From this she drew the erroneous form-critical conclusion that while the Magnificat is a 'song of thanksgiving', the Benedictus, which summons people to worship, is a 'hymn' (using the categories of Gunkel). The psalm is not a summons to worship even if a subjunctive is supplied. As we have seen, the berakah is the most common declarative response to a saving act of God (pp. 71, 77, 175n.39 above).

38. Plummer, *Luke*, 40; Brown, *Birth*, 370.

39. Deichgräber, *Gotteshymnus*, 30-32; D. Milling, *Doxology*, argued that Deichgräber's study had not been thorough enough and that the evidence actually shows an even greater preponderance of the indicative than

Deichgräber allowed. See also BD, 71, who advocated the use of the indicative in these formulae.

40. Deichgräber, *Gotteshymnus*, 31, lists the examples.

41. Jones, 'Psalms', 29.

42. In that verse the word appears in parallel with 'remember' and in close connection with 'thy people' and 'salvation', all concepts which reappear in the Benedictus. The verb 'to visit' reappears in connection with an occasion of God's favour at Lk. 7.16; 19.44; Acts 15.44.

43. In Lk. 1.68 God is the subject of the verb but in Lk. 24.21 it is Jesus.

44. Sahlin, *Messias*, 288. Cf. Jones, 'Psalms', 29. The Lukan expression may, therefore, be a 'non-LXX Hebraism'.

45. See above, pp. 95-96. Cf. SB, II, 110-11; Ps. 18.3, 132.16-17; 1 Sam. 2.10; Ezek. 29.21.

46. Harnack, *Physician*, 206. Gnilka's suggestion, 'Hymnus', 221, that the use of ἤγειρεν represents a Lucan alteration, fails to convince. That the exact phrase ἤγειρεν κέρας does not appear in the LXX is irrelevant.

47. Cf. Acts 13.22; Judg. 3.9. See also the description of the coming of the Teacher of Righteousness, 1QS I.5-12.

48. Jones, 'Psalms', 30; Benoit, 'L'Enfance', 187 n. 7; Jeremias, *TDNT*, V, 703.

49. Lohfink, *Sammlung*, 27.

50. See above, pp. 57-58.

51. See Völter, *Erzählungen*, 270; Schürmann, *Lukas*, 87; Gnilka, 'Hymnus', 220.

52. Wilcox, *Semitisms*, 74-75; Marshall, *Luke*, 90. Cf. Ernst, *Lukas*, 95; Jones, 'Psalms', 31.

53. Brown, *Birth*, 383.

54. Burger, *Davidssohn*, 131. Burger drew from this observation the conclusion that the verse must, therefore, be an insertion into the original 'eschatological hymn'. That the hymn is 'eschatological' in that sense is doubtful.

55. See Plummer, *Luke*, 41; Schürmann, *Lukas*, 37 n. 37; Klostermann, *Lukas*, 27.

56. So Jones, 'Psalms', 31; Lagrange, *Luc*, 59.

57. So Marshall, *Luke*, 91. Cf. Gaston, *Stone*, 263, 271.

58. Cf. Lk. 9.31. See Manek, 'New Exodus'.

59. H. Schürmann, *Lukas*, 87.

60. Brown, *Birth*, 389.

61. Brown, *Birth*, 371-72; Lagrange, *Luc*, 60.

62. See Marshall, *Luke*, 92. Brown, *Birth*, 372, would rather see them as infinitives showing the result of God's actions.

63. See above, p. 29.

64. μετά appears to mean 'to' our fathers. It is a 'Hebraizing expression'. See BD, 163.

65. See Grundmann, *Lukas*, 72.
66. Cf. Mic. 7.20; 1 Macc. 4.10.
67. So Jones, 'Psalms', 31-32.
68. 1 Macc. 1.15, 63. Cf. Jones, 'Psalms', 32; and cf. the term 'holy prophets'.
69. 'Attractio inversa' (BD, 153); Klostermann, *Lukas*, 27; Marshall, *Luke*, 92. Lagrange denied that there is 'attractio inversa' here, calling this expression 'a Hebraism' (*Luc*, 60). It may well be a Hebraism, but so to label the expression does not explain the alteration in Greek cases in the words dependent on διαθήκης.
70. Klostermann, *Lukas*, 27; Sahlin, *Messias*, 290-91. See above, pp. 42-45.
71. Cf. Jer. 11.5; Mic. 7.20.
72. Schürmann, *Lukas*, 88.
73. Jones, 'Psalms', 32.
74. Marshall, *Luke*, 92. There are 19 occurrences of τοῦ + infinitive in Luke and 17 in Acts.
75. So Brown, *Birth*, 372.
76. Schürmann, *Lukas*, 88. Jones, 'Psalms', 33, offered a very neat parallel to this verse from 1QH XVII.14. Unfortunately there are too many lacunae in the text at this point to be sure that the reconstruction on which Jones depends is accurate. Cf. Mansoor, *Hymns*, 108.
77. The Benedictus reads ἐν ὁσιότητι καὶ δικαιοσύνῃ, the LXX of Jos. 24.14 ἐν εὐθύτητι καὶ ἐν δικαιοσύνῃ. This may be a 'non-LXX' allusion to the OT for the pair in the Benedictus could be a literal translation of the Hebrew בתמים ובאמת. ὁσιότητι is a perfectly acceptable translation of תמים. Cf. 1 Kings 9.4 where ὁσιότητι appears in parallel with εὐθυτήτι but the former translates תמים.
78. See above, pp. 130-31.
79. See above, pp. 93-94, 134.
80. Schürmann, *Lukas*, 90; Schmithals, *Lukas*, 34. This is the prophecy implied by 1.67.
81. Plummer, *Luke*, 42.
82. See, for example, Brown, *Birth*, 372.
83. Vielhauer, 'Benedictus', 36.
84. Perhaps the use of the verb 'to go' in v. 76 is due to the influence of Lk. 1.17. The Greek verbs are not, in fact, the same, however.
85. See above, pp. 93-94.
86. See above, p. 94.
87. See above, pp. 130, 179n.29.
88. Klostermann, *Lukas*, 28; Lagrange, *Luc*, 61; Schürmann, *Lukas*, 91.
89. Marshall, *Luke*, 93. Gnilka, 'Hymnus', 235-36, noted that Test. Levi 2.11 calls the Messiah 'Lord'.
90. Vielhauer, 'Hymnus', 38.
91. Jones, 'Psalms', 36. Nor does the expression occur in the material

covered by Wahl, *Clavis*.

92. So Marshall, *Luke*, 93. The controversy described in Lagrange, *Luc*, 61-62, over the word to which ἐν ἀφέσει... should be attached, to 1) salvation, 2) knowledge or 3) to give, seems an empty one. It is through forgiveness of sins that knowledge of salvation exists in any of the three cases.

93. It cannot be found in the OT but occurs in 1 Enoch 12.5.

94. Sahlin claimed that ἄφεσις here means renunciation rather than forgiveness of sins (*Messias*, 294). Cf. Lewis, 'Baptism', 226. While this interpretation may be linguistically possible it hardly seems the most likely reading in Lk. 1.77.

95. On the meaning of this word see especially Jacoby, ''Ανατολή', and Gnilka, 'Hymnus', 227-32. See also the summary of positions in Marshall, *Luke*, 94-95.

96. See above, p. 34.

97. See not only the Shemoneh Esreh but the other examples listed in SB, II, 113. See also 4Qpatr 3 and 4QFlor. I.11.

98. Justin Martyr, *Dialogue*, 121.2: 'Anatolē is his name' (cf. Brown, *Birth*, 40). Perhaps another reference to the ἀνατολή can be found in Melito of Sardis according to Gnilka, 'Hymnus', 232.

99. See above, pp. 34-35.

100. That which rises, either a sun (cf. Mal 4.22 LXX) or a star (cf. Num. 24.17; 1QM XI.6; Test. Levi 18.3; Test. Jud. 24.1) could be called an ἀνατολή.

101. We may safely leave aside the idea of Lambertz, 'Sprachliches', 84, that the presence of ἀνατολή stems from the misunderstanding of the liturgical direction 'Selah'. Likewise, Zahn's suggestion, *Lukas*, 118, that ἀνατολή is not the subject of the verb but a mere 'Satzapposition' (cf. σωτηρίαν in v. 71) can be rejected. ἀνατολή is clearly subject of the verb 'to visit' (cf. Jacoby, ''Ανατολή', 207).

102. ἐξ ὕψους does not necessarily imply pre-existence as Jacoby thought (''Ανατολή', 207).

103. Cf. Ezek. 29.21 where two of these images again are combined: 'On that day I will cause a horn to spring forth to the house of Israel' (Gk. ἀνατελεῖ κέρας, Hebrew אצמיח קרן).

104. See Plummer, *Luke*, 43.

105. Cf. Marshall, *Luke*, 93. In the original hymn it would have followed on v. 75, 'all our days through the heartfelt mercy of our God...' The interpolation had to come before rather than after the prepositional phrase because of its close links with v. 78b, ἐν οἷς, that is, the 'heartfelt mercy', σπλάγχνα ἐλέους.

106. Vielhauer attached 'to guide' (v. 79b) to 'to give' (v. 77), making John the subject of both infinitives ('Benedictus', 35-36). Both, he claimed, are articular infinitives and therefore should be connected despite the intervening

appearance of the non-articular infinitive in v. 79 of which ἀνατολή is the subject. But the variation between articular and non-articular infinitives in vv. 72-74 does not indicate change of subject; God is subject of the three infinitives in these verses. There appears, therefore, to be no reason to break the apparent parallelism between the two infinitives in v. 79. The ἀνατολή is subject of both (Brown, *Birth*, 374).

107. Marshall, *Luke*, 95, noted that the text of this verse is closest to the 'non-LXX rendering of Is. 8.23–9.1 MT in Mt. 4.15f.'. Cf. Stendahl, *School*, 105 n. 2, who suggests that Matthew's rendering of Isaiah's text emanated from the Hebrew but was influenced by traditional Greek translations.

108. *TDNT*, II, 415.

109. Klostermann, *Lukas*, 29.

The Nunc Dimittis

1. Gaston, *Stone*, 273.

2. As we have seen, p. 66 above, the 'net score' of this section of the narrative is markedly less Semitic than is ch. 1.

3. Spitta, 'Hymnen', 310.

4. Bultmann, *History*, 296, and Grundmann, *Lukas*, 88, have argued that the universalism of v. 32 points to the secondary insertion of the hymn.

5. Leaney, *Luke*, 99.

6. This expression was used in later Jewish writing to describe the time of Messianic salvation (SB, II, 124-26).

7. All commentators note this structure.

8. See Marshall, *Luke*, 119. Ernst, *Lukas*, 117, compared the Nunc Dimittis to the *Sterbgebet* of pious Jews but offered no convincing example of such a prayer.

9. Ernst, *Lukas*, 117 (*Lobspruch*); Schürmann, *Lukas*, 125 (*Lobpreis*); Lohfink, *Sammlung*, 29 (*Lied*). Gurney, *Nunc Dimittis*, 42, 'It is indeed rather a Thanksgiving than a prayer'.

10. See below, p. 146.

11. *APOT*, II, 76.

12. Jones, 'Psalms', 40.

13. Jones, 'Psalms', 48.

14. Jones, 'Psalms', 40.

15. McNamara, *Targum*, 243.

16. See the table of OT parallels in Brown, *Birth*, 458. See also Miyoshi, 'Darstellung', 94-98.

17. Plummer, *Luke*, 67.

18. Navone, *Themes*, 183.

19. Bauer, *Lexicon*, 96.

20. Marshall, *Luke*, 119-20. Cf. Brown, *Birth*, 439; Leaney, *Luke*, 99.

21. Sahlin, *Messias*, 253.

22. Cf. Acts 15.32; and cf. SB, II, 138.

23. Gen. 15.2; Num. 20.29; Tob. 3.6, 13; 2 Macc. 7.9

24. Schürmann, *Lukas*, 125 n. 202. Cf. Lk. 10.23.

25. Josephus, *War* 1.79; Ernst, *Lukas*, 117.

26. See Grundmann, *Lukas*, 98, who suggested that Simeon is here liberated from hard and onerous service. The analogy should not be pressed too far, however; Simeon expects no release from the service of this 'Master' (Schürmann, *Lukas*, 125).

27. Wilcox, *Semitisms*, 73.

28. Foerster, *TDNT*, II, 415.

29. Grundmann, *Lukas*, 90.

30. Marshall, *Luke*, 120; Lohfink, *Sammlung*, 29; Grundmann, *Lukas*, 90.

31. The language of Acts 28.28 is reminiscent of Ps. 67.2.

32. The subject of the verb 'to prepare' is here God rather than John the Baptist as in Lk. 1.17, 76; 3.4.

33. Jones, 'Psalms', 42.

34. Cf. Lk. 1.55, 70, 73.

35. Kilpatrick, 'Λαοί', 127.

36. Marshall, *Luke*, 121.

37. See further D. van Winkle, *Universalism and Nationalism in Deutero-Isaiah* (Ph.D. Cambridge, 1983).

38. Cf. Is. 60.1, 19, where light and glory also appear in parallel in the period of eschatological salvation. Glory also pertains to Israel in Ps. 89.17. See also Rom. 9.4.

39. The linking of the concepts 'light' and 'glory' led Gryglewicz, 'Herkunft', 267ff., to posit an origin for this hymn in Johannine circles. This seems unlikely; the hymn's links are with Isaiah, not John.

40. See the discussion in Plummer, *Luke*, 69.

41. Sahlin, *Messias*, 254.

42. גָּלוֹת piel infinitive, גְּלוּת 'dispersion'.

43. Aytoun, 'Hymns', 275.

The Significance of the Hymns

1. See above, pp. 21-28.

2. To look for themes which recur later in Luke–Acts is to reject Conzelmann's well-known view that these narratives are irrelevant or even contrary to the theology of Luke (*Theology*, 16 n. 3). Conzelmann has been rebuked quite thoroughly for ignoring Luke 1–2, so no attack on his theory is necessary here. See especially Minear's important article 'Luke's Use', 120ff., and two essays which attempt (with little success in my opinion) to fit Luke 1–2 into Conzelmann's three-part division of salvation history: Tatum,

'Epoch', and Oliver, 'Birth Stories'.

3. The most important such expression is 'salvation', σωτηρία (1.69, 71, 77), σωτήριον (2.30), and 'saviour' (1.47). See the treatment of the theme in Marshall, *Historian*, 92ff. Marshall claimed that 'the idea of salvation supplies the key to the theology of Luke' (*Historian*, 92). It is true that the theme is especially prominent in the infancy narratives (*Historian*, 96ff.). The members of the 'salvation' word group do not, however, occur with nearly the same frequency in the remainder of Luke–Acts. (See the figure given by Marshall himself [*Historian*, 92 n. 4].) But while the word 'salvation' is perhaps not prominent in Luke–Acts as a whole the idea conjured up by that word, that God has acted decisively to save his people, is a keynote both of the infancy hymns and the rest of Luke's work.

4. See above, pp. 122-24.

5. See above, pp. 100-102.

6. See the exegesis of the verses in question.

7. This may, however, be too distinct a division. The past too has had its share of fulfilment, the Exodus, the career of David, etc., and the present period still contains promise, e.g. the promise of the annunciation to Mary (Lk. 1.30ff.), and of the parousia (Acts 1.11).

8. Cf. Mk 1.2-3.

9. The hymns only respond to the fulfilment already described in the narrative.

10. See, for example, Cadbury, *Luke–Acts*, 303ff.; Conzelmann, *Theology*, 157-63; Lohse, 'Heilsgeschichte', 261ff., esp. 264; Vielhauer, 'Paulinism', 43, 46-47. The most important statement of the theme was by Schubert, 'Luke 24', esp. 173ff. (There the theme is called 'proof from prophecy'.)

11. See Wilson, *Gentiles*, 53-54; Franklin, *Christ the Lord*, 60, 69ff., 119ff.; Dahl, 'Abraham', 152, 157 n. 54; Minear, 'Luke's Use', 117-20. Cf. Jervell, *People*, 42, 70 n. 9; Kurz, 'Historiography', 285. But Conzelmann himself recognized this motif (see n. 10 above) and obviously must have felt that it was not incompatible with his three-epoch analysis of Luke's view of history.

12. See also Lk. 7.24ff.; Acts 1.16; 2.25, 34; 3.18ff.; 4.25; 8.32ff.; 9.22; 15.16ff., 18.

13. As we shall see, Gaston, *Stone*, 298ff., assigned the interest in the parallel theme of the restoration of Israel to 'Proto-Luke', i.e. the original form of Lk. 1—Acts 15 (*Stone*, 254).

14. There is no trace whatsoever of Paul's doctrine that all who have faith are offspring of Abraham. Those who used these psalms were offspring of Abraham 'after the flesh' (cf. Dahl, 'Abraham', 140).

15. See Flender, *Theologian*, 107-35; Franklin, *Christ the Lord*, 77-115; Gaston, *Stone*, 298-334; George, *Luc*, 87-124; Gnilka, *Verstockung*, esp. 141-55; Lohfink, *Sammlung*, 17-62; O'Neill, *Theology*, 77ff.; Richardson, *Israel*, 160-65; Schmitt, 'Restauration'; van Goudoever, 'Israel'; Wainwright, 'Restoration', and the surveys of Eltester, 'Israel', and Bovon, *Luc*, 342-61.

16. See van Goudoever, 'Israel', on the problem of the place of Israel in the Gospel of Luke. He concluded, 'Luke was not prepared to exclude Israel from salvation' ('Israel', 123). It is interesting to note, however, that even van Goudoever interpreted the pericopes with which he dealt in light of the missionary thrust of Acts ('Israel', 112-13).

17. O'Neill, *Theology*, 98-99.

18. Haenchen, *Acts*, 101. Cf. Gnilka, *Verstockung*, 130: 'Die von Isaias vorausgesagte Verstocktheit der Juden, die sich in der Gegenwart erfüllte, hat den Weg des Evangeliums zu den Heiden jetzt vollständig und endgültig freigemacht'. See also Wilson, *Gentiles*, 232-33, and Haenchen's theological opposite, Bruce, *Acts*, 282, 533-34.

19. Jervell, *People*. In this collection of essays Jervell set forth a number of interrelated propositions, that the early church was interested in and preserved traditions about the missionary endeavour, that early Jewish-Christians were represented by Luke as faithful to the law, etc. Although these essays are of great value they are outside the scope of the present study. I shall concern myself here only with the material discussed in chapter 2, 'The Divided People of God', (*People*, 41-74). Other scholars have also noted that Luke represents a considerable number of Jews accepting the Gospel. Cf. Schmitt, 'Restauration'; Gaston, *Stone*, 298ff.; Dahl, 'Abraham', 151.

20. Jervell, *People*, 41-42.

21. Acts 2.41 (47); 4.4; 5.14; 6.17; 9.42, 12.24; 13.43; 14.1; 17.10ff.; (19.20); 21.20. Cf. Jervell, *People*, 44.

22. Acts 11.21, 24; 14.1; 17.4; 18.8. Cf. Jervell, *People*, 44-45.

23. Jervell, *People*, 45-46.

24. Jervell, *People*, 46.

25. Jervell, *People*, 47-48.

26. See Wilson, *Gentiles*, 232-33; Bovon, *Luc*, 354-56; Richard, 'Divine Purpose', 279. See also Wainwright, 'Restoration', 77, and W. Eltester, 'Israel', 122-25. Wainwright criticized Jervell strongly for suggesting that Israel's restoration is in the past. Jervell doubtless does not adequately consider the possibility that God has yet more in store for Israel but Wainwright's argument is no more than a corrective. It does not deal with the substance of Jervell's position. Eltester's objection concerned the application of the name 'Israel'. He insisted that it belongs not to the Jewish-Christians alone but to the Church as a whole. The use of the term 'Israel' in the infancy hymns would seem to contradict Eltester's position. There, the Gentile believers are clearly differentiated from Israel (Lk. 2.32).

27. Jervell, *People*, 51-54.

28. Jervell, *People*, 53.

29. Jervell, *People*, 55.

30. Jervell, *People*, 53.

31. According to Jervell's analysis of Acts 3.11-26 (*People*, 54).

32. Jervell, *People*, 64.

33. Jervell, *People*, 68.
34. Gaston, 'Tradition and Redaction'.
35. Gaston, 'Tradition and Redaction', 209, 214. Cf. *Stone*, 254.
36. This is the conclusion of Martin, *Syntactical Evidence*, 97. It should be noted, however, that some of the material in Acts which Martin considered to be Semitic has a 'net score' similar to that of the material I studied in which Luke was dependent on Mark. See Table 6, p. 66 above. Jervell's essay, 'The Problem of Traditions in Acts' (*People*, 19-39), also concerns the problem of sources in Acts. Jervell considered terms used by Paul to describe what he had heard about the churches to which he was writing and concluded that these terms indicate that stories about the foundation of churches and other apostolic activity formed part of early Christian preaching.
37. Jervell, *People*, 46.
38. This verse alludes to Is. 49.6, which is explicitly quoted by Paul when he turns to the Gentiles (Acts 13.47).
39. There is likewise no hint that the Jews have permanently cut themselves off from Israel or that the mission to Jews is completely over. This is, perhaps, the least persuasive part of Jervell's argument. Luke could not have supposed that the mission to the Gentiles concluded with Acts 28. Why would he have thought that the church no longer preached to the Jews? It may be that in the evangelist's day the mission to the Jews was meeting with little success but there seems no reason to suppose that Luke had given up all hope for unrepentant Israel.

BIBLIOGRAPHY

Aquinas, St Thomas, *Catena Aurea: Commentary on the four Gospels collected out of the works of the Fathers*, ed. J.H. Parker, Oxford, 1841-44.

Auffret, Pierre, 'Note sur la structure littéraire de Lc 1:68-79', *NTS* 24 (1978), 248-58.

Aytoun, R.A., 'The Ten Lucan Hymns of the Nativity in their Original Language', *JTS* 18 (1917), 274-88.

Barns, T., 'The Magnificat in Niceta of Remesiana and Cyril of Jerusalem', *JTS* 7 (1906), 449-53.

Baur, W., *Orthodoxy and Heresy in Earliest Christianity*, London: SCM, 1972.

Bauer, W., Arndt, W., Gingrich, F.W., *A Greek-English Lexicon of the New Testament and Other Early Christian Literature*, Chicago: Univ. of Chicago, 4th edn, 1952.

Baur, F.C., *The Church History of the First Three Centuries*, London: Williams & Norgate, 1878.

Benko, S., 'The Magnificat: A History of the Controversy', *JBL* 86 (1967), 263-75.

Benoit, P., 'L'enfance de Jean-Baptiste selon Luc 1', *NTS* 3 (1956-57), 169-94.

Bernard, J.H., 'The Magnificat', *Expositor*, Seventh Series, 3 (1907), 193-206.

Black, M., *An Aramaic Approach to the Gospels*, 3rd edn, Oxford: Clarendon, 1967.

Bornhäuser, K., *Die Geburts- und Kindheitsgeschichte Jesu*, Gütersloh: Bertelsmann, 1930.

Bovon, F., *Luc le Théologien*, Neuchâtel & Paris: Delachaux & Niestlé, 1978.

Bowen, C.R., 'John the Baptist in the New Testament', *AJT* 16 (1912), 90-106.

Box, G.H., *The Virgin Birth of Jesus*, London: Williams & Norgate, 1916.

—'The Gospel Narratives of the Infancy and the Alleged Influence of Heathen Ideas', *ZNW* 6 (1906), 80-101.

Brandon, S.G.F., *The Fall of Jerusalem and the Christian Church*, London: SPCK, 1951.

Brown, R.E., *The Birth of the Messiah*, Garden City, NY: Doubleday, 1977.

Bultmann, R., *The History of the Synoptic Tradition*, Oxford: Blackwell, 1972.

Burger, C., *Jesus als Davidsohn*, Göttingen: Vandenhoeck & Ruprecht, 1970.

Burkitt, F.C. 'Who Spoke the Magnificat?', *JTS* 7 (1906), 220-27.

Burney, C.F., *The Aramaic Origin of the Fourth Gospel*, Oxford: OUP, 1922.

Burrows, E., *The Gospel of the Infancy and other Biblical Essays*, London: Burns Oates & Washbourne, 1940.

Cadbury, H.J., *The Making of Luke–Acts*, New York: Macmillan, 1927.

—*The Style and Literary Method of Luke: The Diction of Luke and Acts*, Harvard Theological Studies, 6, Cambridge, Mass.: Harvard University, 1919.

Calvin, J., *Commentary on a Harmony of the Evangelists Matthew, Mark, Luke*, I, Edinburgh: T. & T. Clark, 1920.

Charles, R.H., *The Apocrypha and Pseudepigrapha of the Old Testament in English*, Oxford: Clarendon, 1912.

—*The Revelation of St. John* (ICC), Edinburgh: T. & T. Clark, 1920.

Chatfield, C., *Statistics for Technology: A Course in Applied Statistics*, 2nd edn, London: Chapman & Hall, 1978.

Conzelmann, H., *The Theology of St. Luke*, New York: Harper, 1960.

Creed, J.M., *The Gospel according to St. Luke*, London: Macmillan, 1930.

Cross, F.M., *The Ancient Library of Qumran and Modern Biblical Studies*, London: Duckworth, 1958.

Dahl, N.A., 'The Story of Abraham in Luke–Acts', *SLA*, 139-58.

Dalman, G., *The Words of Jesus*, Edinburgh: T. & T. Clark, 1902.

Dancy, J.C., *The Shorter Books of the Apocrypha*, Cambridge: CUP, 1972.

Daniélou, J. (ed.), *Aspects du Judéo-Christianisme*, Travaux du Centre d'Études Supérieures Specialisé d'Histoire des Religions de Strasbourg, Paris: Presses Universitaires, 1965.

Daniélou, J., *The Theology of Jewish Christianity*, London: Darton, Longman & Todd, 1964.

Danker, F.W., *Jesus and the New Age according to St. Luke*, St. Louis: Clayton, 1972.

Daube, D., *The New Testament and Rabbinic Judaism*, New York: Arno, 1973.

Davies, J.G., 'The Ascription of the Magnificat to Mary', *JTS* 15 (1964), 307-308.

Davies, P.R., *The War Scroll from Qumran: Its Structure and History*, Rome: Pontifical Biblical Institute, 1977.

de Catanzero, J., 'Fear, Knowledge, and Love: A Study in Old Testament Piety', *CJT* 9 (1963), 166-73.

Deichgräber, R., *Gotteshymnus und Christushymnus*, Göttingen: Vandenhoeck & Ruprecht, 1967,

Delcor, M., 'Cinq nouveaux psaumes esséniens', *RQ* 1 (1958-59), 85-102.

Delling, G., *Worship in the New Testament*, London: Darton, Longman & Todd, 1962.

Dibelius, M., *From Tradition to Gospel*, New York: Scribner's, 1935.

—'Jungfrauensohn und Krippenkind: Untersuchungen zur Geburtsgeschichte Jesu in Lukas-Evangelium', in *Botschaft und Geschichte*, Tübingen: Mohr, 1953.

—*Die urchristliche Überlieferung von Johannes dem Täufer*, Göttingen: Vandenhoeck & Ruprecht, 1911.

Dreyer, A.G.D., *An Examination of the Possible Relation between Luke's Infancy Narratives and the Qumran Hodayot*, Amsterdam: 1962.

Drury, J., *Tradition and Design in Luke's Gospel*, London: Darton, Longman & Todd, 1976.

Durand, A., 'L'origine du Magnificat', *RB* 7 (1898), 74-77.

Eissfeldt, O., *The Old Testament, An Introduction*, Oxford: Blackwell, 1965.

Ellis, E.E., *The Gospel of Luke*, London & Edinburgh: Nelson, 1966.

Eltester, W., 'Israel im lukanischen Werk und die Nazarethperikope', in E. Grässer et al., *Jesus in Nazareth*, Berlin: Töpelmann, 1972, 76-147.

Emmet, C.W., 'Should the Magnificat be Ascribed to Elizabeth?', *Expositor*, Seventh Series, 8 (1909), 531-39.

Erdmann, G., *Die Vorgeschichte des Lukas und Matthäus-Evangeliums und Vergils vierte Ekloge*, Göttingen: Vandenhoeck & Ruprecht, 1932.

Ernst, J., *Das Evangelium nach Lukas*, Regensburg: Pustet, 1976.

Farrar, F.W., *The Gospel according to St. Luke*, Cambridge: CUP, 1895.

Farris, S.C., *The Christology of Luke's Infancy Hymns*, unpublished Th.M. project paper, Union Theological Seminary in Virginia, 1978.

—'On Discerning Semitic Sources in Luke 1-2', in R.T. France and D. Wenham (eds.), *Gospel Perspectives*, II, Sheffield: JSOT, 1981, 201-37.

Figueras, P., 'Symeon et Anne ou la témoignage de la loi et des prophètes', *Nov Test* 20 (1978), 84-99.

Fitzmyer, J.A., *The Genesis Apocryphon of Qumran Cave 1*, Rome: Pontifical Biblical Institute, 1966.

—*A Wandering Aramaean*, Missoula: Scholars Press, 1979.

Flender, H., *St. Luke, Theologian of Redemptive History*, Philadelphia: Fortress, 1967.

Flood, E., 'The Magnificat and the Benedictus', *Clergy Review* 51 (1966), 205-10.

Forestell, J.T., 'Old Testament Background of the Magnificat', *Marian Studies* 12 (1961), 205-44.

Franklin, E., *Christ the Lord*, London: SPCK, 1975.

Gaechter, P., *Maria im Erdenleben*, Innsbruck: Tyrolia, 1953.

Gaston, L., *No Stone on Another*, Leiden: Brill, 1970.

—'Lucan Birth Narratives in Tradition and Redaction', *SBL Seminar Papers 1976*, 209-17.

Geldenhuys, N., *Commentary on the Gospel of Luke*, London & Edinburgh: Marshall, Morgan and Scott, 1950.

George, A., *Études sur l'Oeuvre de Luc*, Paris: Gabalda, 1978.

Gertner, M., 'Midrashim in the New Testament', *JSS* 7 (1962), 267-92.

Gnilka, J., 'Der Hymnus des Zacharias', *BZ* 6 (1962), 215-38.

—*Die Verstockung Israels*, Munich: Kösel-Verlag, 1961.

Goguel, M., *Au Seuil de l'Évangile, Jean-Baptiste*, Paris: Payot, 1928.

Goulder, M., *The Evangelists' Calendar*, London: SPCK, 1979.

Goulder, M., and Sanderson, M., 'St. Luke's Genesis', *JTS* 9 (1957), 12-30.

Gray, G.B., *The Forms of Hebrew Poetry*, New York: Ktav, 1972 (reprint with prolegomenon by D.N. Freedman).

—*Isaiah 1–39* (ICC), Edinburgh: T. & T. Clark, 1912.

Grundmann, W., *Das Evangelium nach Lukas*, Berlin: Evangelische Verlag, 1966.

Gryglewicz, F., 'Die Herkunft der Hymnen des Kindheitsevangelium des Lukas', *NTS* 21 (1974-75), 265-73.

Gunkel, H., *Einleitung in die Psalmen*, completed by J. Begrich, Göttingen: Vandenhoeck & Ruprecht, 1933.

—'Die Lieder in der Kindheitsgeschichte Jesu bei Lukas', in A. von Harnack, *Festgabe*, Tübingen: Mohr, 1921, 43-60.

—*The Psalms: A Form Critical Introduction*, Biblical Series 19, Facet Books, Philadelphia: Fortress, 1967.

Gurney, T.A., *Nunc Dimittis or the Song of the Watcher for the Lord's Christ*, London: Longmans, Green & Co., 1906.

Gutierrez, G., *A Theology of Liberation*, Maryknoll, NY: Orbis, 1973.

Haenchen, E., *The Acts of the Apostles: a Commentary*. Philadelphia: Fortress, 1971.

Hahn, F., *The Titles of Jesus in Christology*, London: Lutterworth, 1969.

—*The Worship of the Early Church*, Philadelphia: Fortress, 1972.

Hamel, E., 'Le Magnificat et le renversement des situations. Réflexion théologico-biblique', *Gregorianum* 60 (1979), 55-84.

Haupt, P., 'Magnificat and Benedictus', *American Journal of Philology* 40 (1919), 64-75.

Harnack, A. von, *Luke the Physician, The Author of the Third Gospel and the Acts of the Apostles*, New York: Putnam's 1907.

—'Das Magnificat der Elisabeth (Luk 1.46-55) nebst einigen Bemerkungen zu Luk 1 und 2', *Sitzungberichte der Königlichen Preussischen Akademie der Wissenschaften zu Berlin* 27 (1900), 538-66.

Hatch, E. and Redpath, H., *A Concordance to the Septuagint*, Oxford: Clarendon, 1897.

Hawkins, J.C. *Horae Synopticae: Contributions to the Study of the Synoptic Problem*, Oxford: Clarendon, 1899.

Hendrickx, H., *The Infancy Narratives*, Manila: East Asian Pastoral Institute, 1975.

Hennecke, E., *New Testament Apocrypha*, ed. W. Schneemelcher, London: Lutterworth, 1963.

Hilgenfeld, A., 'Die Geburts- und Kindheitsgeschichte Jesu, Luc 1.5–2.52', *Zeitschrift für die Wissenschaftliche Theologie* 44 (1901), 177-235.

Hort, F.J.A., *Judaistic Christianity*, London: Macmillan, 1898.

Hunzinger, C.-H., 'Fragmente einer älteren Fassung des Buches Milḥama aus Höhle 4 von Qumran', *ZAW* 69 (1957), 131-51.

Jacobé, F., See under Loisy, A.

Jacoby, A., 'Ἀνατολὴ ἐξ ὕψους', *ZNW* 20 (1921), 205-14.

James, M.R. and Ryle, H.E., *The Psalms of the Phrarisees, commonly called: Psalms of Solomon*, Cambridge: CUP, 1891.

Jellicoe, S. (ed.), *Studies in the Septuagint*, New York: Ktav, 1974.

Jeremias, J., *Die Sprache des Lukasevangeliums*, Göttingen: Vandenhoeck & Ruprecht, 1980.

Jervell, J., *Luke and the People of God*, Minneapolis: Augsburg, 1972.

Johnson, L.T., *The Literary Function of Possessions in Luke's Gospel*, Missola: Scholars Press, 1977.

Jones, D.R., 'The Background and Character of the Lukan Psalms', *JTS* 19 n.s. (1968), 19-50.

Kahle, P., *The Cairo Geniza*, Oxford: Blackwell, 1959.

Kaiser, O., *Isaiah 13–39*, London: SCM, 1974.

Kilpatrick, G.D., 'Λαοί at Luke II 23 and Acts IV 25, 27', *JTS* 16 (1965), 127.

Klijn, A.F.J., 'The Study of Jewish Christianity', *NTS* 20 (1974), 419-31.

Klijn, A.F.J. and Reinink, G.J., *Patristic Evidence for Jewish Christian Sects*, Supplements to Novum Testamentum, 36, Leiden: Brill, 1973.

Klostermann, E., *Das Lukasevangelium*, Handbuch zum Neuen Testament, 5, Tübingen: Mohr, 1929.

Knox, W.L., *The Sources of the Synoptic Gospels*, II, Cambridge: CUP, 1957.

Koontz, J.V.G., 'Mary's Magnificat', *Bibliotheca Sacra* 116 (1959), 336-49.

Kraeling, C.H., *John the Baptist*, New York: Scribner's, 1951.

Kraft, C.H., 'Poetic Structure in the Qumran Thanksgiving Hymns', *Biblical Research* 2 (1957), 1-18.

Kraft, R.A., 'In Search of "Jewish Christianity" and its "Theology". Problems of Definition and Methodology', *RSR* 60 (1972), 81-92.

Lagrange, M.-J., *L'Évangile selon St. Luc*, Paris: Lecoffre, 1948.

Lambertz, M., 'Sprachliches aus Septuaginta und Neuen Testament', *Wissenschaftliches Zeitschrift Univ. Leipzig* (1952-53), 79-84.

Laurentin, R., *Structure et Théologie de Luc I–II*, Paris: Lecoffre, Gabalda, 1957.

—'Traces d'allusions etymologiques en Luc I–II', *Biblica* 37 (1956), 435-56.

—'Traces d'allusions etymologiques en Luc I–II', *Biblica* 38 (1957), 1-23.

Leaney, A.R.C., *A Commentary on the Gospel according to St. Luke*, London: A. & C. Black, 1957.

Lehman, M.R., 'Talmudic Material Relating to the Dead Sea Scrolls', *RQ* 1 (1958-59), 391-404.

Leivestad, R., 'Ταπεινός—ταπεινόφρων', *Nov Test* 8 (1966), 36-47.

Lewis, A.S., 'Did John Preach Baptism for the Remission of Sins?', *Expositor*, Fifth Series, 7 (1898), 223-27.

Lohfink, G., *Die Sammlung Israels*, München: Kösel, 1975.

Lohse, E., 'Lukas als Theologe der Heilsgeschichte', *EvTh* 14 (1954), 256-75.

Loisy, A., *L'Évangile selon Luc*, Paris: Nourry, 1924.

—*Les Évangiles Synoptiques*, Ceffonds: chez l'auteur, 1907-1908.

—(under the name of F. Jacobé), 'L'origine du Magnificat', *Revue d'Histoire et de Littérature Religieuses* 2 (1897), 424-32.

Luce, H.K., *The Gospel according to St. Luke*, Cambridge: CUP, 1949.

Lührmann, D., 'Ein Weisheitspsalm aus Qumran (11Q Ps^a xvii)', *ZAW* 80 (1968), 87-98.

Machen, J.G., 'The First Two Chapters of Luke', *PTR* 10 (1912), 212-77.

—'The Hymns of the First Chapter of Luke', *PTR* 10 (1912), 1-38.

—*The Virgin Birth of Christ*, New York: Harper, 1930.

McHugh, J., *The Mother of Jesus in the New Testament*, Garden City, NY: Doubleday, 1975.

McNamara, M., *The New Testament and the Palestinian Targum to the Pentateuch*, Rome: Pontifical Biblical Institute, 1978.

MacNeill, H.L., 'The Sitz im Leben of Luke 1.5–2.20', *JBL* 65 (1946), 123-30.

Magne, J., 'Le Psaume 154 et le Psaume 155', *RQ* 9 (1978), 95-111.

Manek, J., 'The New Exodus in the Books of Luke', *Nov Test* 2 (1957), 8-23.

Mann, C.S., 'The Historicity of the Birth Narratives', in his *Historicity and Chronology in the New Testament*, London: SPCK, 1965, 46-58.

Manson, T.W., *The Teaching of Jesus*, Cambridge: CUP, 1951.

Manson, W., *The Gospel of Luke* (Moffatt's NT Commentary), London: Hodder & Stoughton, 1930.

Mansoor, M., *The Thanksgiving Hymns, Studies on the Texts of the Desert of Judah*, III, Leiden: Brill, 1961.

Marshall, I.H., *The Gospel of Luke, A Commentary on the Greek Text*, Exeter: Paternoster, 1978.

—*Luke: Historian and Theologian*, Exeter: Paternoster, 1970.

Martin, R.A., 'Some Syntactical Criteria of Translation Greek', *Vetus Testamentum* 10 (1960), 295-310.

—'Syntactical Evidence of Aramaic Sources in Greek Documents', LXX and Cognate Studies 3, Missoula: Scholars Press, 1974.

Studies on the Testament of Joseph, ed. G.W.E. Nickelsburg, Jr, Missoula: Scholars Press, 1975.

—'Syntax Criticism of the LXX Additions to the Book of Esther', *JBL* 94 (1975), 65-72.

—'Syntax Criticism of the Testament of Abraham', in *Studies on the Testament of Abraham*, ed. G.W.E. Nickelsburg, Jr, Missoula: Scholars Press, 1976.

Marty, J., 'Étude des textes cultuels de prières contenus dans le Nouveau Testament', *Revue d'Histoire et de Philosophie Religieuses* 9 (1929), 234-68, 366-76.

Mealand, R., *Poverty and Expectation in Luke's Gospel*, London: SPCK, 1980.

Milling, D.H., *The Origin and Character of the New Testament Doxology*, unpublished PhD dissertation, Cambridge: 1972.

Minear, P., 'Luke's Use of the Birth Stories', *SLA*, 111-30.

Mingana, A., 'Christian Documents in Syriac, Arabic and Garshuni', *BJRL* 11 (1927), 494-99.

Miyoshi, M., 'Jesu Darstellung oder Reinigung im Tempel unter Berück-sichtigung von Nunc Dimittis, Lk ii 22-38', *Annual of the Japanese Biblical Institute* 4 (1978), 85-110.

Morgenthaler, R., *Die Lukanische Geschichtsschreibung als Zeugnis*, Zurich: Zwingli, 1949.

Morris, L., *The Gospel according to St. Luke*, London: IVP, 1974.

Moulton, J.H., *A Grammar of New Testament Greek*, vol. I, 3rd edn, *Prolegomena*, Edinburgh: T. & T. Clark, 1908. Vol. II, *Accidence and Word Formation*, with W.F. Howard, Edinburgh: T. & T. Clark, 1929.

Moulton, W.F. and Geden, A.S., *Concordance to the Greek Testament*, 4th edn, Edinburgh: T. & T. Clark, 1963.

Mowinckel, S., *The Psalms in Israel's Worship*, Oxford: Blackwell, 1962.

—'Some Remarks on Hodayot 39:5-20', *JBL* 75 (1956), 265-76.

Munck, J. 'Israel and the Gentiles in the New Testament', *JTS* 2 (1951), 3-16.

—'Jewish Christianity in Post-Apostolic Times', *NTS* 6 (1959-60), 103-16.

—'Jewish Christianity', in J. Daniélou (ed.), *Aspects du Judéo-Christianisme*.

Murray, R., 'Defining Judaeo-Christianity', *Heythrop Journal* 15 (1974), 303-10.

Myers, J.M., *I Chronicles* (The Anchor Bible), Garden City, NY: Doubleday, 1965.

Navone, J., *Themes of St. Luke*, Rome: Gregorian University Press, 1977.

Noth, M., 'Die fünf syrische überlieferten apocryphen Psalmen', *ZAW* 48 (1930), 1-23.

Oliver, H.H., 'The Lucan Birth Stories and the Purpose of Luke–Acts', *NTS* 10 (1963-64), 202-26.

O'Neill, J.C., 'The Synoptic Problem', *NTS* 21 (1974-75), 273-85.

—*The Theology of Acts in its Historical Setting* 2nd edn, London: SPCK, 1970.

Osten-Sacken, P. von der, *Gott und Belial*, Göttingen: Vandenhoeck & Ruprecht, 1969.

Philo Judaeus, *Philo* (Loeb Classical Library), ed. F.H. Colson, London: Heinemann, Cambridge, Mass.: Harvard, 1941.

Philonenko, M., 'L'origine essénienne des cinq Psaumes syriaques de David', *Semitica* 9 (1959), 35-48.

Plummer, A., *The Gospel according to St. Luke* (ICC) 5th edn, Edinburgh: T. & T. Clark, 1901.

Quispel, G., 'The Discussion of Judaic Christianity', *Vig Christ* 22 (1968), 81-93.

Ragg, L., *St. Luke* (Westminster Commentaries), London: Methuen & Co., 1922.

Ramaroson, L., 'Ad Structuram Cantici Magnificat', *Verbum Domini* 46 (1968), 30-46.

Reicke, B., *The Gospel of Luke*, London: SPCK, 1965.

Rengstorf, K.H., *Das Evangelium nach Lukas* (Das Neue Testament Deutsch), Göttingen: Vandenhoeck & Ruprecht, 1949.

Resch, A., *Das Kindheitsevangelium nach Lukas und Matthäus*, Texte und Untersuchungen, 10, Leipzig: Hinrichs, 1897.

Richard, E., 'The Divine Purpose: The Jews and the Gentile Mission', *1981 SBL Seminar Papers*, 267-82.

Richardson, P., *Israel in the Apostolic Church*, Cambridge: CUP, 1969.

Riegel, S., 'Jewish Christianity: Definitions and Terminology', *NTS* 24 (1977-78), 410-15.

Rienecker, F., *Das Evangelium des Lukas*, Wuppertal: Brockhaus, 1974.

Robertson, A.T., *A Translation of Luke's Gospel*, New York: G.H. Doran, 1923.

Robinson, J.A.T., 'Elijah, John and Jesus: An Essay in Detection', *NTS* 4 (1957-58), 343-48.

Robinson, J.M., 'Die Hodajot-Formel in Gebet und Hymnus des Frühchristentums', in *Apophoreta*, Festschrift für E. Haenchen, Berlin: Töpelmann, 1964.

Ruddick, C.T., Jr, 'Birth Narratives in Genesis and Luke', *Nov Test* 12 (1970), 343-48.

Ryle, H., and James, M., *The Psalms of Solomon*, Cambridge: CUP, 1891.

Sabourin, L., *The Psalms, Their Origin and Meaning*, New York: Alba House, 1974.

Sahlin, H., *Der Messias und das Gottesvolk*, Uppsala: Almqvist, 1945.

Sanders, J.A., *The Psalms Scroll at Qumran Cave 11*, Discoveries in the Judaean Desert, IV, Oxford, 1965.

Schille, G., *Frühchristliche Hymnen*, Berlin: Evangelische Verlaganstalt, 1965.

Schmid, J., *Das Evangelium nach Lukas*, Gütersloh: Mohn, 1981.

Schmitt, J., 'L'Église de Jérusalem ou la "Restauration d'Israel"', *Revue des Sciences Religieuses* 27 (1953), 209-18.

Schnackenburg, R., 'Das Magnificat, seine Spiritualität und Theologie', *Geist und Leben* 38 (1965), 342-57.

Schneider, G., *Das Evangelium nach Lukas*, Gütersloh: Mohn, Würzburg: Echter, 1977.

Schoeps, H.J., *Jewish Christianity*, Philadelphia: Fortress, 1969.

Schonfield, H., *The Lost Book of the Nativity of John*, Edinburgh: T. & T. Clark, 1929.

Schoonheim, P.L., 'Der alttestamentliche Boden der Vokabel ὑπερηφάνους, Lukas 1.51', *Nov Test* 8 (1966), 235-46.

Schotroff, L., 'Das Magnificat und die älteste Tradition über Jesus von Nazareth', *EvTh* 38 (1978), 298-313.

Schubert, P., 'The Structure and Significance of Luke 24', in *Neutestamentliche Studien für Rudolph Bultmann*, Berlin: Töpelmann, 1957, 165-86.

—*Studies in Luke–Acts*, ed. L.E. Keck and J.L. Martyn, London: SPCK, 1968.

Schüpphaus, J., *Die Psalmen Salomos*, Leiden: Brill, 1977.

Schürer, E., *The Jewish People in the Age of Jesus Christ*, revised G. Vermes *et al.*, Edinburgh: T. & T. Clark, 1979.

Schürmann, Heinz, *Das Lukasevangelium* (Kommentar zu 1:1–9:50), Freiburg: Herder, 1969.

Scobie, C.H.H., *John the Baptist*, Philadelphia: Fortress, 1964.

Seccombe, D.P., *Possessions and the Poor in Luke–Acts*, unpublished PhD dissertation, Cambridge, 1978.

Skehan, P.W., 'Again the Syriac Apocryphal Psalms', *CBQ* 38 (1978), 143-58.

Smitmans, A., 'Die Hymnen der Kindheitsgeschichte nach Lukas', *Bibel und Kirche* 21 (1966), 115-18.

Sparks, H.F.D., 'The Semitisms of St. Luke's Gospel', *JTS* 44 n.s. (1943), 129-38.

Spitta, F., 'Die chronologischen Notizen und die Hymnen in Lc 1 u. 2', *ZNW* 7 (1906), 281-317.

—'Das Magnificat. Ein Psalm der Maria und nicht der Elisabeth', in *Theologische Abhandlung für H.J. Holtzmann*, Tübingen und Leipzig: Mohr, 1902.

Starcky, J., 'Psaumes apocryphes de la grotte 4 de Qumran', *RB* 73 (1966), 353-71.

Stendhal, K., *The School of St. Matthew and its Use of the Old Testament*, 2nd edn, Philadelphia: Fortress, 1968.

Strack, H. and Billerbeck, P., *Kommentar zum Neuen Testament aus Talmud und Midrasch*, München: Beck, 1922-28.

Strugnell, J., 'Notes on the Text and Transmission of the Apocryphal Psalms 151, 154, 155', *HTR* 69 (1966), 257-81.

Stuart, D.K., *Early Hebrew Metre*, Missoula: Scholars Press, 1974.

Sweet, J., *Revelation*, London: SCM, 1979.

Talbert, C.H., *Literary Patterns, Theological Themes, and the Genre of Luke–Acts*, Missoula: Scholars Press, 1974.

—*Perspectives on Luke–Acts*, Edinburgh: T. & T. Clark, 1978.

Tannehill, R.C., 'The Magnificat as Poem', *JBL* 93 (1974), 263-75.

Tatum, W.B., 'The Epoch of Israel: Luke I–II and the Theological Plan of Luke–Acts', *NTS* 13 (1966-67), 184-95.

Thompson, G.H.P., *The Gospel according to Luke*, Oxford: Clarendon, 1972.

Thyen, H., 'Βάπτισμα μετανοίας εἰς ἄφεσιν ἁμαρτιῶν', in *Zeit und Geschichte*, Festschrift für R. Bultmann, Tübingen: Mohr, 1964, 97-125.

Tinsley, E.J., *The Gospel according to St. Luke*, Cambridge: CUP, 1965.

Torrey, C.C., *The Apocalypse of John*, New Haven: Yale University Press, 1958.

—*The Four Gospels, A New Translation*, London: Hodder & Stoughton, 1933.

—'Medina and Πόλις and Luke 1:39', *HTR* 17 (1924), 83-91.

—*Our Translated Gospels, Some of the Evidence*, London: Hodder & Stoughton, 1936.

Turner, C.H., 'Niceta of Remesiana', *JTS* 24 (1923), 225-52.

Turner, N., 'The Relation of Luke I and II to Hebraic Sources and the Rest of Luke–Acts', *NTS* 2 (1955-56), 100-109.

van den Berghe, P., ' 'Ani et 'Anaw dans les Psaumes', in *Le Psautier*, Louvain: Publications Universitaires, 1962.

van Goudoever, J., 'The Place of Israel in Luke's Gospel', *Nov Test* 8 (1966), 111-23.

Vanhoye, A., 'Structure du "Benedictus"', *NTS* 12 (1965-66), 382-89.

van Winkle, D., *Universalism and Nationalism in Deutero-Isaiah*, unpublished PhD dissertation, Cambridge, 1983.

Vielhauer, P., 'Das Benedictus des Zacharias', reprinted in his *Aufsätze zum Neuen Testament* (Theologische Bücherei), München: Kaiser, 1965, 28-46.

—'On the Paulinism of Acts', *SLA*, 33-50.

Vogels, W., 'Le Magnificat, Marie et Israël', *Église et Théologie* 6 (1975), 279-96.

Völter, D., 'Die Apokalypse des Zacharias im Evangelium des Lucas', *Theologisch Tijdschrift* 30 (1896), 244-69.

—*Die evangelischen Erzählungen von der Geburt und Kindheit Jesu kritisch untersucht*, Strasbourg: Heitz, 1911.

Wainwright, A.W., 'Luke and the Restoration of the Kingdom to Israel', *ExpTim* 89 (1977), 76-79.

Wahl, C., *Clavis librorum Veteris Testamenti apocryphorum philologica*, reprinted, Graz: Akademische Druck und Verlag, 1972.

Weiss, B., *The Life of Christ*, 3 vols., Edinburgh: T. & T. Clark, 1890-92.

Weiss, J., *Die Schriften des Neuen Testaments*, I, 2nd edn, Berlin: Reimer, 1911.

Wellhausen, J., *Einleitung in die drei ersten Evangelien*, 2nd edn, Berlin: Reimer, 1911.

Werner, E., *The Sacred Bridge*, London: Dennis Dobson, New York: Columbia University, 1959.

Westermann, C., *The Praise of God in the Psalms*, London: Epworth, 1966.

Wilcox, M., *The Semitisms of Acts*, Oxford: Clarendon, 1965.

Wilson, R. McL., 'Some Recent Studies in the Lucan Infancy Narratives', in *Studia Evangelica* (1957), ed. K. Aland, Berlin, 1959.

Wilson, S., *The Gentiles and the Gentile Mission in Luke–Acts*, Cambridge: CUP, 1973.

Wink, W., *John the Baptist in the Gospel Tradition*, Cambridge: CUP, 1968.

Winter, P., 'The Cultural Background of the Narrative in Luke I and II', *JQR* 45 (1954), 159-67, 230-42, 287.

—'On Luke and Lukan Sources', *ZNW* 4 (1956), 217-42.

—'Magnificat and Benedictus—Maccabaean Psalms?', *BJRL* 37 (1954-55), 328-47.

—'The Main Literary Problem of the Lucan Infancy Story', *Anglican Theological Review* 40 (1958), 257-64.

—'On the Margin of Luke I, II', *Studia Theologica* 12 (1958), 103-107.

—'The Proto-Source of Luke 1', *Nov Test* 1 (1956), 184-99.

—'Some Observations on the Language in the Birth and Infancy Stories of the Third Gospel', *NTS* 1 (1954-55), 111-21.

Winter, P., 'Two Notes on the Theory of Imitation Translation Greek', *Studia Theologica* 7 (1953), 158-65.

Wragg, J., *St. Luke's Nativity Narrative with Special Reference to the Canticles in the Light of the Jewish and Early Christian Background*, unpublished PhD dissertation, Manchester, 1965.

Yadin, Y., *The Scroll of the War of the Sons of Light against the Sons of Darkness*, Oxford: OUP, 1962.

Zahn, T., *Das Evangelium des Lucas*, 4te Auflage, Leipzig: Deichert, 1920.

Zimmermann, H., 'Evangelium des Lukas, Kap. 1 und 2: Ein Versuch der Vermittlung zwischen Hilgenfeld und Harnack', *Theologische Studien und Kritiken* 76 (1903), 247-90.

Zorell, F.X., 'Das Magnificat, ein Kunstwerk hebräischer oder aramäischer Poesie?', *Zeitschrift für die katholische Theologie* 29 (1905), 754-58.

INDEXES

INDEX OF BIBLICAL REFERENCES

INDEX OF AUTHORS

220   *The Hymns of Luke's Infancy Narratives*

Schmid, J. 184n42
Schmithals, W. 162n5, 193n80
Schmitt, J. 197n15, 198n19
Schoeps, H. 181n62
Schonfield, H. 90, 179n34
Schoonheim, P. 188n110
Schotroff, L. 116, 185n49, 189n125
Schubert, P. 197n10
Schüpphaus, J. 178n13
Schürer, E. 175n32
Schurmann, H. 109, 116, 119, 130-31,
    153n51, 153n55, 153n59, 162n3,
    183n12, 183n23, 184n38, 184n41,
    185n49, 185n50, 186n71, 186n81,
    187n84, 187n105, 189n138, 190n18,
    191n18, 191n19, 191n24, 193n72,
    193n76, 193n80, 193n88, 195n9,
    196n24
Scobie, C. 90, 179n34, 188n115,
    188n116, 189n127
Skehan, P. 177n61
Sparks, H.F.D. 15, 36, 162n7, 167n35
Spitta, F. 22-23, 164n30, 183n7, 183n19,
    195n3
Starcky, J. 176n46, 177n64, 177n65
Strecker, G. 181n62
Strugnell, J. 177n61
Stuart, D. 171n100
Sweet, J. 173n29

Talbert, C.H. 105, 182n18
Tannehill, R. 15, 46, 113, 116, 162n9,
    170n89, 184n35, 184n36, 185n49,
    185n53, 187n105, 187n109,
    188n114, 189n138
Tatum, W. 167n40, 196n1
Thyen, H. 92, 179n40, 179n43
Tinsley, E. 15, 162n7
Tischendorff, C. 128
Torrey, C.C. 35, 37-40, 167n43, 167n44-
    46, 168n48-54, 170n86, 173n27,
    173n29
Turner, C. 182n5

Turner, N. 15, 36, 40-41, 162n7, 167n35,
    168n63, 168n66, 168n70, 168n71,
    169n72, 172n7

van den Berghe, P. 188n115
van Goudoever, J. 197n15, 198n16
van Winkle, D. 196n37
Vanhoye, A. 128-129, 190n1
Vielhauer, P. 92-94, 130, 139, 179n28,
    179n40, 179n44, 180n45, 180n47,
    180n48, 190n16, 191n18, 191n24,
    193n83, 193n90, 194n106, 197n10
Vogels, W. 185n51, 186n76
Volter, D. 89-92, 178n25, 179n34-37
Volter, D. 182n4, 192n51

Wainwright A. 198n26
Weiss, B. 186n75
Wellhausen, J. 37, 167n43
Werner, E. 161n3
Westermann, C. 10, 67-69, 71-73, 75, 97,
    129, 161n5-8, 174n4, 174n6, 174n7,
    174n11, 174n15-20, 175n22-27,
    176n41, 181n63, 184n39, 187n93
Wilcox, M. 96, 180n57-59, 192n52,
    196n27
Wilson, S. 197n11, 198n18, 198n26
Wink, W. 170n88, 178n22, 180n50, 182n4
Winter, P. 34, 40-42, 86-88, 130, 163n24,
    166n20-22, 167n35, 168n53,
    168n60-62, 168n64, 168n65,
    168n67-69, 168n71, 169n73, 169n75,
    170n88, 177n3, 177n5, 177n6,
    177n8, 178n10, 180n50, 185n45,
    187n100, 190n16
Wragg, J. 128, 162n3, 190n1, 191n37

Yadin, Y. 80, 165n53, 176n51, 176n52

Zahn, T. 183n15, 183n17, 183n19,
    194n101
Zorrell, F.X. 46, 48, 49, 171n91, 171n93,
    171n95

JOURNAL FOR THE STUDY OF THE NEW TESTAMENT
Supplement Series